FORGOTTEN PATHS

FORGOTTEN PATHS

Etymology and the Allegorical Mindset

Davide Del Bello

The Catholic University of America Press

Washington, D.C.

The paper used in this publication meets the minimum requirements

of American National Standards for Information Science—Permanence

of Paper for Printed Library Materials, ANSI z39.48-1984.

∞

Library of Congress Cataloging-in-Publication Data

Del Bello, Davide, 1964–

   Forgotten paths : etymology and the allegorical mindset /
Davide Del Bello.

      p. cm.

   Includes bibliographical references and index.

   ISBN-13: 978-0-8132-1484-9 (cloth : alk. paper)

   ISBN-10: 0-8132-1484-X (cloth : alk. paper)   1. Language and
languages—Etymology—History.   2. Allegory.   I. Title.

   P321.D45 2007

   121'.68—dc22   2006021104

Neque instantia, neque futura

Ai miei genitori

CONTENTS

ILLUSTRATIONS

ACKNOWLEDGMENTS

During the years that went into the preparation of this book, I have incurred countless debts on both sides of the Atlantic. A note of sincere appreciation goes to John Schaeffer, Susan Deskis, and David Gorman at Northern Illinois University, who originally fostered my project: without their unrelenting assistance, this manuscript would not have been possible. Special thanks are also due to Nicole Clifton, whose knowledge of Latin and medieval literature was helpful in many respects, and to John Mulryan and Alva V. Cellini at St. Bonaventure University for their expert advice and unflagging encouragement. The Library and the Rare Books Room at the University of Illinois at Urbana-Champaign provided the ideal research environment; I am especially thankful to Robert Cagle and Kathleen Kluegel at the English Library for their help and unostentatious expertise. Other libraries have also been most welcoming: the Founders Memorial Library at Northern Illinois, the Friedsam Library at St. Bonaventure, the Widener Library at Harvard, the Biblioteca Angelo Mai, and the Biblioteca di Lingue e Lettere in Bergamo.

My recent and past research abroad was helped immeasurably by the Dipartimento di Linguistica e Letterature Comparate at Bergamo University. I am most grateful to Alessandra Marzola and Stefano Rosso for furthering my plans and for bearing with my endless qualms. And I wish to thank Maria Vittoria Molinari, Pierluigi Cuzzolin, Alberto Castoldi, Mario Corona, Francesca Guidotti, Rossana Bonadei, Giuliano Bernini, Giovanni Bottiroli, and Flaminia Nicora for their trust and support. In the painful task of editing this manuscript, invaluable help has come from Erik Scherpf, who put up with early drafts

and checked my translations; and from Carole Sutton, who provided
much-needed suggestions on style. To both I send my gratitude and
my affection. And affection goes to my many unmentioned friends
and to the members of my family: Renata, Giovanni, Fabiola, Tiziana,
Adolf, Erika, and Erik to whom my debt is deepest. My solitary work
would have been much harder if their patience had not been great and
their love unconditional.

INTRODUCTION

Amicus, per derivationem, quasi animi custos. Dictus autem proprie: amator turpitudinis, quia amore torquetur libidinis: amicus ab hamo, id est, a catena caritatis. (X,2)

[*Amicus* is formed by derivation, almost as *animi custos*. Hence it is properly said: *lover* (*amator*) of foulness, because one is tormented by libidinous love, but *amicus*, from *hamo*, that is, from the shackles of charity.]

This etymology appears at the beginning of Book X (*De Vocabulis*) in Isidore of Seville's *Etymologiarum Sive Origines Libri XX*. It is a prime example of the kind of medieval etymologizing that seems almost flauntingly at variance with a persistent notion of "scientific etymology," the *Sprachwissenschaft*—or Science of Language—pioneered by nineteenth-century German scholars and tacitly endorsed to this day. Confronted with etymologies of the Isidorian kind, one is inclined to be condescending, on account of the methodological sophistication that sets modern lexicography apart from "quaint" medieval naïveté. Premodern etymologies seem at best intriguing instances of rhetorical wordplay, open to a number of critical approaches (linguistic, psychoanalytic, new-historicist, or deconstructionist). At worst, and with very few exceptions, they simply "deserve" the epithets of "foolish" and "insipid trifling" authoritatively applied to them by German historian Ernst Robert Curtius.

Yet, the line of etymological thinking that through Plato's *Cratylus* reaches the Middle Ages and the Renaissance hardly disappears with the advent of science. After the speculations of Giambattista Vico, Ernesto Grassi, and Martin Heidegger (to name but a representative few), the etymological mode eventually resurfaces in the postmodern literary experiments of Jacques Derrida's *différance* and Paul de Man's *allegories*. As early as 1976, French critic Gérard Genette "recognized the . . . echo" of Socrates's (and Cratylus's) analysis of naming in "other texts from various periods" and set general lines of "a survey of the posterity of *Cratylus*" that listed names like Marcel Proust, Gaston Bachelard, and Jean-Paul Sartre.[1]

The present study is meant as a foray into the rough terrain of Western etymologizing. I do not set out to provide full coverage or thorough analyses of the many etymological practices that inhabit the cultural and literary tradition of the West. In the presence of such looming figures as Plato and Isidore, and at the outskirts of the critical *silva* that their works have fostered for millennia, I am going to mark routes of interpretation, which may in time contribute to full-scale maps of the role that etymologizing has had, and continues to have, in the history of Western culture. I am particularly interested in etymology and allegory as complementary modes of thought: while much has been written on allegory as a knowledge tool, i.e., as a device that acts more as a cultural and philosophical *forma mentis* than sheer literary form, I find that similar functions to be found historically in etymological discourse remain largely uncharted. Arguably, the rhetorical, argumentative impact of etymology has always been acknowledged, at least as far as prominent ancient and medieval scholars are concerned. But appreciation for such etymologies seems to me to have been granted invariably with strong reservations about their literary or cognitive worth. Etymologies of the Isidorian kind continue either to be cited as curious specimens of scientific antiquarianism or to be altogether dismissed on the grounds of semantic and phonological inaccuracy.

With this scenario in mind, I turn to classical, medieval, and Renaissance texts to draw suggestions and general notes about the inter-

1. Gérard Genette, *Mimologics = Mimologiques: voyage en Cratylie*, trans. Thaïs Morgan (Lincoln: University of Nebraska Press, 1995), 6.

action between etymological and allegorical ways of knowing, thinking, writing, and arguing. These notes may serve to bring into sharper
focus the hazy contours of the "*figura etymologica*" with respect to allegory; to claim and assess the viability of classical and medieval etymologizing as a dynamic, cognitive tool; and to appraise the persistence
of an etymologico-allegorical *modus operandi* from the late Enlightenment to postmodernism.

The study consists of eight chapters. Chapters 1 and 2 tackle major scholarly issues on the subject of "etymology and allegory," while
chapters 3 to 7 focus on etymologico-allegorical works (both literary
and theoretical) across time, and chapter 8 sets forth a theory of etymological thought, especially in an allegorical context. Chapter 1 charts
the evolution of "scientific" etymology from the eighteenth century to
the present. By postulating and analyzing sets of historical or theoretical reasons that might have led first to the affirmation of etymology as
a science and then to its current unpopular status, this chapter paves
the way to a full-scale reappraisal of prescientific etymologizing. The
structure is chronological, with divisions borrowed from Yakov Malkiel: I start with pre-1900 etymologizing, move on to consider the first
half of the twentieth century, and then conclude with an overview of
etymological practices from the 1950s to the present. Occasionally, I
have found it necessary to digress on questions that I thought relevant
to my purpose, as for example in my expanded treatment of Ferdinand
de Saussure and the issue of linguistic arbitrariness. And to signpost
these digressions, I have marked them off with subheadings.

I have based my research on five main monographs on etymology: Malkiel's *Etymology*,[2] Elmar Seebold's *Etymologie*,[3] Zamboni's
L'etimologia,[4] Guiraud's *Structures étymologiques du lexique français*,[5] and

---

2. Yakov Malkiel, *Etymology* (Cambridge: Cambridge University Press, 1993).
3. Elmar Seebold, *Etymologie: Eine Einführung am Biespiel der deutschen Sprache* (Munich: Beck, 1981).
4. Alberto Zamboni, *L'etimologia* (Bologna: Zanichelli, 1976).
5. Pierre Guiraud, *Structures étymologiques du lexique français*, 2nd ed. (Paris: Larousse, 1967).

Vittore Pisani's *L'etimologia: storia questioni metodo*.[6] These have been selected because of their breadth of coverage and depth of analysis but also by virtue of their chronological distribution, which should reflect etymology's fortune at different points of recent history.[7] Observations on pre-1800 etymology are deliberately left to subsequent chapters.

Chapter 2 sets up the wider theoretical framework around etymology, by discussing some of the philosophical issues at stake in the quest for "original" etymons, as well as various ways in which the quest has been hailed or maligned, exhumed, or refurbished. I draw attention to instances where the form, the process, or the ends of etymology and allegory seem to overlap (namely in the philosophical and argumentative arenas). Chapters 3 to 5 describe a number of etymologico-allegorical schemes from classical Greece (Plato), the Roman world (Varro), and the Middle Ages (Isidore). The chapters' focus is on works whose form, content, or function may typically graph etymology's evolution over the span of almost sixteen centuries. Chapter 6 sketches allegory's and etymology's fortune in the Renaissance, while chapter 7 puts the contributions of de Man, Derrida, and Vico side by side against and within the empirical objectivism promoted by scientific discourse.

Finally, chapter 8 assesses etymologizing as a cognitive tool: as a discourse linked to allegory and mnemotechnique and suspended between rhetoric and science. Among other things, I try to reestablish etymology's jurisdiction beyond the scope of structuralist linguistics (phonology, morphology, lexicography) and examine etymology's prowess at constructing or interpreting knowledge and desire "allegorically." All translations are mine, unless otherwise indicated.

6. Vittore Pisani, *L'etimologia: Storia, questioni, metodo* (Brescia: Paideia, 1967).
7. One work that has only too recently become available, and that I was therefore unable to discuss profitably in this study, is Walter Belardi's thorough study on etymology in Western culture. Belardi sets out "to rectify incorrect opinions about etymology, to propose a number of new etymologies, and, besides and above all, to contribute to stating the role that etymology has had in the cultural history of our Western world" ["a rettificare opinioni non corrette intorno all'etimologia, a proporre qualche etimologia nuova, e oltre a ciò, anzi soprattutto, contribuire a dichiarare il ruolo che l'etimologia ha avuto nella storia culturale del nostro Occidente"]. Walter Belardi, *L'etimologia nella storia della cultura occidentale*, 2 vols. (Rome: Dipartimento di Studi Glottoantropologici Università di Roma "La Sapienza," Editrice il Calamo, 2002), 1:8.

FORGOTTEN PATHS

CHAPTER 1

THE SCIENCE OF ETYMOLOGY
From "Sound" Laws to Plausible Conjectures

IS ETYMOLOGY A SCIENCE? Nineteenth-century German scholars would not have doubted that the study of word origins is a *Wissenschaft*, the kind of exact knowledge that is based on predictable linguistic laws. In 1852, Ernst Förstemann claimed that word origins followed *strenge Lautgesetze* (strict sound laws). Two decades later he maintained that these laws were *ausnahmslos* (exceptionless).[1]

Contours are not quite so sharp if one looks at the role etymology is granted today. To be sure, the number of current books involving "word origins"—collections, dictionaries, lexicons—would seem to indicate that etymology thrives.[2] And such lasting popular interest in etymology reflects an ongoing interest on the part of lecturers, critics, writers, lawyers, historians, and politicians, who consistently refer to etymology to further their claims. Etymologizing is bound to feature prominently whenever definitions are at stake: not only, then, in the tenuous realms of philosophy, poetry, or literary criticism, but also—and more vehemently—in scientific, legal, and political arenas. Social scientists may draw inspiration from Sigmund Freud, who often used etymology to articulate his thought, as in his famous 1919 essay on *The*

1. Ernst Förstemann, "Über deutsche Volksetymologie," *Zeitschrift für vergleichende Sprachforschung* I (1852): 1–27, in Malkiel, *Etymology*, 21. See also Belardi, *L'etimologia*, 333ff.
2. An offhand search for etymology-related books at the Amazon bookseller website (http://www.amazon.com; accessed 3 November 2004) returns a plethora of popular (and intriguing) titles, ranging from traditional, "comprehensive" etymological dictionaries to semiplayful or satiric books on word origins and their possible uses. Oxford, Cambridge, Chambers, or Merriam-Webster dictionaries belong to the first group. An instance from the latter group is Richard McKee's bestseller *The Clan of the Flapdragon and Other Adventures in Etymology, by B. M. W. Schrapnel, Ph.D.* (Tuscaloosa: University of Alabama Press, 1997).

Uncanny; or from Frederick Engels, who elaborated upon the etymology of "family" in *The Origin of the Family, Private Property, and the State*.[3] Medical doctors might unexpectedly be found dabbling in word origins as they consult a reference work like Mohammad Diab's *Lexicon of Orthopaedic Etymology*.[4] And with the intent of sharing some of their findings, physicists may well decide to emulate Ralph Baierlein, who thought it worthwhile to speculate on the etymologies of *molecule* and *thermodynamics* in his 1999 volume on *Thermal Physics*.[5] Instances of etymologizing in legal, political, and religious publications abound. The supposed origin of countless terms (like "revolution," "democracy," "freedom," "law," "marriage," "family," "church," "state," "pagan," "heretic") is invoked and then supported or debunked in order to revise definitions, substantiate pleas, and serve specific agendas.[6]

---

3. Sigmund Freud, *The Uncanny*, trans David McLintock (New York: Penguin Books, 2003).

"The original meaning of the word 'family' (*familia*) is not that compound of sentimentality and domestic strife which forms the ideal of the present-day philistine; among the Romans it did not at first even refer to the married pair and their children, but only to the slaves. *Famulus* means domestic slave, and *familia* is the total number of slaves belonging to one man. As late as the time of Gaius, the *familia*, *id est patrimonium* (family, that is, the patrimony, the inheritance) was bequeathed by will. The term was invented by the Romans to denote a new social organism, whose head ruled over wife and children and a number of slaves, and was invested under Roman paternal power with rights of life and death over them all." Friedrich Engels, *The Origin of the Family, Private Property, and the State* [Ursprung der Familie, des Privateigentums und des Staats], in *Marx Engels Werke*, Band 21 (London: Electric Book Co., 2001), II:2.3.22. Within the field of the social sciences, one may of course just as effectively consider recent influential developments, as provided namely in the works of Jacques Lacan or Michel Foucault. Their ample recourse to etymology, however, is more self-conscious and has already been the object of extended attention. See for instance Jacques Lacan, *Speech and Language in Psychoanalysis*, trans. Anthony Wilden (Baltimore: Johns Hopkins University Press, 1981). Also Michel Foucault, *Fearless Speech*, ed. Joseph Pearson (Los Angeles: Semiotext(e), 2001). For a deconstructive use of etymology in literary criticism see especially Joseph Miller's "The Critic as Host," in Harold Bloom et al., *Deconstruction and Criticism* (New York: Seabury Press, 1979).

4. Mohammad Diab, *Lexicon of Orthopaedic Etymology* (Amsterdam: Harwood Academic Publishers, 1999).

5. Ralph Baierlein, *Thermal Physics* (Cambridge: Cambridge University Press, 1999).

6. A typical formula for arguments based on etymology will be something like "the original meaning/sense of the word/term x was." That is often the starting point from which inferences are drawn and claims made as to the efficacy, the appropriateness, or the political correctness of the word(s) being discussed. It is on the basis of such claims that definitions and redefinitions are then advocated. And, far from being the preserve of scholars or politicians, arguments from etymology are ubiquitous: even a search limited to online forums or Internet

Despite—or perhaps because of—all this, the prognosis of linguists is negative. Yakov Malkiel succinctly explains that "etymology no longer enters into mainline linguistics, except obliquely via diachrony, and the mere mention of it is redolent of irretrievable past enthusiasms, of something quaint, rather than of truly relevant present-day concerns and the common interests of keen minds."[7] The *International Encyclopedia of Linguistics* informs us that "etymology—as an aspect of linguistics, a scholarly activity, or a specimen of such activity—is widely recognized, but it is not a proper field in itself."[8] More explicitly, *The Encyclopedia of Language and Linguistics* warns that "the reputation of etymology among professional students of linguistic science has conceivably at no earlier juncture been so ill-defined and self-contradictory as it happens to be as the 1990s begin."[9]

Weblogs returns thousands of engaging instances, often to do with controversial, current issues, from war to same-sex marriage. A couple of examples from two disparate fields will suffice. In her 1981 essay *The Critical Difference*, Barbara Johnson used etymology to argue as follows: "Deconstruction is not synonymous with 'destruction,' however. It is in fact much closer to the original meaning of the word analysis itself, which etymologically means 'to undo'—a virtual synonym for 'to deconstruct.' The deconstruction of a text does not proceed by random doubt or arbitrary subversion, but by the careful teasing out of warring forces of signification within the text itself. If anything is destroyed in a deconstructive reading, it is not the text, but the claim to unequivocal domination of one mode of signifying over another. A deconstructive reading is a reading which analyses the specificity of a text's critical difference from itself." Barbara Johnson, *The Critical Difference: Essays in the Contemporary Rhetoric of Reading* (Baltimore: Johns Hopkins University Press, 1981). In an altogether dissimilar showground, an anonymous blog writer recently used a presumed, and intentionally suppressed, etymological link between "church" and "circus" to attack the club-like, controlled elitism of congregations: "Some years ago I did a research on the word church, and found that it came from a root word meaning circle, that the word was the basis of the word circus, because a circus used a circle/ring to perform their events. Hence, the word church means circle, it is where the people are brought together, and controlled as a group. That is the opposite of the word ecclesia which is called out from. I believe it is this difference between the two concepts that has allowed so much evil to exist today. Churches are more interested in their memberships, tithes and control than in a separated life to God. Oh by the way I might add the Bible dictionary I used was old, the new ones seem to have dropped that definition . . . happy hunting . . ." http://weblog.theviewfromthecore.com/2004_04/ind_003415.html (accessed 5 April 2004). The link between "church" and "circus" seems, in fact, unattested.

7. Malkiel, *Etymology*, 135.

8. The International Encyclopedia of Linguistics, ed. William Bright (Oxford: Oxford University Press, 1992).

9. The Encyclopedia of Language and Linguistics, ed. R. E. Asher and J. M. Y. Simpson (Oxford: Pergamon Press, 1994).

One can start to qualify these statements by running a computerized search of etymological entries in the second edition of the Oxford English Dictionary (OED) on CD-ROM.[10] Results show that more than 2,700 etymologies are defined as "obscure" and more than 1,200 carry the qualification of "uncertain," often in phrases like "of uncertain derivation." Around 1,300 are listed as "unknown," 748 as "doubtful," and a good number include conjectural adverbs like "probably." Given the approximate count of 290,500 lexical entries for this electronic edition of the OED, one may conservatively estimate that at least 3 percent of the total English corpus eludes rigorous etymological categorization.

However negligible this percentage may seem, it does more, I believe, than point to areas of language that still need to explained from the point of view of morphology, phonology, or semantics. For one, these "mysterious" etymologies remind us that conjectural practices survive—healthily—in the pages of an authoritative source such as the OED. More importantly, these etymologies point to the theoretical issues, the problems, and the inner tensions that etymology qua scientific discipline has faced and is still facing. The numerous, vexing questions recounted by Malkiel in connection with the low contemporary status of etymology bear witness to a continuing struggle.[11]

It is no coincidence that Pierre Guiraud (1912–1983), one of the controversial figures of twentieth-century etymology should begin his *Dictionnaire des étymologies obscures* in these words: "Obscure etymologies are numerous. We find 1,500 in a dictionary of 16,000 entries, 10,000 of which are learned words that do not pose a problem in terms of origin. Hence, the origin of twenty-five percent of entries in the French vocabulary (1,500–6,000) remain unexplained or poorly explained."[12]

10. *The Oxford English Dictionary on Historical Principles on CD-ROM*, 2nd ed. rev. (Oxford: Oxford University Press, 2002).
11. Malkiel, *Etymology*, 135–42.
12. Pierre Guiraud, *Dictionnaire des étymologies obscures* (Paris: Payot, 1982), 7.

Guiraud's work is, in a sense, already a symptom of the "malaise" and "loss of status" Malkiel diagnoses at the heart of etymological studies in the second half of the twentieth century.[13] The meaning and the repercussions of Guiraud's momentous endeavor will be tackled later. Here, drawing upon Malkiel's research, and with the aim to understand and contextualize etymology's current loss of prestige, I am going to look at salient vicissitudes that, in the course of the last two centuries, have given shape to what Alberto Zamboni called the "romance of etymology."[14]

Etymologizing before 1900

The birth of scientific etymology coincides with the rise of historical, or "diachronic," phonetics as practiced by German and Scandinavian scholars: the "Neogrammarians" of the late nineteenth century. Neogrammarians equated etymology with the one-way, strictly chronological reconstructions of "roots," which they unearthed by collating similar words at different evolutionary stages. Such roots were then organized hierarchically on the basis of predictable patterns of sound changes. Jacob Grimm's phonological "laws" are, in Malkiel's eyes, the single most influential factor of nineteenth-century scholarship: phonetics displaces morphology and marks "the rise to unprecedented prominence of linguistics."[15]

Despite differing priorities and shifts of focus, scholars like Franz Bopp (1791–1867), Friedrich Diez (1794–1876), Friedrich Pott (1802–87), Wilhelm Meyer-Lübke (1861–1936), and Michel Bréal (1832–1915) contributed to the *Sprachwissenschaft* that, at its zenith in 1900, comfortably straddled the realms of historico-comparative grammar and etymology. From Malkiel's thick description we can derive three main features of late nineteenth-century etymology to be dealt with below

13. Malkiel, Etymology, 135.   14. Zamboni, L'etimologia, 125.
15. Malkiel, Etymology, 7.

under separate headings: analytical stringency, chronological linearity, and reliance on morphology as opposed to meaning.

Analytical Stringency and Folk Etymology

When faced with the analytical rigor of the Neogrammarians, one must remember that academic etymology at the time relied on the empirical method and on theoretical positivism of the kind found in the prestigious realm of natural science. In Malkiel's words, "the transmutation of etymology into an esteemed and even admired academic discipline was . . . not exclusively, but to a large extent, due to this rapid expansion of its academic underpinning, which made progress time-consuming and subject to controls, and thus sharply curtailed the margin of free-wheeling, spontaneous guesswork."[16] Friedrich Diez's definition of etymology, juxtaposing a *kritische Methode* to an *unkritische Methode*, is symptomatic in this respect:

The task of etymology is to trace (*zurückzuführen*) a given word back to its origins. However, the method used to fulfill this task is not always the same. One can easily discern a critical (*kritische*) and an uncritical (*unkritische*) method. The uncritical method derives its interpretation randomly from a superficial similarity of forms or forces an interpretation if the similarity is only vague. Even when there is complete dissimilarity, interpretation is forced through a series of arbitrarily created middle-terms. Such a fundamentally flawed procedure, which nevertheless has some success where wit and divination abound, has in the eyes of many brought discredit on the whole art of etymology. The uncritical method endears itself to others thanks to its easiness, to which untrained people are inclined. . . . Unlike the uncritical method, the critical method is subject to the principles and rules that have been discovered in phonetics. No deviation is allowed from these principles, unless clear, factual exceptions demand otherwise. . . . The critical method weighs each letter and attempts to determine the individual worth that each letter should be accorded.[17]

Förstemann's comment on sound laws, cited at the beginning of this chapter, must be understood in the light of Diez's assertions. And to Förstemann's rigor must also be traced the current prejudice

---

16. Ibid., 16.

17. Quoted in Pierre Swiggers, "Le travail étymologique: typologie historique et analytique, perspectives, effets," in *Discours étymologiques*, ed. Jean-Pierre Chambon and Georges Lüdi (Freiburg: Max Niemeyer Verlag, 1991), 34.

against "popular" etymology. In his 1852 paper on "German Folk Etymology," Förstemann proposed that we distinguish between *gelehrte Etymologie* (scholarly etymology) and *Volksetymologie* ("popular etymology," mostly used to name strategies of semantic stretching and borrowing found in place-names).[18] Classic examples of the latter are the explication—or remotivation—of the Latinate and unintelligible "asparagus" into of the self-explanatory "sparrow grass" or, in a felicitous encounter of etymology and entomology, the Spanish "cucaracha," assimilated to a more Germanic-sounding "cockroach." The distinction between popular and learned etymology, liberally adopted by Anglophone and Francophone linguists, survives to this day in the tacit understanding of folk etymology as "false" or inferior to rigorous etymologizing.[19]

Of course, narrow characterizations of Neogrammarianism should be avoided, as Malkiel cautiously warns in his account of the historical events that turned etymology into a full-fledged discipline. While we cannot ignore the bias of scholars who later came to be named disparagingly *Lautschiebers* (soundshifters),[20] in the terrain of late nineteenth-century scholarship we should also be able to find the seeds of twentieth-century conjectural lexicology. So, for instance, by virtue of his groundbreaking work on onomastics, onomasiology, and phonosymbolism, Friedrich Pott must be credited at once with furthering Neogrammarian historicism and with having laid "the cornerstone for modern-day, 'pure etymology.'"[21] Pott's achievement exhibits the kind of complexity that combines "private conceptions of linguistics with ethnography, mythology, and other disciplines,"[22] relatively unpopular among *die Junggrammatiker*.[23]

---

18. Förstemann, "Über deutsche Volksetymologie," 1–27.
19. Malkiel, *Etymology*, 20.
20. Raimo Anttila, *Historical and Comparative Linguistics*, Amsterdam Studies in the Theory and History of Linguistic Science, Series IV: Current Issues in Linguistic Theory. 2nd rev. ed. (Philadelphia: Benjamins, 1989), 342.
21. Malkiel, *Etymology*, 14.   22. Ibid., 12.
23. One egregious exception is Jacob Grimm's *Deutsche Mythologie*, which employs lin-

Chronological Linearity

Late nineteenth-century scholars were convinced that etymology consisted of a thorough reconstruction of the chronological links a given word had entertained with other words over a period of time. And Neogrammarians took on the habit of using genealogical and botanical models to describe this kind of progression. In so doing, they were actually reviving a convention dating back to Latin grammarians of the fourth and fifth centuries AD, a convention that had been inherited by medieval scholastics and was now being incorporated, with suitable emendations, into "scientific etymology." More specifically, what nineteenth-century etymologists did was to integrate genealogical and botanical analogs into the models of "families" and of "tree diagrams," used to chart the chronological progress of a given linguistic "root" (the kind of one-line descent normally marked with the sign << or >>).[24]

Tree diagrams, it is true, soon proved inadequate. As early as 1856, Johannes Schmidt tried to address their shortcomings by proposing a "wave model," which envisioned relations between languages and words in terms of their arrangement along geographical or chronological boundaries (isoglossae). But despite Schmidt's innovative proposal, tree diagrams continued to prosper, are still common in historical linguistics,[25] and convey a chronological stringency that scholars have happily achieved by "purifying" premodern models. We might

---

guistics in the service of mythography. Jacob Grimm, *Deutsche Mythologie* (Berlin: Dummlers, 1875).

24. As a matter of fact, the key concept of "root" was already present in Indian scholarly speculations around the fifth century BC. See Alberto Zamboni, *L'etimologia*, 12–13. The concept came to the fore in conjunction with nineteenth-century comparatistic studies of Sanskrit; it anticipated the intensely morphological bent of some modern etymological endeavors, hence, for instance, the twentieth-century Russian custom of using *etimologija* as a synonym for morphology. And, in its systematic focus on morphology, historical linguistics led to the early-twentieth-century substitution of "derivation" for "etymology." As for the term "family tree," it is usually said to have been introduced by the German scholar August Schleicher in the middle of the nineteenth century. For an analysis of these and other terms see Robert Lawrence Trask, *Historical Linguistics* (London: Arnold, 1996), 182–87.

25. Trask, *Historical Linguistics*, 185.

say that Neogrammarians appropriated well-established metaphors and pruned their rhetorical implications and their philosophical ramifications to serve a rigorously quantitative analysis. One instance of this attitude survives in the preference, common among contemporary linguists, for a term like "lexical change" over the vague "etymology."[26] Peaceful but subtly significant coercions of this kind mark attempts to achieve a "neutral" language, purged of valuative biases and grounded in objectivity.

Importance of Form over Meaning

Most nineteenth-century scholars saw etymologizing as a painstaking, one-way, chronological reconstruction of links between words. What needs to be emphasized here is the quality of such links. For the third major trend in pre-1900 etymology consists in privileging form over meaning, in highlighting formal links (phonological, morphological, or semantic) at the expense of a range of historically bound senses. I am not of course trying to set up a dichotomy between form and meaning. What I am arguing is that linguistics, and in particular pre-1900 historical linguistics, precisely because of its "scientific" thrust, may have made opaque, or limited, the cognitive scope of meaning by reducing it to a series of formal features. And this is turn may have lead to etymologizing that is procedurally accurate but semantically faulty.

Let's look at one notorious example of this "faulty" etymologizing: Meyer-Lübke's etymology of *planta*,[27] criticized by Wartburg and Baldinger[28] and later mentioned by Zamboni.[29] Although "impeccable" from a phonological viewpoint, Meyer-Lübke's etymology is, as Baldinger notes, "false."[30] Italian *pianta*, Sardinian *pranta*, French

26. Terry Crowley, *An Introduction to Historical Linguistics*, 2nd ed. (Auckland: Oxford University Press, 1992), 37.
27. Wilhelm Meyer-Lübke, *Romanisches Etymologisches Wörterbuch*, 3d ed. (Heidelberg: Winter, 1930–1935), 6565.
28. Walther von Wartburg, *Etymologica* (Tübingen: Niemeyer, 1958).
29. Zamboni, *L'etimologia*, 28.
30. "Prenons l'exemple de *plante* et ouvrons notre Meyer-Lübke: il énumère les dérivés

plante, Provençal and Catalan *planta*, Spanish *llanta*, Portoguese *chan-ta*, and even German *Pflanze* and Old High German *Pflanza* do invite a transparent phonological (and semantic) deduction from the Latin word *planta*. But the Latin *planta* is not semantically congruent to *plant*. Unlike the abstract generic word *arbor* (tree), *planta* seems to have con-veyed the localized meaning of "scion" or "cutting." By adhering to a stringent comparatist method, Meyer-Lübke disregards the crucial se-mantic fact that French *plante* is not directly related to the classical Lat-in *planta*. Rather, *plante* derives from a later process of semantic gen-eralization that is grounded in the history of botanical science during the thirteenth and fourteenth centuries. One can, of course, excuse Meyer-Lübke's "error" as an instance of oversimplification. But one must also, inevitably, recognize the limits of his phono-semantic anal-ysis, removed from the historical events that, in Baldinger's words, are the background of word-biographies (*la biographie du mot*).[31] Baldinger claimed that one of the hardest tasks etymology will have to undertake is precisely establishing the creative milieu (*le milieu créateur*), the set of social, political, geographical circumstances that make the histories of words as convoluted and as fascinating as the histories of individu-al human beings: "It is a question of finding the link between the his-tory of the word and the history of humans as historical, social, and cultural beings."[32]

Along the same lines, Zamboni complained that the relationship

---

romans du latin *planta* 'Pflanze.' Un point, c'est tout! Pour Meyer-Lübke il n'y avait plus de problème étymologique, puisque du point de vue phonétique tout était en règle. Seulement, le latin *planta* 'Pflanze, plante' n'existe pas! . . . l'étymologie de Meyer-Lübke est *fausse* mal-gré la déduction phonétique impeccable." [Let us take the example of *planter* and open our Meyer-Lübke. It lists the Roman derivatives of the Latin *planta* (plant). Everything is settled in one point. For Meyer-Lübke there are no more etymological problems to discuss, since from a phonetic viewpoint everything works. The fact is that the Latin *planta* (plant) does not exist! . . . Meyer-Lübke's etymology is false despite his impeccable phonological deduction.] Kurt Baldinger, *Festschrift Walther von Wartburg zum 80. Geburtstag. 18 Mai 1968* (Tübingen: Niemeyer, 1968).

31. Kurt Baldinger, "L'étymologie hier et aujourd'hui," in *Die Faszination der Sprachwissen-schaft: ausgewählte Aufsätze zum 70. Geburtstag* (Tübingen: Niemeyer, 1990), 46.

32. Baldinger, "L'étymologie," 74.

between language and culture, albeit never denied, has been "put into the shade by certain streams of modern linguistics."[33] The relation to history does remain one of the major cruces of contemporary linguistics, torn between its quintessentially scientific, technical mission and the pressure of historical perspectives that break it up into multiple complementary branches: sociolinguistics, ethnolinguistics, psycholinguistics. To cite Zamboni, "while it is true that historicist trends are inherent in the methods [of scientific etymology], they remain, however, limited for the most part to the reconstruction of historical phases via linguistic phases" without due attention to the simultaneous presence (*covarianza*) of the two phases.[34] And once we accept Zamboni's critique of a strictly linguistic understanding of "history," rigorous nineteenth-century labels like "comparatist historicism" or "historical grammar" come to sound subtly deceptive.[35]

The *Wörter und Sachen* Experience: Etymology between 1900 and 1950

As we move to the first half of the twentieth century, we witness a perceptible shift from exacting *historische Wortforschung* to the kind of "etymological notes" adumbrated in Popp and embodied in the cultural-historical journal *Wörter und Sachen*. Launched in Heidelberg by Carl Winter in 1909, the journal reflected the controversial views of Hugo Schuchardt (1842–1927), "the scourge *par excellence*, of Neogrammarianism."[36] Lexis was given priority over phonetics; ethnography, mythology, archaeology, and folklore joined forces in the production of etymological word histories, conveniently published with "finely drawn pictures" and photographs documenting the "real things" sup-

33. Zamboni, *L'etimologia*, 148.

34. Zamboni, *L'etimologia*, 147.

35. For a discussion of the synchronic notion of history sanctioned by linguistics, namely in the Saussurean *Cours*, see Derek Attridge, *Peculiar Language: Literature as Difference from the Renaissance to James Joyce* (London: Methuen, 1988), 105.

36. Malkiel, *Etymology*, 24.

posedly signified in the given words. Concern with *realia* and attention to meaning were the two prevailing attitudes at the time: they underlie the lexicocentric studies of Jules Gilliéron (1854–1926), the witty etymological anecdotes of John Orr (1885–1966), and the monumental compilation of Walther von Wartburg's (1920–1970) *Französiches etymologisches Wörterbuch*. Scholars gradually abandoned strict diachronic phonetics because they could count on a wealthier and more sophisticated reading public, willing to be "titillated by colorful, exotic, or amusing anecdotal word histories."[37] By the first decade of the twentieth century, phonological laws were invoked only indirectly, and various hypotheses dealing with multiple causation gained momentum. Etymologists started to explore phenomena such as collision of homonyms, false restoration (or regression), phonosymbolic effects, or even playful alteration. At the same time, they developed a new "historical" perception of etymological events grounded in geography, onomastics, and topology, a perception that marked the appearance of "extra-heavy documentation," unknown in the previous century but uncompromisingly embraced by early twentieth-century scholars. Reactions to this new etymologizing by anecdotes started to circulate soon and found authoritative voices in the work of Antoine Meillet and his eminent colleagues from the Parisian circle: Alfred Ernout, Émile Benveniste, Michel Lejeune. Their influential views sanctioned the ongoing assimilation of etymology to lexicology, the latter term increasingly preferred to the ontologism and romantic amateurishness evoked by the former. Toward the middle of the century, figures like Edward Sapir and Otto Jespersen drew converts to linguistics. And in Malkiel's view, the prestige of linguistics, de facto relegating etymology to lexicological analysis, is one of the decisive forces whereby etymology starts to be treated with condescension.

All the factors seen so far finally converge in the composite landscape of contemporary etymological studies. The current prevailing

37. Ibid., 43.

sentiment among scholars is that "etymological curiosity and skill represent something definitely old-fashioned, passé, a quaint orientation reconcilable, at best, with John Orr's odd scale of values but not with a modernist, progressive view of language research traceable, in the final analysis, to Ferdinand de Saussure's *Cours de linguistique générale*."[38] And the unfaltering prestige of Saussure's work certainly calls for some extended consideration before we direct our attention to contemporary etymology.

De Saussure and the Arbitrariness of Signs

The notion of "arbitrariness" that we are going to examine in this section has to do with the concept of "folk etymology," to which Saussure in his *Cours* devotes more than a passing mention (TRC: 3, VI). Among the examples of "*étymologie populaire*," Saussure listed Old French *soufraite* ("deprivation," from the Latin *suffracta << subfrangere*), giving the adjective *souffreteux* (sickly), often erroneously related to *souffrir* (suffer), "with which it has nothing in common" (CGL: 174). Lexical adaptations of this kind, Saussure noted, are not as haphazard as they may appear. Rather, they are "crude attempts to explain refractory words by relating them to something known" (CGL: 173), hence the appellation "*étymologie populaire*" (TRC: 3 VI, al. 2). Saussure's approach is interesting because it attempts to explain the difference between *étymologie populaire* and *analogie*—both due to a process of morphological association—via a typology of folk etymologies and not

38. Ibid. Since a few relevant passages are absent from the standard English edition by Bally and Sechehaye (*Course in General Linguistics*, ed. Charles Bally and Albert Sechehaye, trans. and annot. Roy Harris, with the collaboration of Albert Riedlinger [LaSalle, Ill.: Open Court, 1986]), I will cite three sources with reference to Saussure's *Cours*: (1) Ferdinand de Saussure, *Cours de linguistique générale*, ed. Rudolf Engler (Wiesbaden: Harrassowitz, 1967); henceforth COURSL. (2) Ferdinand de Saussure, *Course in General Linguistics*, trans. Wade Baskin (London: Fontana, 1974); henceforth CGL. (3) Ferdinand de Saussure, *Troisième cours de linguistique générale (1910–1911): d'apres les cahiers d'Emile Constantin. Saussure's third course of lectures on general linguistics (1910–1911): from the notebooks of Emile Constantin*, ed. Eisuke Komatsu (Oxford: Pergamon Press, 1993); henceforth TRC. References for citations from the English translation are appended to the corresponding passages in French, given in notes.

simply in terms of a dichotomy between "rational" and "haphazard." A first category comprises those numerous folk etymologies that affect the meaning of a word without changing its form explicitly (CGL: 174–75, and TRC: VI, al. 4), as in the case of colloquial German *durchbläuen* (to thrash soundly), often related to *blau* (blue, possibly on account of the bluish bruises left by flogging) but actually originating from Old High German *bliuwan* (to flog, from *bleuel* mallet). Other categories include instances of suffixal adaptation by analogy with common endings (as in the French *homard* [lobster] with a final -d inserted by analogy with the common -*ard* suffix), or recombination of foreign-sounding terms into familiar elements (as in the German *Trampeltier*, dromedary, recombined as *trampeln* plus *Tier*). The common denominator ("pure and simple interpretations of misunderstood forms in terms of known forms")[39] would seem to imply that analogy and folk etymology are both strategies of reinterpretation (*Umdeutung*). Yet, Saussure brilliantly notes that analogy is based on the forgetting (*oubli*) of a previous form, while folk etymology is based on remembering (*souvenir*) an anterior form: "Thus, the fact that in one case remembering and in the other forgetting are at the base of analysis, builds up an insurmountable barrier between folk etymology and analogy."[40]

For one thing, Saussure highlights the peculiarity of folk etymology as a process that occurs only under *conditions particulières*, with borrowings, technical jargon, or rare words imperfectly assimilated by a speaker. And his remarks on the memorative quality of etymology will be useful when I assess the cognitive scope of allegorical etymology. On the other hand, Saussure bluntly dismisses *étymologie populaire* in favor of analogy. *L'étymologie populaire est un phénomène pathologique*, almost *vicieux*, Saussure concludes, and as such it must be emphatically

---

39. [Interprétations pures et simples de formes incomprises par des formes connues] (TRC: 3 VI, al.7)(CGL: 175).

40. [Donc le fait que dans l'une c'est l'oubli et dans l'autre le souvenir <<qui est à la base de l'analyse>> dresse une barrière infranchissable entre l'etymologie populaire et l'analogie.] (TRC: I, R 3.10)

(*soigneusement*) distinguished from analogy, which instead "belongs to the normal functioning of language" [appartient au fonctionnement normal de la langue].[41] Only analogy, the creative principle of language, deserves to be called "formation." Folk etymology, on the contrary, is stigmatized as a "*déformation*" (TRC: I R 3.11).

Given the influence to this day of Saussure's work on linguistic practice, these comments on folk etymology are compelling. Equally significant is the fact that etymology itself should figure in the critical edition of Saussure's *Cours* only in a four-page appendix to section three, covering "*linguistique diachronique*." Even in its formal layout, Saussure's work foreshadows the current relegation of etymology, whose existence is hardly acknowledged beyond (or even within) the all-embracing domain of linguistics. In Saussure's definition, etymology is not a discipline or even a fraction of a discipline: "Etymology is neither a distinct discipline nor a division of evolutionary linguistics. It is only a special application of the principles that relate to synchronic and diachronic facts. It goes back into the history of words until it finds something to explain them."[42]

The word "etymology," he asserts, brings to mind "the origin or provenance of a word" [origine ou provenance d'un mot], but in so doing it reveals a fundamental ambiguity, whereby diachronic and synchronic explanations are improperly fused. Phonetic alteration, semantic alteration, and phonosemantic alteration (as French *chair* <<flesh>> from Latin *caro*; or French *labourer* <<to till>> from Latin *laborare* <<to work>>) establish links between previously unrelated words across time. Yet, grammatical derivation (as in French *pommi-*

41. (CGL: 78)(TRC: 3 VI, al. 10 and I, R 3.3) Noting this same passage, later expunged by the editors from the final version of the course, Derek Attridge comments upon the "unexpected animus" shown by Saussure toward folk etymology and spelling pronunciation. Attridge, *Peculiar Language*, 112–13).

42. [L'étymologie n'est ni une discipline distincte ni une partie de la linguistique évolutive; c'est seulement une application spéciale des principes relatifs aux faits syncroniques et diachroniques. Elle remonte dans le passé des mots jusqu'à ce qu'elle trouve quelque choses qui les explique.] (CGL: 189)(COURSL: App. C, al. 1)

er from French *pomme*) functions *within* the language system and does not imply provenance from an earlier form. Because etymology establishes synchronic and diachronic links between words, and because, by virtue of the famous Saussurean axiom (CGL: 67, and CRS: I 2 al.1; I 2 al.3), words as linguistic signs are essentially arbitrary, Saussure concludes that etymology is a purely linguistic phenomenon: "the explaining of words through the historical study of their relationship with other words."[43] Just like linguistics, etymology describes linguistic facts, but it is woefully blemished by a lack of method as it borrows information haphazardly from phonetics, morphology, or semantics. It even lacks linguistics' metalanguage, its ability to reflect on the linguistic operations one performs when one makes etymological reconstructions.

Ultimately, Saussure's dismissal of etymology is rooted in the ambiguous notion of "arbitrariness," the cornerstone of modern linguistic theory. "The sham of arbitrariness," as John Joseph argued in his brilliant *Limiting the Arbitrary*, is in fact but one of the cruxes in "a work which, with its complex textual history, offers no end of problems and inconsistencies."[44] Joseph has convincingly exposed the treacherous workings of Saussurean arbitrariness by showing how it is in fact jarringly tied to the competing dogma of systematicity.[45] The link that unites a given concept (signified) to its acoustic image (signifier) is "radically (*radicalement*) arbitrary. Everyone agrees" (CGL: 76).[46]

---

43. (CGL: 189). The English translation introduces the ambiguous term "historical research" where the French has only "recherche de rapports": "l'explication des mots par la recherche de leurs rapports avec d'autres mots." (COURSL: App. C, al. 4).

44. John Joseph, *Limiting the Arbitrary: Linguistic Naturalism and Its Opposites in Plato's Cratylus and the Modern Theories of Language* (Amsterdam: Benjamins, 2000).

45. Joseph remarks that Saussure puts "these two things, arbitrariness and systematicity, in direct opposition to one another, such that the one represents the limitation of the other." This is the starting point for Joseph's insightful analysis of the common pattern underlying the history of Western linguistics from ancient times to the present. For Joseph, Saussure's own theory is yet another instance of the dichotomizing attitude at work in the protracted, unsolved "debate over whether language is natural or conventional." Joseph, *Limiting the Arbitrary*, 1.

46. Joseph acutely notes that "Saussure and his contemporaries no longer discourse

The link does not imply any kind of "interior," mimetic analogy between language and the conceptual world. Even writing obeys linguistic laws that go beyond individual or collective motivations and follow language's own "fatal evolution" (TRC: G 1.2).

It comes as no surprise therefore that the concept of arbitrariness (the core of the Saussurean approach to language) should have undergone, in the hands of more or less orthodox followers, considerable alterations. Following an increasingly multidisciplinary trend, linguists (especially those ethnographically trained) seem willing to acknowledge with greater emphasis, for instance, the impact that motivational, mimological patterns have on word formation and change.[47] As Joseph put it, "modern linguistics talks the conventionalist talk, but walks the naturalist walk."[48]

Saussure himself was not blind to the mimetism inherent in sym-

---

openly about the 'natural' in language; it seems too vague, even spiritualistic a notion in their positivistic age. Overtly, the CGL passes beyond conventionalism to assert the radical arbitrariness of language." Joseph, Limiting the Arbitrary, 126.

47. Kurt Baldinger, for instance, distinguishes between primary and secondary motivation: "In most words, the motivation is not primary, that is, they are not motivated by reality. Nevertheless, we must quickly add that secondary motivations are extremely frequent." Baldinger, L'étymologie, 10. Raimo Anttila notes that "arbitrariness is outside the nucleus of the sign itself—it is in the outer shape and the semantic range." Anttila, Historical and Comparative Linguistics, 13–14. The issue is still controversial, although most scholars seem to agree that the doctrine of arbitrariness tout court in the case of linguistic signs is untenable. For a discussion of how Saussurean arbitrariness bears upon historiography, see Derek Attridge's "Language as History/History as Language: Saussure and the Romance of Etymology," in Post-Structuralism and the Question of History, ed. Geoff Bennington and Robert Young, 90–126 (Cambridge: Cambridge University Press, 1989). Joseph recently noted the dubious practice whereby linguists tend to set up a distinction between "marked" and "unmarked" language, while at the same time professing full adherence to a supposedly Saussurean principle of arbitrariness. Joseph, Limiting the Arbitrary, 2ff. For a comprehensive account of the mechanisms involved in language change, one should turn to April McMahon's Understanding Language Change (Cambridge: Cambridge University Press, 1994). Chapter 7, pages 174–90, of McMahon's book, on semantic and lexical change, is especially relevant to our discourse, although her discussion of arbitrariness (176–77) somehow perpetuates the haziness that Joseph detected in Saussure's own treatment of the subject. Sociolinguistic mechanisms involved in language change are analyzed in Jean Aitchison's Language Change: Progress or Decay? (Cambridge: Cambridge University Press, 2001).

48. "First, while it is true that linguists claim to be in consensus about the arbitrariness of language, if you look at the rest of what they actually teach and write, you find them treating language as not arbitrary at all, but determined by, or grounded in, something outside itself." Joseph, Limiting the Arbitrary, 2.

bols and warned linguists against the danger of using "symbol" as a synonym for "sign": "the linguistic symbol is never empty; there is at least a rudimentary connexion between the idea and that which acts as its sign."[49] De facto, however, Saussure's *Cours* asserts a linguistic doctrine that places arbitrariness "right at the top" of a true hierarchy from which most linguistic considerations, like "hidden consequences of that truth," originate (TRC: 76). Hence, perhaps the present reluctance among linguists to allow for extrasystemic factors—such as the ones entertained by etymology—that threaten to pollute its scientific nature. Hence, also, the distrust among literary schools variously indebted to linguistics, of approaches that contravene those tacit assumptions.[50] What happens is that a legitimate intrasystemic claim about the relation of phonetic sequences to a supposed meaning is made to bear only on extrasystemic matter, on concepts and on the perceptual *realia* that these supposedly denote.[51]

In her work on historical semantics, Eve Sweetser has addressed the "areas of interdependency between cognition and language."[52] Arguing against the overextension of Boolean feature-based phonetics to the realm of semantics, she has observed that, while "to many linguists, the non-phonological side of etymology appears inherently non-scientific,"[53] research corroborates the commonsensical notion

49. [Le symbole n'est jamais vide; il y a au moins un rudiment de lien entre l'idée er ce qui lui sert de signe.] (CGL: 76a) For a discussion of the controversial notion of "arbitrariness" in Saussure see also Belardi, *L'etimologia*, 63–84.

50. Albeit from a poststructuralist viewpoint, Derek Attridge seems to corroborate this conclusion when he notes that "it is rare to find a linguist who accepts that changes in language, or resistances to change, which result from prescriptivism, of however misguided a variety, are as much part of the evolution of language as any other change, and who accepts that to think otherwise is to introduce prescriptivism into linguistics itself." Attridge, *Peculiar Language*, 115.

51. The intrasystemic/extrasystemic dichotomy is, of course, purely methodological, but it does go against the grain of much current, poststructuralist critique of Western binary logic, most prominently voiced in the works of Paul de Man and Jacques Derrida. I discuss poststructuralism with regard to etymology in chapter 6.

52. Eve Sweetser, *From Etymology to Pragmatics: Metaphorical and Cultural Aspects of Semantic Structure*, Cambridge Studies in Linguistics 54 (Cambridge: Cambridge University Press, 1990), 7.

53. Ibid., 23.

that "our linguistic system is inextricably interwoven with the rest of our physical and cognitive selves" and that "humans . . . share a great deal of prelinguistic and extralinguistic experience which is likely to shape language rather than to be shaped by it."[54] On arbitrariness, Sweetser comments:

> . . . in I see the tree, it is an arbitrary fact that the sequence of sounds which we spell see . . . is used in English to refer to vision. But, given this arbitrary fact, it is by no means arbitrary that see can also mean "know" or "understand," as in I see what you're getting at. There is a very good reason why see rather than, say, kick or sit, or some other sensory verb such as smell, is used to express knowledge and understanding. Such motivated relationships between word meanings are as much a part of the study of semantics as inference. But the fact that see can also mean "know" has little to do with truth conditions.[55]

Again, arbitrariness may well be one of the distinctive features of a sign's shape,[56] but we cannot fail to "see in every language a slow but certain progress in adaptation to the forms of experience."[57] If it seems reasonable, as Lev Vygotsky claimed in 1934, that thought and speech are inseparably interwoven, both phylogenetically and ontogenetically, it must also be granted that an exclusively linguistic approach to language offers only a partial view.

Punning on Saussure's own words, one can reverse his statement and submit that often the signifier/signified link in fact turns out to be "radically" (radicalement, i.e., etymologically) nonarbitrary, implicated as it is with vicissitudes of history, culture, and time. As Raimo Anttila says, "the makeup of the linguistic sign is not arbitrary, but necessary. . . . What is arbitrary is that a particular sign be connected with a particular element of the 'real world.' The connection itself is not arbitrary."[58]

54. Ibid., 6–7.

55. Ibid., 5. A full discussion of Sweetser's model can be found in chapter 8.

56. Anttila, Historical and Comparative Linguistics, 13.

57. Leonard Bloomfield, An Introduction to the Study of Language, Amsterdam Studies in the Theory and History of Linguistic Science, Series II, Vol. 3, Classics in Psycholinguistics, new ed. (Amsterdam: Benjamins, 1983), 253.

58. Anttila, Historical and Comparative Linguistics, 13 (his emphasis). See also Giovanni Bot-

Obscure Words: Etymologizing from 1950 to the Present

Returning to an overview of etymology's history in the course of the twentieth century, we cannot fail to notice that it is precisely with unconcealed aversion to the Saussurean dogma that Pierre Guiraud undertook the heterodox task of "wading through the by-ways of lexis"[59] and clarifying muddled etymologies. His *Structures étymologiques du lexique français* and his *Dictionnaire des étymologies obscures* rely on a multidimensional notion of etymological phenomena, a notion resulting from the compromise between several hypothetical processes (blending, borrowing, rapproachment, derivation, suffixation, homonymy, phonosymbolism). Although, Guiraud argues, "the problem of the arbitrariness of signs has lost much of its urgency" after the revisionist interventions of Emile Benveniste (*Nature du signe linguistique*) and Roman Jakobson (*A la recherche de l'essence du langage*), the issue of motivation "constitutes one of the fundamental postulates of [his present] study" [la motivation du signe constitue un des postulats fondamentaux de notre etude].[60] Three important observations follow. The first has to do with the notion of motivation. Etymology is often criticized for attempting to establish patterns of motivation, be they intra- or extralinguistic, and folk etymology is held to be the most notorious culprit in a practice that flies in the face of linguistics' pledge to "study language in and for itself."[61] However:

If the sign is very often arbitrary at the level of second articulation, at the level of first articulation (the level of monemes), the sign is always motivated; i.e., there is always a relation between the form of the signifier and that of the signified. Having granted that, we find that this etymological motivation may become obscure—and it does in a large number of cases—but this accidental *demotivation* at the level of the sign construct is an altogether different thing from the *arbitrariness* at the level of phonemes.[62]

---

tiroli's intriguing comments on Saussurean arbitrariness in *Jacques Lacan: Arte, Linguaggio, Desiderio* (Bergamo: Bergamo University Press, 2002), 19ff.

59. Malkiel, *Etymology*, 127.   60. Guiraud, *Structures*, 195.
61. Ibid., 232.
62. Ibid., 195. [Le problème de l'arbitraire du signe a perdu de son acuité. . . . Mais la

Secondly, Guiraud establishes that motivation is double ("la mo-tivation, donc, est double: semiologique et étymologique"). Besides semiotic motivation (motivation sémiologique), we encounter etymological moti-vation (motivation étymologique), as the sign relates to the etymon from which it derives through the mechanisms of morphology (affixation), semantics (change in meaning), or onomatopeia.[63] Finally, Guiraud proposes that a given etymon functions as a third term of mediation, a sort of catalyst, between the signifier and the signified. "Motiva-tion integrates the etymon into signification: its makes the sense pass through an etymon which constitutes a third term, mediating between the signifier and the signified and functioning as a relay, at once signi-fier and signified."[64]

Guiraud rehabilitates motivation as part of his wider effort "to re-duce the gap between descriptive linguistics and historical linguis-tics."[65] As the title of his Structures étymologiques du lexique français indi-cates, Guiraud employs structuralist concepts but rejects a one-way structuralist approach and highlights its shortcomings "which bring into question the traditional concepts of langue-parole, diachrony-synchrony, arbitrariness-motivation, system-history."[66] The same con-cern is present ten years later in his Dictionnaire: "One can see then how, while structuralism has removed the impasses of historical lin-guistics, it has also found itself hindered within its own limits, limits which new grammars (transformational, generative) attempt to over-come. We attempt to overcome it in history, through the integration

motivation du signe constitue un des postulats fondamentaux de notre étude... Si le signe est très souvent arbitraire en deuxième articulation, en première articulation (au niveau des monèmes), il est toujours motivé; c'est-à-dire qu'il ya a toujours une relation entre la forme du signifiant et celle du signifié. Ceci dit, cètte motivation étymologique peut s'obscurcir—et s'obscurcit dans une grande partie des cas—mais cette démotivation accidentelle au niveau du signe construit est tout autre chose que l'arbitraire au niveau des phonèmes.] In linguistics, the concept of double articulation refers to "duality in language: that is, the coexistence of systems like the two sides of a coin, the medium (either speech or writing) and the message (grammar lexis)." The Oxford Companion to the English Language, ed. Tom McArthur (Oxford: Oxford Univer-sity Press, 1992), v. articulation.

63. Guiraud, Structures, 195–96.   64. Ibid., 197.
65. Ibid., 7.   66. Ibid., 189.

of external data within the structural model."[67] Similar lines of inquiry, crowned with the continued academic success of which Guiraud was unjustly deprived, are followed by Bruno Migliorini (1896–1975). Despite different slants, Migliorini and Guiraud share an interest in neologisms and literary history: they both shun strictly phonological analyses in favor of fragmentary, vignette-like etymological essays.

Fragmentation could very well be taken as the main feature of late twentieth-century etymology, riddled by "irreconcilably conflicting ideas"[68] and simultaneously marked by the demise of German scholarship and the rise of competing national schools (French, Italian, Spanish, British) mainly devoted to the vernacular. Zamboni concluded his discussion of modern etymology with the remark that "probably no other science is so tightly linked to contingent limitations, a fact that is largely responsible for the adventurous, individual tinge of etymological research."[69] Etymology must take into account numerous and varied parameters. While its technical roots are canonically linguistic, it is obvious that etymology presupposes "a specific knowledge of abstract or concrete referents" involving, above all, history in its various forms: geography, politics, economics, et cetera.[70]

As a defensive strategy, Zamboni recommends emphasizing the "internal necessity of etymology" [la necessità interna dell'etimologia] and, despite undeniable "anomalies" [anomalie], its essentially linguistic character. In fact, subordination of etymology to a history of culture must be avoided as detrimental both to linguistics and to etymology. The scientific bases of etymology must be strengthened and its methodological tools refined to stave off "the realm of vagueness and subjectivity" [il dominio del vago e del soggettivo] to which several—otherwise even appreciable—speculations have fallen prey. But twenty years after Zamboni's pronouncements, the status of scientific etymology does not seem to have improved. Nor does linguistics seem

67. Guiraud, Dictionnaire, 170.   68. Malkiel, Etymology, 105.
69. Zamboni, L'etimologia, 100.   70. Ibid.

to have exerted the kind of benign influence that he predicted. Robert Trask gives us an idea of etymology's current plight when, in his 1996 textbook *Historical Linguistics*, he introduces a five-page section on etymology by noting that he knows "of no other textbook which devotes any space to the subject" and "of no single textbook on etymology." The reason has to be sought, he says, in the fact that etymology forces us to come to grips with details and the particular, while most linguists favor general principles. Having candidly acknowledged that etymology is a fascinating subject, Trask laments the "very peripheral position" to which etymology is relegated in the discipline and comments on the scarcity of space allotted to etymologies and etymologists in major journals of linguistics.[71]

A more thorough analysis of the factors responsible for etymology's "rapid loss of status" is found at the end of Malkiel's book. Among these factors we find (1) a general scholarly preference for synchrony over diachrony, at the expense of "dead languages"; (2) the lack of tightly phrased, technical language in etymological studies; (3) the relative lapse of disciplines traditionally allied with etymology (e.g., archaeology, mythology) in favor of more fashionable pursuits (e.g., logic, statistics, mathematics, cognitive theory); (4) the subjectivity inherent in etymological conjectures; (5) the staggering number of variables to be accounted for, as well as "the complexity of their patterns of intertwining in the procreation of a given lexeme."[72] The description of the "pure etymologist," which concludes the long list compiled by Malkiel, paints an eloquent portrait of the etymologist's position in the present world: "unpleasantly enough [the pure etymologist] runs the risk of adversely impressing the community of scholars to which he inescapably belongs as a belated romantic, a sort of straggling daydreamer and intuitivist who is out of tune with the rationally organized and smoothly functioning academic environment."[73]

71. Trask, *Historical Linguistics*, 345.   72. Malkiel, *Etymology*, 135–36.
73. Ibid., 140.

There have been attempts to boost etymology's prestige by hold-
ing it to strict quantitative standards. One of the most recent is Gereon
Franken's book, appropriately entitled *Systematische Etymologie: Untersuchungen einer 'Mischsprache' am Beispiel des Shakespeare-Worstchatzes*. Franken contends that "etymology is loosening its ties from a diachronic,
historical-comparative linguistics and is increasingly coming under
the influence of a systematically oriented, synchronic linguistics."[74] He
welcomes an etymological approach based on the synchronic analysis
of whole sets of lexemes (*der Wortschatz als ganz*), rather than on word
histories, on the basis of their distribution. Through a painstaking
computation of many lexical mechanisms (e.g., loan, loan-derivation,
compound, alternation, conversion) within Shakespeare's corpus,
Franken draws statistically based charts of "etymological" occurrences
that give Shakespeare's plays their often-noted aspect of lexical diversity (*Mischsprache*).

However commendable, Franken's study obviously fails to account
for the many, and arguably more crucial, sides of Shakespearean etymology that are not computable—sides that, enmeshed in the dense
network of Shakespeare's text, so powerfully alter and shape its rhetorical contours.[75] If anything, the rigor of Franken's analysis highlights the fact that etymology can only be equated with computational
lexicography at the price of the same severe curtailment of jurisdiction
to which it has been long subjected.

There have also been attempts, in the field of literary criticism,
to vindicate the power of etymology as "a versatile ideological weapon" by celebrating its fluid rhetoricity, its "status as imaginative storytelling" that makes it so similar to all historical writing. These are
Derek Attridge's views as expressed in "Language as History/History

74. Gereon Franken, *Systematische Etymologie: Untersuchungen einer 'Mischsprache' am Beispiel
des Shakespeare-Wortschatzes*, Anglistische Forschungen 228 (Heidelberg: Universitartsverlag C.
Winter, 1995), 25.

75. These have been discussed in part by Marvin Spevack in "Etymology in Shakespeare,"
in *Shakespeare's Universe: Renaissance Ideas and Conventions: Essays in Honour of W. R. Elton*, ed. John
M. Mucciolo, 187–94 (Aldershot, England: Scolar Press, 1996).

as Language: Saussure and the Romance of Etymology," an essay intended as a "story" of Saussure's ambiguous views on etymology with a view to refuting accusations against his "balefully ahistorical" synchronic theory.[76] According to Attridge, Saussure's merit lies in the fact that his theory replaces mythic notions of an authentic meaning "[with] the meanings possessed for a specific group at a specific time," thereby "open[ing] the door to history."[77] On the contrary, "philological etymology" (of the kind entertained up to the twentieth century) simply "drains [history] of its heterogeneity and materiality[,] substituting the myth of Progress for the myth of the Golden Age which inspired earlier etymological adventures."[78] Thus, Attridge concludes, Saussure's synchronic theory has paved the way for a consideration of etymology, and of history, that is not naïvely teleological but can be used to challenge authority without unwanted truth claims.[79] While I sympathize with Attridge's questioning of scientific and historical objectivism and welcome his rediscovery of etymology's rhetorical prowess, I disagree with his conflation of history and culture with language. Insofar as—in his "problematizing" of history—Attridge tout court equates etymology with wordplay and history with contingent storytelling (both more or less ideologically charged and more or less socially subversive), his assumptions seem to me very much entrenched within the pan-synchronism that they purport to expose. In this sense, his appropriation of etymology is not very different from Franken's objectivist stance.

It remains to be considered whether etymology has any standing at all outside of linguistics (within which it has almost completely lost its voice) and whether and how, after linguistics' apparent dis-

---

76. Attridge, *Peculiar Language*, 120–21. 77. Ibid., 101.
78. Ibid., 104.
79. "Etymology can be used, as we have seen, to confirm a dominant ideology, to deny the possibility of purposeful change, to reinforce the myth of objective and transcendent truth; but it can also be used to unsettle ideology, to uncover opportunities for change, to undermine absolutes and authority—and to do so without setting up an alternative and equally challengeable truth-claim." Ibid., 122.

owning of etymology as a science, etymology can continue to figure as a legitimate line of inquiry. These questions require for one thing that we touch upon some of linguistics' claims with regard to the relation between language and culture, and also that we reassess the fuzzy, rhetorical elements inherent in the rigorously scientific schema of which etymology falls so disgracefully short. The debate surrounding language and culture is as old as history itself, and it is certainly not my intention to map the maze of disquisitions spun on the subject over centuries of scholarship. Yet, etymology's curious bracketing of language and history calls for a few comments. Among linguists, reluctance to trace ample correlations between language and culture in favor of a more systematic, predominantly phonological approach may have been justified by the impressionistic excesses of early nineteenth-century idealism. Yet, as Anttila pointed out and more linguists seem willing to admit, it must be recognized that "the Neogrammarians' emphasis on the independent linguistic side has led to a historical linguistics without history"[80] and that linguistics cannot continue to gloss over one aspect of its subject just because it eludes systematic formalization. If, as is apparently happening, historical and cultural factors are brought to bear upon linguistics *qua* science, then it will also be necessary to reconsider the position and the importance of disciplines like philology and etymology *independently* of purely linguistic, phonological dictates. As Ottavio Lurati puts it, "we are less and less content with a phonetic etymology. We must move on with determination to an etymology of cultural type, anxious to link more systematically linguistic data with particular forms of human existence."[81] And even stronger would be the justification for philology and etymology in the unlikely event that linguistics, confident in its formalistic thrust, should renounce all claims to an understanding of culture. An entire chapter in Zamboni's monograph is devoted

80. Anttila, *Historical and Comparative Linguistics*, 323.
81. Ottavio Lurati, "Étymologie et anthropologie culturelle," in Chambon and Lüdi, *Discours étymologiques*, 315.

to a number of theoretical perspectives that challenge or complement linguistics' views of etymology along the lines of inquiry already established in 1846 by A. G. Schlegel when he distinguished between philosophical etymology, grammatical etymology, and historical etymology.[82] One could view modern etymology—in its morphological and phonological emphasis—as the result and the systematization of grammatical etymology, always present in the linguistic speculations of premodern scholars, as in Varro's De Lingua Latina. It should be kept in mind, however, that premodern notions of grammar were never completely severed from the historical, philosophical, and rhetorical factors which influential branches of modern linguistics are so careful to shun. The definition of "etymology" provided by Eric Hamp in the *International Encyclopedia of Linguistics* seems to follow this aspiration to scientific asepticity: the etymology of a word is supposed "to respect, but not to explicate, its synchronic grammatical constitution, and primarily to trace its form and meaning back in time or forward from a stated point." In aptly technical terms, "an etymology is an excerpt, over a selected bundle of morphonological and semantic features, from the known historical grammar(s) of a set of culturally connected language stages."[83] History is admitted to etymological research only via metalinguistic, and more specifically grammatical, utterances.[84] Still, it suffices to recall the contributions to a sociology of language made in the nineteenth and early twentieth centuries by Durkheim, Bally, Vossler, Vendryès, and Devoto or the previously cited geographical studies of Gilliéron to realize the importance and the currency of the question

82. Auguste-Guillaume Schlegel, De l'étymologie en général (Leipzig, 1846), cited by Zamboni, L'etimologia, 1.

83. International Encyclopedia of Linguistics, 426.

84. See for instance the definition given by Theodora Bynon, Historical Linguistics (Cambridge: Cambridge University Press, 1977), 62: "The etymology of a word is thus its formal and semantic history traced back in time until an earlier grammar, or the grammar of a donor language is reached, the productive rules of which can fully account for it. . . . The establishment of an etymological connection between words of different languages or language states thus demands that the sound correspondences be regular and that the semantic developments be plausible."

surrounding the "tight connection between etymology and history of culture."[85] The kind of *approche étymologique transversale* championed by Lurati in his article on etymology and cultural anthropology rediscovers Baldinger's idea of the creative milieu (*milieu créateur*) in which given words emerge.[86] Etymologizing is therefore not only, and not much, positing well-formed phonological or morphological cross-references. It is, rather, tracing the copresence of different etymological senses, within ample conceptual groups that gives us a measure of the ideological and cultural momentum of given lexical units.[87]

Neologisms provide fertile ground for this kind of inquiry and justify the claims for an extension of the etymological field beyond linguistics. Lurati cites the Italian locution *angelo del ciclostile* (angel of the copy machine), an ideological formation (Kristeva's *idéologème*) coined by Italian feminists in the 1960s to denounce the secondary role assigned to women within the student movement. The polemic nuances of this expression, clearly parodying bourgeois role prescriptions, point to semantic mechanisms apparently at work both in traditional *topoi* like the nineteenth-century coinage "struggle for life" and in neologisms such as "surrogate mother" or "latchkey children," for which Lurati finds equivalents in French, Spanish, German, and Italian. At the core of this confluence between language and history are the "problem of linguistic relativity" [il problema della relatività linguistica] and the "influence of ambience on lexis" [l'influenza dell'ambiente sul lessico].[88] Leonard Bloomfield voiced an old but sensible opinion when he argued that "the history of words, etymology, is interesting to the student of civilization and culture" since "often the only trace of changes in a nation's mode of life is in semantic changes," and that "change in language is thus due to the inevitable conditions under which speech is carried on."[89]

85. Lurati, "Étymologie et anthropologie culturelle," 310.
86. Ibid., 315.
87. See suggestions made by Lurati in this direction, in Lurati, "Étymologie et anthropologie culturelle,", 316.
88. Zamboni, L'etimologia, 148.   89. Bloomfield, An Introduction, 251.

Even more complex are the ties that connect etymological investigation to philosophy and to rhetoric. Once again, linguistics seems more inclined to take over the central role of logic in philosophy, and thereby reconfigure philosophical uses of etymology in linguistic terms, rather than allow for etymology's philosophical scope.[90] Yet etymological philosophizing boasts a venerable tradition, from early Jewish exegetes and Alexandrian scholars, to Homeric commentaries and pre-Socratic dialogues, and all the way through the thread of exegetical inquiry that from classical, medieval, and Renaissance scholars passes into the philosophical tapestries of such dissimilar thinkers as Vico, Heidegger, Proust, Lacan, and Derrida.[91]

In view of its historical, its philosophical, and its rhetorical and ideological implications, etymology, even beyond the exacting jurisdiction of linguistics, can no longer be underestimated. There is more at stake behind etymology's unsolvable "esoterism" than a passion for linguistic curiosity or a psychological drive for analogical, universal motivation.[92] In their introduction to the Acts of the International Colloquium on Etymology organized in 1988 for the centenary of the birth of Walther von Wartburg, Jean-Pierre Chambon and Georges Lüdi epitomized the thrust of the numerous scholarly contributions as a

"deliberate displacement" [déplacement délibéré] of scientific etymology, an overt contestation of the tendency, on the part of scientific etymology, to conceive itself in a space and an order radically separated from "pre-" or "nonscientific" traditions, taken as suspicious intrusions of what is commonly baptized "popular etymology." . . . To interrogate etymology as a plural discourse, as a practice which is both linguistic and "epilinguistic" [is] to demonstrate that the scientific discourse of modern etymology does not encompass the whole terrain (indeed possibly only a very meager portion of it). . . . It is time to open up the wider and richer field of la chose étymologique, a multifaceted phenomenon expressed in diverse epochal and cultural manifestations.[93]

90. Zamboni has interesting observations on the subject. Zamboni, L'etimologia, 154ff.
91. Vico and Derrida are discussed in chapter 6. Heidegger and Proust must be left for discussion elsewhere.
92. Alan S. C. Ross, Etymology: With Especial Reference to English (Fairlawn, N.J.: Essential Books, 1958), 15.
93. Chambon and Lüdi, Discours étymologiques, 1–2.

At the outskirts of the scientific establishment the etymologist, in turn astute investigator or knowledgeable foxhunter, historian or archeologist, philosopher or rhetorician, perseveres: "The ingenuity of the etymologist and his power of invention and combination cannot be replaced by mechanical rules. The etymologist like any other archaeologist or historian may stumble on his subject accidentally."[94] To conclude with an example of this investigative attitude, at once systematic and intuitive, I call to mind the work of Vittore Pisani. Despite its age, Pisani's *L'etimologia* continues to figure as a significant contribution to etymological inquiry. Both the *International Encyclopedia of Linguistics* and the *Routledge Dictionary of Language and Linguistics* list it as a major bibliographic reference.[95] Besides providing an impressively detailed introductory account of ancient etymology, the "history and concept of etymology,"[96] Pisani's work charts contemporary trends in etymological research, with special attention to the role of "borrowing" (imprestito; replaced in current practices by the more neutral "lexical diffusion"), the concept of "the hereditary" [ereditario], and the theory of "linguistic geography" [geografia linguistica]. In Pisani's words, the role of the modern etymologist is "to establish the formal materials employed by those who first created a given word, as well as to determine the concept which they intended to express through that word."[97] Of particular interest is his distinction between two lexical categories that clarify the role and the intent of etymological inquiry: descriptive (*descrittivo*) words and denominative (*denominative*) words. Descriptive words still bear traces of the semantic, morphological, or phonological models whereby they were historically coined; these are still "alive" [vivi] in the usage of speakers or interpreters. An example of this in English could be the eponymous use of the neologism *bobbit*

94. Anttila, *Historical and Comparative Linguistics*, 331.
95. *Routledge Dictionary of Language and Linguistics*, Hadumod Bussmann, ed. and trans. Kerstin Kazzazi and Gregory Trauth (London: Routledge, 1996).
96. Pisani, *L'etimologia*, 11–48.
97. Ibid., 79–80.

colloquially used as a synonym of "severing" or "cutting."[98] Denominative words, on the other hand, evoke concepts that are presented with the absolute voice of received tradition, their models having been obscured by disparate factors (semantic or phonetic change, assimilation and so on). Onomatopoeic expressions or lexical borrowings are part of this second category. Pisani maintains that "the interpretative activity performed by a common speaker in relation to both types of words is the foundation of etymological science."[99] Therefore, both the etymological constructs and the etymological analyses speakers or scholars conduct on them are interpretations.

What is most striking about Pisani's contribution is his sustained focus on the complex historical connection between external (phonetic, morphological) and internal (semantic) forms of language, as well as his awareness of the weight that extralinguistic phenomena have on such a connection: a theoretical stance certainly not new but rarely expounded or embraced by twentieth-century etymologists. Pisani does not hesitate to conclude his section on semantics with the remark that etymology also comes to bear upon the "spiritual part of the word, that which gives the word value and life and that of which the external, acoustic form is but a concrete manifestation in the physical realm."[100] Pisani's statement can easily be written off as antiquated idealism of the Crocean kind. I would rather assert that it depicts one of the most challenging tasks facing present-day linguists, who, despite a diligent application of phonetic principles to semantic fields, remain "ill-equipped" to cope with semantic irregularities and to pro-

98. Robertson Cochrane, *Wordplay: Origins, Meanings, and Usage of the English Language* (Toronto: University of Toronto Press, 1996), v. *bobbit*. The full incident is recounted on Wikipedia: "On the night of June 23, 1993, Bobbit cut off her husband's penis with a kitchen knife as he lay sleeping in their Manassas, Virginia, home. She then drove off with the severed appendage and flung it out her car window. Police performed a diligent search and located it, and it was then surgically reattached." (Wikipedia contributors, "bobbit," *Wikipedia, The Free Encyclopedia*, http://en.wikipedia.org/w/index.php?title=John_and_Lorena_Bobbitt&oldid=45415412; accessed March 31, 2006).

99. Pisani, *L'etimologia*, 43.

100. Ibid., 180.

duce convincing formalizations.[101] Pisani's comment sheds light on
the symbolic, rhetorical, ideological, cognitive, and value-making aspects of human language that one-way scientism must disregard, but
that nonscientific etymology, a practice "older than Western linguistics,"[102] has always endeavored to investigate.

In this chapter we have surveyed modern etymology from its pioneering steps in the nineteenth century to the morass of the late
twentieth. We started with the strict phonological rules endorsed by
comparatist grammarians and based on genealogical and familial analogs. We detected the shift to the anecdotal, ethnographic study of
word histories epitomized by the *Wörter und Sachen* movement. And
we witnessed the crises and self-contradictions of present-day etymology, whose shaky identity falters as its two initial currents continue to be diluted into the mainstream of contemporary linguistics.
In the sweeping formula offered by Pierre Swiggers, nineteenth- and
twentieth-century etymology appears as a discipline concerned with
the paleontological or biological history of words (*l'étymologie comme
histoire—pàleontologique ou biologique—du mot*).[103] It is also a discipline
permeated by diverse practices of transition (*practiques de transition*),
such as the nineteenth-century change of course from impressionistic comparatism to rigorous philology founded on grammar. Indeed,
where one might have expected a discipline shaped in the clear-cut
mold of science, a discipline finally purged of "spurious" word explanations, one encounters a hybrid domain: still very much an art—in
the post-Romantic sense of the word—a praxis more and more conscious of the ties that it entertains with the erratic speculations of its
past.[104] The chapters that follow come to grips with these "dated" at-

---

101. In Anttila's words, "Linguists are still not equipped to talk about semantics, and the
term 'abstract' . . . has been used as a justification for ignorance." Anttila, *Historical and Comparative Linguistics*, 4–5.

102. Ibid., 326.

103. Swiggers, "Le travail étymologique," 35.

104. At the end of her recent, detailed analysis of etymologizing, Marina Benedetti notes
that "it does not seem possible, at the present juncture, to talk about an explicit general theory
of etymologizing" partly because of the "extreme variety of factors" that etymology must ac-

tempts and, after considering some among the manifold factors that
linguistics has elected to expunge, venture to find "methods" that organize numberless, wondrous specimens of etymological madness.

---

count for (255). Etymology, she grants, still holds theoretical value within the empirical and
inductive framework of linguistics. Yet its "peculiarity . . . lies in the fact that it does not rely
on a clear-cut or confined theoresis, but comprises and includes [. . .] multiple aspects that
pertain to linguistic knowledge in general" (256). She encouragingly concludes by advocating
etymological inquiries based on the collaborative efforts of linguistics, philology, and cultural history; inquiries whose "success does not depend on adherence to the dogmas of any one
discipline or trend, but on our receptiveness to the clues and suggestions that may come from
diverse sources." Marina Benedetti, "Etymology between Typology and History," in *Il cambiamento linguistico*, ed. Marco Mancini (Rome: Carocci, 2003), (255–56).

CHAPTER 2

NOMEN EST OMEN
Etymology and Allegory

A FIFTH-CENTURY COMMENTARY on Plato's *Cratylus*, the *Explicatio Cratyli* of the Neoplatonic philosopher Proclus, offers a clue to the tangled destinies of etymology and allegory. The passage in question is number LXXXVIII among the 185 *scholia*, or short chapters, which give us Proclus's exegesis of a large section from Plato's dialogue (338a–407c). Although Proclus's comments are not arranged systematically, they address specific paragraphs of the *Cratylus* and respond to two main philosophical goals: to explain the workings of the soul and to extol the attributes of the gods as inferred from their names.[1]

I will use Proclus's commentary to try to make sense of Plato's *Cratylus* and of the controversy between φύσει and θέσει (the nature or convention of linguistic signs) in chapter 3. Here, I am going to focus on Proclus's coining of one word, apparently not attested elsewhere in the known corpus of ancient Greek texts.[2] The word is *etymegorein* (ἐτυμηγορεῖν), and this is one of five passages where it appears:

---

1. That is what Francesco Romano says in his introduction to the Italian translation of Proclus: "Scopo del Cratilo è di 1) mostrare l'attività generatrice e assimilatrice dell'anima; 2) celebrare le proprietà degli ordinamenti degli dèi cosí come è possibile desumere dai loro nomi." In Proclus, *Lezioni sul "Cratilo" di Platone*, trans. Francesco Romano, Symbolon 7 (Catania: Università di Catania, 1989), 45, xviii.

2. See Henry George Liddell and Robert Scott, *A Greek-English Lexicon*, new 9th ed., with a 1996 supplement (New York: Oxford University Press, 1940), v. *etymegoreo*. Both *etymegoreo* and *etymegoreia* refer to Proclus's *In Cratylum* as their only source (pages 43 and 45, respectively). *Etymegoreia* is given as a synonym of *etymologeia*. The variant *etymegoros*, found in *Orphica*, is listed with the more poetic sense of "speaking truth" and does not seem to have had the philosophical import of Proclus's isolated usage. *Orphica Argonautica*, ed. E. Abel (Leipzig: 1885), A4, 1178. The 1996 supplement to Liddell-Scott also includes the words *etymofanos* (ἐτυμόφανος) and *etymofas* (ἐτυμοφᾶς), taken from poetry word lists and both of dubious origin.

As a matter of fact, while fathers name their children after what they remember, what they hope for, or similar such things, it is chance that decides whether or not there should be consistency between the lives of these [i.e., children] and the names given to them on different criteria [i.e., those of things remembered or hoped for]. Let then Agamemnon name his son "Orestes" not so much because of his mountaineer disposition, but on account of his vehemence and swiftness in hurling himself forward [i.e., not by derivation from ὄρος = mount, but from ὀρούω = I hurl myself]; either because he actually finds in him evidence of this nature, or because he wants him to become so. In any case, chance will always assign to Orestes, with different criteria, such name as is most true, because it reveals his life in its entirety. That is why Socrates deems it appropriate to etymegorize (ἐτυμηγορεῖν) the name "Orestes" in accordance with the latter cause [i.e., chance] and not instead in accordance with the more human one [i.e., the remembrance or hope of his father].[3]

This instance of etymegoreo as a verb is closely followed, two pages later, by the noun etymegoreiai, used twice as a synonym of etymologies:

Once again in his etymologies (ἐτυμηγορίαις) Plato shows first what the thing reveals of itself, then what it is similar to, by virtue of the syllables that form its name. For instance, in the case of Orestes, he first mentions his ferine and wild nature (i.e., the way Orestes actually is); then he adds his being "like a mountaineer" (i.e., the sign that is similar to him), as seen in the syllables forming his name. And regarding Agamemnon, he first talks about his being perseverant and tenacious, then adds these words: "that this man should be admired for his persistence is shown by the name Ἀγαμέμνων and similarly for the name which follows."[4]

Morphologically, etymegorein is fairly straightforward: it combines the common Greek forms etymon (true) and agoreuein (to argue) and is generally taken as a synonym of etymologein (etymologize).[5] When seen in context, though, Proclus's coinage lends itself to some interesting notes. First of all, the term etymegoreo, visibly linked to the verb agoreuein (to argue, speak in public), brings to the fore one sense of etymologizing that scientism has tended to obscure.[6] It unveils and af-

---

3. Quoted by Romano in Proclus, Lezioni, 18–29. English translations for this and other passages from Romano are mine. The five instances of etymegoreo/ein are at 43.29; 45.14 and 23; 53.7; 76.17.

4. Proclus, Lezioni, 45.14–22.

5. Romano translates it as "etymologize." So does Alberto Zamboni, who mentions Proclus's curious coinage in his introductory remarks on etymology. Zamboni, L'etimologia, 1.

6. Liddell-Scott lists first the meaning of etymologeo as "argu[ing] from etymology," fol-

firms the argumentative, rhetorical thrust of etymologizing, beside, and possibly even before, the demands of a more technically mind-ed science of word origins (ἡ ἐτυμηγορική). Secondly, as hinted at in the passage from Proclus below, *etymegoreo* qualifies a kind of ety-mologizing that, in its attention to "the form of life" over "matter," is more germane to the process of hermeneutics, or interpretation: "Pla-to, who in his etymologies (ἐτυμηγορίαις) despises matter and ad-heres above all to form, says that the name Agamemnon comes from the word ἀγαστός and not from the word ἄγαν. Grammarians, on the other hand, being mostly concerned with the matter and not the form of life, probably etymologize (ἐτυμολογήσουσιν) in reverse."[7] It is as if *etymegoreo* and *etymologeo* conveyed the two opposed practices undertaken, with regard to "true meanings"—or *etyma*— by Plato and by the grammarians (*grammatikoi*), respectively.[8] What matters here is that for Proclus *etymegoreo* seems to allow precisely for the kind of in-terpretive freedom with respect to *etyma* that *etymologeo* strives to elim-inate.[9] *Etyma* may be accessible, but they are so only through the by-ways of history, where straight genealogical lines are diffracted into a plethora of equally "true" conjectures.

The hermeneutic fuzziness of *etymegoreia* prompts an immedi-ate comparison. *Etymegoreia* is morphologically (and etymologically) similar to another far more fortunate if not less controversial word: *allēgorein*, in Latin *allēgoria* or, in two of the many loan translations, *diversiloquium*, *alieniloquium*. Modern English descendants include "al-

---

lowed by the more dated but now prevalent sense of "analyz[ing] a word and find[ing] its ori-gin."

7. Proclus, *Lezioni*, 45.23–28.

8. Other instances of *etymologein/etymologia* in Proclus are found at 45.5; 39.12.21; 40.21; 42.14; 45.28; 40.23.

9. Ascribing rhetorical indeterminacy to Plato's work may at first seem flawed, if one has in mind Plato's idealistic positing of immutable ideal forms. But the issue is strictly connected with the *fusei/thesei* controversy, over which Plato's position remains far from clear. Giovanni Reale is among the growing number of critics who—against accepted views of Plato's essen-tialism—are intrigued by the "relativism" of his late myths. Giovanni Reale, *Per una nuova in-terpretazione di Platone: Rilettura della metafisica dei grandi dialoghi alla luce delle "Dottrine non scritte,"* 11th ed. (Milan: Vita e Pensiero, 1991).

legory," "allegorize," "allegoresis," "allegorical," "allegorism." The formal analogy between *allegorein* and *etymegorein*—despite the fact that occurrences of the latter are statistically negligible—suggests, I think, that some overlap exists between the two: they have both, after all, stirred the interests of hard-core linguists and literary theorists.

But to locate intersections between the paths of allegory and etymology, we need to shed light on some of the issues surrounding allegory. And I propose to do so via etymology—a good opportunity to survey in practice what we will be maintaining in theory. Allegory has long been at the center of heated controversy, a controversy raging over its dual role—allegory as figure of speech and allegoresis as interpretive practice—its semantic provisionality, its referential deviousness, and its manifold historical applications.[10] I am going to trace some etymological synapses of "allegory" and see how they pattern a view of language that is at once nominalist and realist, existentialist and essentialist, secular and eschatological.[11]

One of the most comprehensive treatments of allegory is given by Jon Whitman in *Allegory: The Dynamics of an Ancient and Medieval Technique.*[12] The first known instance of "allegory" as a figure of speech, he says, is in the *De Elocutione*, written by a rhetorician by the name of "Demetrius." Unfortunately, the dating of the work remains open to question, and scholars place it anywhere from 270 BC up to the first century AD. It is not until the work of Philodemus, around 60 BC, that the word allegory appears "as a familiar trope (*tropos*) and is linked with metaphor" in a Greek rhetorical treatise;[13] yet, by this time, a par-

10. See the entry "allegory" in Alex Preminger and T. V. F. Brogan, eds., *The New Princeton Encyclopedia of Poetry and Poetics* (Princeton, N.J.: Princeton University Press, 1993): "Allegory (Gr. *allos*, 'other,' and *agoreuein*, 'to speak') is a term that denotes two complementary procedures: a way of composing literature and a way of interpreting it. To compose allegorically is to construct a work so that its apparent sense refers to an 'other' sense. To interpret allegorically (allegoresis) is to explain a work as if there were an 'other' sense to which it referred" (31).

11. I use all these terms in their general OED definitions.

12. Jon Whitman, *Allegory: The Dynamics of an Ancient and Medieval Technique* (Oxford: Clarendon, 1987). See especially his appendix "On the History of the Term 'Allegory'" (263–68).

13. Ibid., 264.

allel Latin translation of the term had already appeared in the *Rhetorica Ad Herennium*.[14] Through the subsequent works of Cicero, who defines it as "a continuous stream of metaphors" (*cum fluxerunt continuae plures tralationes* [sic]) in his *De Oratore* (III, xli, 166), we get to Quintilian's definition of *allēgoria* as "continuous metaphor" ("*allēgorian* facit continua *metaphora*": *Institutio Oratoria* IX, II, 46) or "inversio" (VIII, vi, 44). It is Quintilian's influential definition, coupled with the tradition of Homeric allegoresis, that informs medieval and Renaissance debates on "allegory" at least until the Romantic diatribe. Romantics will once and for all juxtapose what they perceive as the mechanistic, multilayer structuring of allegory to the organic immediacy of the "symbol."[15]

For our purposes, there are two key points in Whitman's account. First, there does not seem to be conclusive evidence in any existing Greek texts of "allegory" as "meaning something other than what one says." The definition is indeed Aristotle's, but as Whitman notes, Aristotle applied it to *hyponoia* (underlying sense) and not to "allegory."[16] Latin rhetoricians, perhaps as a result of translation, may have been responsible for the later emphasis on "the Other."[17] Second, the Greek use of *allēgoria* as a substitute for the word *hyponoia*, or underlying sense, in the exegetical practice that gains currency by the first century AD and is recorded by Plutarch, may well be due to the rising influence of Roman culture.[18] Even if we accept *allēgoria* as a possible back-

---

14. Cicero, *Ad. C. Herennium de ratione dicendi*, trans. Harry Caplan (London: Heinemann, 1954), 224.

15. See Tzvetan Todorov, *Theories of the Symbol*, trans. Catherine Porter (Ithaca, N.Y.: Cornell University Press, 1982).

16. Whitman, *Allegory*, 264.

17. Mentions of the "Other" abound in poststructuralist discourse but tend to be cryptic at best. Often the "Other" is conjured up to dramatize Derridian "différance" or de Man's allegorizing (see chapter 6). References to the "Other" in this study are not directly meant to address deconstructionist issues, although obviously my insistence on allegorical etymology as a cognitive tool and a figure of unity calls for appraisals of language and difference that resist Derrida's suggestions.

18. As Jean Pépin notes, "The word *allegoria* is relatively recent in the Greek language. Yet it translates a very old idea, expressed above all in the word *hyponoia*. The primary sense of *hyponoia* is 'supposition' or 'conjecture.' It presupposes a relation between two different mental concepts. On the one hand a concrete datum is presented to perception; on the other, *hyponoia*

formation, partly ascribable to Roman rhetoricians, we still need to shed light on its history. Here's what Whitman has to say about the verb *agoreuein* in his analysis of the compound *(allos agoreuein)*: "*Allēgoria* has two component parts in Greek. The first of these parts, coming from the word *allos*, means 'other'; it inverts the sense of the second component. This second component is the verb *agoreuein*, originally meaning 'to speak in the assembly,' in the *agora*. Though already in Homer this verb has the original meaning 'to speak,' throughout its history it retained the original sense of discoursing in public, speaking in the open."[19] After this important remark, he goes on to explain that "the second component of the word 'allegory' . . . had historical connections both with official, political address and with everyday, common speech," and concludes that "when this component was combined with the inverting word *allos*, the resulting composite connoted both that which was said in *secret*, and that which was *unworthy* of the *crowd*. These two connotations of the word 'allegory'—guarded language and elite language—become explicit parts of allegorical theory and practice."[20] It is at this point that etymology can be invoked, to take Whitman's remarks a step further. Even though the secretive, elitist aura he mentions undoubtedly lingers on in the Western allegorical tradition, I submit that the word *allēgoria* also preserves and entertains references to the public arena of discourse making; to a communal, myth-making kind of epistemology. I reach this conclusion by rereading the two components: ἄλλος conveys the senses of "another," "one besides what has been mentioned," but also "different, diverse," i.e., "condensing more than one feature." The noun *agora* (ἀγορά), from which comes *agoreuein*, comprises the ideas of "assembly," "marketplace," and "public speaking" and functions also as a

---

suggests an idea concerning the future beyond the world of senses." Jean Pépin, *Mythe et allégorie; les origines grecques et les contestations judéo-chrétiennes*, Philosophie de l'esprit (Aubier: Editions Montaigne, 1958), 85. Pépin also warns that "to retrace, even generally, the history of allegorical interpretation of Homer by the Greeks is dangerous, because even though the word *allegoria* is recent, that history covers at least ten centuries." Ibid., 91.

19. Whitman, *Allegory*, 263.   20. Ibid.

chronological marker (ἀγορὰ πλήθουσα—the forenoon).[21] Putting the two together, we get the established meaning of "speaking about the Other" (or "Other speaking") but also of "incorporat[ing] more than one voice at the same time in a public discourse, or narrative." The latter sense is all the more relevant in the iconic, mythological milieu of early Greek culture, which condensed popular narratives in the syncretic attributes of the gods. Jean Pépin provides a remarkable example of this practice: "In his treatise On Isis and Osiris Plutarch says also that 'the Greeks saw in Chronos an allegorical (ἀλληγοροῦσι) designation of time.'"[22] The two senses must be stressed. Allegoria as "speaking about the Other" implies a referential split—something or someone removed from the present discourse to which words obliquely refer. And in this sense, while it purports to be a privileged vehicle of secrets, allegoria in fact exposes the limits of language, the Babel of humans after the Fall. On the other hand, to read allegoria as a "public discourse that incorporates multiple features" implies acknowledging the communal, dialogic setup of meaning making, which begins with the pragmatic utterances of people in the public square—the agora— within the shared day-to-day sphere of human endeavors. The first sense relies on metaphor and permeates essentialist interpretations of Plato's myths, and the second sense relies on metonymy and recalls the polyphony of meanings theorized by Mikhail Bakhtin.[23]

I submit that the richness of allegory as trope, genre, and interpretive tool rests with both meanings and that the history of allegorical traditions is the story of the alternate fortunes of one to the detri-

---

21. Liddell and Scott, 13.   22. Pépin, Mythe et allégorie, 88.

23. I am thinking in particular of Mikhail Bakhtin, Esthétique et théorie du roman, trans. Daria Olivier (Paris: Gallimard, 1978). The copresence of metaphor and metonymy within allegory has been long recognized and variously discussed, but mainly in terms of competing interpretive appropriations on the part of rival epistemologies. Deborah Madsen, for example, notes that "in classical Greek, Roman, and Judaistic models, allegory is identified as a species of rhetoric that operates in the same way as metaphor. But a competing model was developed as a part of the typological explication of the two biblical testaments by the Gospel writers and later patristic exegetes. Competition between these two conceptions of allegory—allegory as metaphor and allegory as metonymy—has been protracted." Deborah Madsen, Rereading Allegory: A Narrative Approach to Genre (New York: St. Martin's, 1994), 1.

ment of the other: the illumination of one sense and the concealment of the other. And the senses we have disclosed in this digression on ἀλληγορία apply just as well to ἐτυμηγορία. The *agoreuein* suffix they share recalls the practical decision making of the agora (the public forum) rather than to exacting discrimination of the philosophers' logos. "Talking about the Other" and "talking about the Truth" may then be taken as the two sides of an ongoing dialogue. This is, I think, the direction taken by Flavia Ursini in her brilliant article on etymology and dialect lexicology, where she convincingly makes a case for the pragmatic, "transitional" character of folk etymologies, the very etymologies unyielding linguists would dismiss as unforgivably false. But, Ursini insists, the notion of a "false semantic interpretation is contradictory [because] meaning is a continuous process of interpretation and mediation of the past" and in popular etymological practice "components that are no longer relevant can be transformed or forgotten without leaving a trace."[24] One should therefore acknowledge that "the falsity of so-called popular etymology comes from the superimposition of a linear codification, made up of historical (phonetic and morphological) rules, onto an evolving process like oral language. But speech eludes diachronic analysis and abstract formalization, because it is inseparable from the global phenomenon of culture."[25] Ursini's study targets language in its pragmatic use and deals with etymology as a speech act involved in communal meaning making. But her remarks also come to bear upon the "scholarly" fields of etymological creation and etymological interpretation. Because one of the most flagrant misappropriations of etymology and allegory, initiated with post-Socratic philosophers and thoroughly sanctioned in Cartesianism, lies in the disregard for their argumentative, rhetorical value in favor of inflexible standards of truth versus falsity. In the post-Cartesian debate, allegory becomes either a predictable two-level device that hides truth

24. Flavia Ursini, *Etimologia, cultura e lessico dialettale* (Macerata: Pacini, 1979), 46.
25. Ibid.

beneath a figurative, mystifying veil (thereby falling short, in Romantic eyes, of the unobtrusive directness of symbols),[26] or a potent, but annihilating, mechanism that parodies its own linguistic trappings and bemoans an unbridgeable gap from an unattainable "Other." Etymology suffers an analogous destiny: it is either written off as the ancient fallacy of "searching for the true meaning of a word"[27] and survives as a dated umbrella term for that part of historical linguistics dealing with lexical change, or it is brandished as a "versatile ideological weapon" used to "undermine absolutes and authority—and . . . do[es] so without setting up an alternative and equally challengeable truth-claim."[28]

Equally disenchanted with etymology's tacit derogation by linguists and with its ideologized exhumation on the part of poststructuralists, I propose to reassess etymology's cultural import in premodern texts and to do so with an eye on the far-reaching rhetorical and cognitive ramifications of allegory, with which, I believe, etymology shares much.

Let me start with some general comments. First of all, both *etymology* and *allegory* are used with reference either to a heuristic method— be it allegoresis or a scientific reconstruction of etymological roots— or to instances of such methods in specific texts. Thus we talk about Isidore's etymology of *homo* as an example of the encompassing practice "medieval etymology." And we cite the Lion, a common allegory for Christ, as an example of the typological gist of medieval allegory. Further, etymology and allegory denote both the writing of texts that exhibit allegorical or etymological features and the interpretation, or exegesis, of these features. That is why etymology and allegory straddle the jurisdictions of rhetoric, where they act as recognizable *figu-*

26. Unlike the symbol, which is a fully realized object in itself, in the eyes of Goethe, Schelling, and Humboldt allegory is heterotelic (to use Todorov's term): it points to something beyond itself and does not imply a motivated relation to its object. See especially Goethe's *Über die Gegenstände der bildenden Kunst* (1797), and Friedrich Schelling's *Philosophie der Kunst* (1802). Both are discussed by Tzvetan Todorov in *Theories of the Symbol*, chapter 6.

27. David Crystal, ed., *Encyclopedic Dictionary of Language and Languages* (Oxford: Cambridge University Press, 1992), v. *etymology*.

28. Attridge, *Peculiar Language*, 22.

rae; of literature, where they identify genres or themes; and of literary criticism, where they inspire and uphold interpretative forays. Finally, since both allegory and etymology make pronouncements about presumably inaccessible, or poorly accessible, origins (*etyma* or *alloi* that with disparate aims they set out to unravel), it seems that they grant or guard access to privileged knowledge, initiatory or not; that they function at once synchronically, yielding vibrant *tranches de vie*,[29] and/or diachronically, tracing genealogical and "original" connections; and that they operate on multiple, more or less correlated, layers or levels.

The Hermetic, mystic, religious quality of both allegory and etymology is widely documented. It figures prominently in the scriptural exegesis of Jewish *midrash*. It finds parallels in the Indian tradition of the Vedic *nirukta* (explication) that merges etymologizing with ritual through the analysis of the mantra, and in the Hindu *mīmāmsa* (reflection), which couples etymology and allegory to search for philosophical truths. It also undergirds the grammatical endeavor of the Arabian *ištiqāq*.[30] Greek Stoicism, to which we owe the word "etymology," is strongly imbued with divinatory practices which later seep into philosophical-linguistic theorizing on the correctness of names (ὀρθότης τῶν ὀνομάτων). Even Latin grammar is not immune from mysticism, as exemplified in the *quartus gradus etymologiae* of Varro and in Cicero's discussion of *veriloquium*. The Middle Ages, populated with allegorical dictionaries, bestiaries, and encyclopedias that use etymology to disclose hidden Christian senses in the Scripture and in the world, mark the fulfillment of a spiritual quest that had been present in various measures and degrees throughout antiquity.

Time is another area of intense and problematic interaction between etymology and allegory. Ancient etymology has often been dismissed as hopelessly achronic, unaware of the historical mechanisms of lexi-

29. In *Les Tropes*, César du Marsais notes that, unlike the *esprit méthodique*, allegory renders an idea through another idea that is striking (*frappante*) and vivid to the senses. César du Marsais, *Les Tropes* (Paris: Belin-le-Prieur, 1818).

30. For a discussion of this and other aspects of etymologizing see Zamboni, *L'etimologia*, especially pages 11–16.

cal change discovered by scientific etymology under the guidance of linguistics.[31] However, long after the limitations of a purely historicist perspective have become evident and historical linguistics is called to retain its own position and credibility against a flood of prestigious synchronic studies, that judgment sounds blatantly biased. Ancient etymology may well look static when seen through the lens of modern historiography. What is neither obvious nor beyond question is the claim that modern historicism is the proper perspective and ought to be applied as a corrective yardstick to the "fanciful" etymologizing of the past.

Friedrich Ohly reminds us that modern etymologizing would have sounded dubious to medieval scholars, limited as it is to the *littera*, or literal sense, of a given word and therefore unwilling to hazard interpretations on "the forms of life" or the world.[32] In fact, ancient etymologists, and especially medieval allegorists after them, seemed conscious of the fiction ingrained in their *historiae*, both in their literal claims and in the secondary senses they drew from allegorical readings. To them the *littera* was never justifiable in and for itself: its historical or denotative scope already echoed the senses to be explored at other interpretive levels—allegorical, typological, anagogical. Similarly, the *voces*—signifiers—never covered the full semantic scope of a given word; not until etymology undertook to put forward their *vis*, their allegorical, typological, or anagogical force.

It is with an eye on the "dynamic stasis" of all historiographic endeavors that etymologists and allegorists in premodern times produce

31. In his excursus on ancient etymology, Zamboni notes that "the Arabs, like everyone else in the ancient world, lack a historical conception of language development . . . and their view is thereby strictly static." Zamboni, *L'etimologia*, 15. Citing etymologist Friedrich Müller, Franco Cavazza agrees that "the major impediment of ancient etymology was the almost complete lack, in all classical authors, of a historical awareness of language." Franco Cavazza, *Studio su Varrone etimologo e grammatico* (Florence: La Nuova Italia, 1981), 18. However, Cavazza agrees with Jan Pinborg that this widespread assessment of ancient etymology should be mitigated: "Die stoische Etymologie ist nicht lautgeschichtlich, sondern begriffsgeschichtlich; das wesentliche am Wort ist der Inhalt." Jan Pinborg, "Das Sprachdenken der Stoa und Augustins Dialektik," *Classica et Mediaevalia* 23 (1962), 18, n. 9.

32. Friedrich Ohly, *Geometria e Memoria: Lettera e allegoria nel Medioevo*, trans. Bruno Argenton (Bologna: Il Mulino, 1985), 263.

detailed descriptions of their respective disciplines in multilayered, hierarchical models. In his influential *De Lingua Latina*, Varro posits four degrees (*gradi*) of etymological inquiry:

Infimus quo populus etiam venit, secundus quo grammatica descendit antiqua, tertius . . . quo philosophia ascendens pervenit, quartus ubi est adytum et initia regis.

> [The lowest is that to which even the common folk has come; . . . the second is that to which old-time grammar has mounted . . . the third level is that to which philosophy ascended . . . , the fourth is that where the sanctuary is, and the mysteries of the high-priest].[33]

These nicely match the fourfold model of patristic exegesis popularized by Augustine of Dacia in the distich:

Littera gesta docet, quid credas allegoria
moralis quid agas, quo tendas anagogia.

> [The letter teaches you the deeds, allegory teaches you what to believe, the moral sense teaches you how to behave, and the anagogy tells you what to strive for].[34]

The four degrees of Varronian etymology at once define and defy the limits of a grammatical approach to language by leading into the mystery of the *quartus gradus etymologiae*, a theory that has not ceased to lure and puzzle scholars.[35] Similarly, the four senses of scriptural exegesis predicate the possibilities of interpretations that invariably exceed their own goals, because they rely on the unquantifiable algorithm of faith, the *regula fidei* still engaging medievalists.

To conclude, we may say that allegorical etymology (*etymegoreia*) is present when a linguistic form, a signifier, is created or is read as

33. Marcus Terentius Varro, *De lingua Latina*, trans. Roland Kent, Loeb Classical Library, rev. and repr. ed. (Cambridge, Mass.: Harvard University Press, 1951), 5, 7–8.

34. In Ohly, *Geometria*, 266. The allegorical dimension of patristic exegesis has been the subject of innumerable studies that would require separate treatment. A significant contribution is Manlio Simonetti's *Biblical Interpretation in the Early Church: An Historical Introduction to Patristic Exegesis*, trans. John A. Hughes (Edinburgh: T. & T. Clark, 1994). See also Alan Hauser and Duane Watson, eds., *A History of Biblical Interpretation* (Grand Rapids, Mich.: William B. Eerdmans, 2003).

35. See chapter 4.

an *allegory* (in the senses of the term expounded above) of its possible meaning(s), or signified(s). We could diagram this allegorical lien with the sign ⇆ indicating mutual approximation:

[Form A] *Amicus* ⇆ *Animi Custos* [Etymology B]

To analytically trained ears, the link between a form A and its allegorical etymology B will sound cheaply homophonic, certainly unfit for serious linguistic consideration. Eloquent examples are the Latin *agnus* (lamb), derived from *agnoscit* (knows) from the fact that the lamb is said to recognize its own mother, or the word *bellum* (battle) antiphrastically etymologized as an unpleasant (*non bellum*) undertaking. Yet allegorical etymology resolutely employs and deploys weak homophonies to bridge semantic gaps, posit areas of semantic overlap between words *and* between concepts, or map argumentative fault lines along which epistemic shifts are likely to occur. I suspect that one objects to etymologies like these not so much on the basis of their phonological naïveté (although a linguist would hasten to point out, for instance, that *agnus* "has nothing to do with" *agnoscit*) but more on account of their essentialist élan and their rhetorical, ideological assertiveness. In the Isidorian example, the form *amicus* is etymologized as *animi custos* by reference to an ideologically bound range of senses (the friend as Christian guardian of your soul). And it is also etymologized as *hamo* with reference to the symbolic shackles of chaste love. What is deplorably lacking is the manageable neutrality of the scientific discourse, and what is irritatingly present is the play of rhetorical permutations, here constrained in commanding ideological patterns.

The fact is that *etymegoreia* treads the fuzzy, contested, liminal zone between words and things, thought and language, eternity and history, spirit and matter—concepts and phenomena that it is expected to reflect but also anticipated to affect. *Nomen est omen. Nomina sunt consequentia rerum.* Our story of etymological allegory is the story of how, in different ways and at different times in history, people have used, conceptualized, and modeled this fundamental duplicity.

CHAPTER 3

THE NAMES OF HEROES
Greek and Alexandrian Etymologizing

SO FAR I HAVE ENDEAVORED to provide a viable model of allegorical etymology. To this end, I dealt first with etymology's loss of prestige within contemporary linguistics and called for a reappraisal of its role: the stress twentieth-century linguists lay on morphology and phonology fails to account for the extralinguistic claims of ancient etymologizing. To narrow the scope of research, I then set up a comparison between etymology and allegory: two rhetorical devices, scholarly and popular, that stray along the controversial divide between language and the world. Janus-like, language concurrently reflects and affects reality, as in the two maxims: Nomen est omen and Nomina sunt consequentia rerum.

It is now time to look for antecedents to these medieval adages in Greek and Alexandrian culture by examining eponyms, proper and common names, in which, I will argue, etymology and allegory coalesce. Eponyms denote characteristics of their bearers—they are a consequentia of them—but also shape their temperament or physical appearance; they work as an omen of the bearers' destiny. Also, eponyms can be said to strive for the kind of "unity in diversity" featured in etymegoreia. We are going to look at samples from Homeric literature and from there move on to Plato's dialogue on the "Correctness of Names": the Cratylus. That section reviews Plato's ideas on names and etymologizing to refute scholars who read his work as an anti-allegorical and anti-etymological manifesto. Final pages are devoted to Philo of Alexandria, who bracketed onomastics with divination and complex philosophical allegorizing.

Etymology and Onomastics

The link between allegory and etymology with regard to ancient onomastics—the study of proper names—is widely mentioned but rather cursorily explored. In his European Literature and the Latin Middle Ages, Curtius did cite numerous instances from the Iliad of "speaking names," that is, names that allegorize physical or moral qualities of their bearers.[1] First, he notes that Homer derived Odysseus's name ("Wrathful one") from the fact that his grandfather was "full of hatred" (ὀδυσσόμενος). Then he explains how Odysseus, before revealing himself, resorted to etymological puns. "He comes from 'Sorrowfield' (Alybas), his name is 'Strife' (Esperitos), and he is the son of 'Hardlife Vexation' (Apheidas Polypemonides)."[2] He even adds examples of many other Homeric eponyms like Hector ("Shielder"), Thersites ("Impudent"), Thoas ("Stormy"), Harmonides ("Joiner"). But Curtius was unwilling to read much in what he ultimately judged as Homer's "indulg[ence]" in "etymological play."[3] And, he was quick to remark, playful etymologizing of this kind occurred just as often in Pindar (who had speculated on the name Themistios as being from θεμόω ἱστία—"Sailspreader") and in Aeschylus (who had allegorized at length over Helen's name, Ἑλήνη). Apart from this hasty dismissal of eponymic etymologies, it now appears that the main shortcoming of Curtius's survey of Greek etymologizing lies in its conflation of separate etymological trends. In the outline proposed by Reitzenstein as early as 1897,[4] and recently endorsed by Zamboni, Greek etymologizing was broken down into four chronological phases.[5] The first centers upon the controversy between the natural and the convention-

---

1. Ernst Robert Curtius, *European Literature and the Latin Middle Ages*, trans. Willard R. Trask (New York: Pantheon Books, 1953).

2. Ibid., 495.

3. Ibid.

4. Richard Reitzenstein, *Geschichte der griechischen Etymologika* (Leipzig: 1897); and *Etymologika*, in "Paulys Real-Encyclopadie der classischen Altertumswissenschaft," 6 vols. (Stuttgart: J. B. Metzler, 1907).

5. Oversimplification in a chronology of this kind is inevitable, but such framing may

al views of language: names either represent reality (physikài eikónes) or are merely artificial labels dictated by custom (technêtai eikónes). This is the phase Zamboni comments on when he says that the philo- sophical search for αἰτία, or ultimate cause, is focused "not much on language, but rather on things themselves."[6] The second phase cen- ters on grammar: it starts with an inquiry into primitive words (πρῶτα ὀνόματα) and a description of their possible combinations. It is at this Alexandrian stage that etymology breaks away from analogy and history to become an autonomous field. The remaining two phases are hard to make out (if not by pure chronology), but they eventually merge into the new, systematic format of the *Etymologicon*.

From this account, it is the Stoics who stand out as the leading etymological school. That is why Stoic allegorism takes a full chapter in Jean Pépin's *Myth et Allégorie*, where we are given notable instances of onomastic etymologizing from Zeno, Cleanthes, and Chrysippus. They interpreted Homer's and Hesiod's poems with the aim of find- ing "behind the names of the gods and the heroes, the physical and psychological realities that they express."[7] Zeno, for instance, is said to have applied etymology to the names of Hesiod's Titans in order "to discern in their adventures pronouncements of general physics."[8] Coeos (Κοῖον) would allude to the quality (τὴν ποιότητα) of the so- lar course, which graphically replaces π with a χ. Hyperion (να) would indicate an ascending movement, via the expression "to go higher" (ὑπεράνω ἰέναι) and Japet (Ἰαπετον) would name that part of the universe where light objects float freely (πίπτειν ἄνω). Of equal inter- est are Cleanthes's comments on the etymological clues that connect Apollo to the Sun. Apollo (Ἀπολλων) represents the Sun because the Sun rises from different points (ἀπ' ἄλλων χαὶ ἄλλων τόπων); it was nicknamed Loxias (Λοξίας) either by virtue of its spiraling trajectory

---

serve the legitimate heuristic purpose of coping with an unwieldy mesh of linguistic data and historiographical inferences.

6. Zamboni, *L'etimologia*, 16–17.   7. Pépin, *Mythe et allégorie*, 131.
8. Ibid., 128.

(λοξαί) or because its rays reach us obliquely (λοξας). And the epithet Dionysus (Διόνυσος) was given to the Sun because, within the space of a day, it fully encircles (διανύσαι) the compass of the skies. But the degree of elaboration Stoic allegorists reached is perhaps more evident in Chrysippus. He takes the initial *alpha* of Ἀπόλλων as a privative prefix and etymologizes Apollo as the one severed from the numerous (πολλῶν) manifestations of fire or, with an etymon that nicely match-es the Latin *solem*, as the one separated (*solus*) from the multitude (ἀ-πολλοί). For Chrysippus, Zeus (Ζευς) owes his name to the fact that he gives sustenance (τὸ ζῆν) to all and is nicknamed Δία because all things exist through him alone (δι' αὐτόν). The earth was named Rhea (Ῥέα) because waters are cooled down (ῥεῖν) on it, and Ares (Ἄρες) derives his name from a moral representation of our own destruc-tive (ἀναιρεῖν) instincts. The Fates (Μοῖρας) drew their names from the fact that a certain destiny has been allotted (μεμερίσθαι) and as-signed to each of us. Their number has to do with the mystic, triadic movement whereby everything is accomplished. Lachesis (Λάχεσις) was named so because she "obtains" (λανχάνειν) for each person what fate has decreed; Atropos (Ἄτροπος) because the destiny each is allotted is immutable (ἄτρεπτον); and Clotho (Κλωθώ) because ev-erything is linked, as if through invisible strings (συγχεχλῶσθαι), to its destiny.[9]

Very much like their Homeric counterparts, these Stoic etymolo-gies are allegorical: the examples given here bring ὑπονοίαι, or "un-dersenses," which hark back to narratives of the moral, physical, or metaphysical worlds.

Etymologies in the *Cratylus*

Stoic etymologizing uses analogy and homophony quite freely, but its ground is semantic and, if we are to believe Dionysius of Halicar-

9. Ibid., 132ff.

nassus,[10] owes much to the work that Baxter places "at the head of the ancient etymological tradition": Plato's *Cratylus*.[11] Although this dialogue has been said by some to occupy a "minor" position in the Platonic corpus,[12] the secondary material is intimidating.[13] It is my conviction that the dialogue is not simply meant as a parody, that its interpretation cannot boil down to an either-or reply about the controversy over the correctness of names, and, most importantly, that *Cratylus's* etymologies shed light on how ancient, and especially Greek, etymologizing worked. I make no claim to originality: each of these statements has in some form or another been tackled. In raising these issues, I am mainly calling attention to some of the strategies of ancient etymology—namely of allegorical etymology—within a philosophical environment that is usually, and I would say misleadingly, perceived as anti-allegorical. The basic issues of Plato's *Cratylus* and the main currents of critical opinion that have sprung from them over the centuries have been brilliantly summed up and robustly argued in a volume by Timothy Baxter: *The Cratylus: Plato's Critique of Naming*. For this reason, and for the sake of coherence, Baxter is the main critical source in my analysis of the *Cratylus*, although I also consider the recent, keen contribution of John Joseph's *Limiting the Arbitrary* and partly draw on that classic "survey of the posterity of the *Cratylus*," Gérard Genette's *Mimologics*.[14]

10. Dionysius of Halicarnassus, *De compositione verborum*. Cited in Timothy M. S. Baxter, *The Cratylus: Plato's Critique of Naming*, Philosophia Antiqua 58 (Leiden: Brill, 1992), 86, n. 1.

11. Subsequent citations refer to the 1926 Loeb Classical Library Fowler edition of the dialogue.

12. See for instance the comment of Harold Fowler in his preface to the 1971 Loeb edition of the *Cratylus*: "The *Cratylus* cannot be said to be of great importance in the development of the Platonic system, as it treats of a special subject somewhat apart from general philosophic theory." Harold Fowler, "Preface," in *The Cratylus*, Loeb Classical Library (Cambridge, Mass.: Harvard University Press, 1971), 4. See also A. E. Taylor, *Plato: The Man and His Work* (London: Methuen, 1960), 78.

13. See for example Cavazza, *Studio su Varrone*, 24, n. 22. An excellent reconstruction of the various traditions of reading the *Cratylus* across disparate "academic constituencies" may be found in Joseph, *Limiting the Arbitrary*, especially pages 8 and following.

14. Genette, *Mimologics*, 6.

The phases of the dialogue are well known.[15] Socrates is called to arbitrate between the views of Cratylus and Hermogenes, who voice the naturalist and the conventionalist theses on language, respectively: is there a necessary, natural link between word and thing, or are names merely based on convention and agreement (ξυθήκη καὶ ὁμολογία)? Socrates at first undermines Hermogenes' conventionalist position by taking it to untenable extremes: if names are not in any way based on nature, then anyone would be free to alter them at will and without consensus (385dff.). If, on the other hand, one considers that a name is an instrument (ὄργανον; 388a) whereby reality is taught and made sense of (388b), one is pressed to recognize that there must be a correct way to use this tool, which in turn implies a specific ability on the part of a skilled name-giver (Νομοθέτης; 388e).[16] Hence, "the giving of names can hardly be . . . a trifling matter, or a task for trifling or casual persons: and Cratylus is right in saying that names belong to things by nature" (390e). Now apparently upholding Cratylus's naturalistic view, Socrates engages in enthusiastic etymologizing that touches upon several categories: proper names, divine names, names conveying physical realities, and names designating human virtues and vices (392aff.). But analysis of these is insufficient: Socrates notes that later names (ὕστερα) are based on earlier ones (πρῶτα) and asks Hermogenes to help him in the arduous task of reconstructing the former (422cff.). As "vocal imitations of that which is imitated" (μίμημα φωνῇ ἐκείνου ὅ μιμεῖται; 423b), names must be investigated according to their phonosymbolic value via their letters and syllables (γράμμασί τε καὶ συλλαβαῖς; 423e). A discussion of the symbolic value of individual sounds ensues: rho seems to express motion and agitation, iota subtleness, lambda smoothness, alpha greatness, and so on (426dff.).[17]

---

15. For a clear outline of issues and subissues dealt with in the Cratylus see Joseph, Limiting the Arbitrary, 87.

16. The contradictions in Socrates' argument have been exposed by Genette in Mimologics, pages 8 and following.

17. For a complete chart of the symbolic values discussed by Socrates, see Genette, Mimologics, 22.

But it is at the height of his oracular pronouncements on language that Socrates feels impelled to abandon Cratylus's "highly promising" mimetic theory. He takes aim at Cratylism by showing etymological inconsistencies between Cratylus's philosophical views and the terms that are supposed to mimic them: for instance, the word "knowledge" (ἐπιστήμη) can be etymologized as "standing still" (ἵστηριν), while in the Heraclitean philosophy supported by Cratylus it ought to designate or recall "flux" (437aff.). With Socrates' admission that "both convention and custom must contribute something towards the indication of our meaning when we speak" (435b), and that "no man of sense can put himself and his soul under the control of names and trust in names and their makers to the point of affirming that he knows anything" (440c), the dialogue comes to an end. Socrates invites Cratylus to join Hermogenes on his trip, a remark that Genette has read as the beginning of a Cratylian voyage across language that lasts to this day.[18] A "canonical" interpretation of the dialogue and of its odd etymologies has yet to be written.

For the purposes of this study, two aspects of the *Cratylus* are worth considering: its broad meaning within Plato's corpus as one of the earliest Western pronouncements on "etymology" and its etymological strategies, as employed by Socrates. The contention between Cratylus and Hermogenes remains unsettled. Some scholars stick to the modern axiom of linguistic arbitrariness and solve the dispute between conventionalism and naturalism in the *Cratylus* with an unqualified subscription to the former. Franco Cavazza voices a widespread opinion in his remark that the *Cratylus* signalled the "serious setback of etymology, which failed to deliver what its very name promised," given the "scientific impossibility [of] reconstruc[ting] the exact etymon of each word."[19] One may hesitate, he argues, to dismiss etymol-

---

18. "A long voyage begins, enlivened by brilliant arguments, ever new, ever the same. A long voyage: it is still going on, or nearly so." Genette, *Mimologics*, 27.
19. Cavazza, *Studio su Varrone*, 25.

ogies in the *Cratylus* as mere wordplay. Yet one cannot deny that "in Plato the possibility of codifying a scientific criterion for etymological research is severely hindered."[20] Timothy Baxter is more attentive to the function of etymologies in the *Cratylus*, which he sees as "a schematized developmental picture of Greek thought,"[21] but his conclusions are similar to Cavazza's: "Plato is attacking a tendency in Greek thought to over-value words."[22] And the implications of Baxter's analysis reach further. For him, Plato undermines etymology to target another culprit: allegory. Etymology is "allegory's handmaiden" because it masks "[the] separation from the surface text" posited by allegorical interpretation. In supporting allegory, etymology—itself an unreliable practice—ends up providing linguistic backing to an even more dubious "scientific" endeavor. Baxter bases his claim on Platonic passages, mainly from the *Republic* (376eff.) and the *Phaedrus* (278b7ff.), that apparently condemn the poet's reliance on "undersenses" (ὑπονοίαι), myths, or for that matter any form of writing conjured up to teach moral, ethical, or physical truths of an essential kind.

Two immediate objections can be raised against Cavazza and Baxter. The first one has to do with the aim of Plato's dialogue. As Genette argues, the assumption that the *Cratylus* is about "etymology" is ambiguous: nowhere in the *Cratylus* or elsewhere in his writings does Plato ever use the term "etymology" or a word conveying the Stoic sense of "looking for the true meaning of a word." The subtitle to the *Cratylus* simply reads "On the Correctness of Names" (ΠΕΡΙ ΟΝΟ-ΜΑΤΩΝ ΟΡΘΟΤΗΤΟΣ). To read the *Cratylus* as a full-length critique of "etymology" is to presume that Plato had in mind a systematic discipline of the sort we only find with the Stoics. And such a presumption is misleading: "The use of this term [etymology] is likely to create a good many misunderstandings, and it has not failed to do so. If one takes the term to mean the search for the true origin of a word, then

20. Ibid.
22. Cavazza, *Studio su Varrone*, 6.

21. Baxter, *The Cratylus*, 92.

it is clear, or at least it should be, that the 'etymologies' in the *Cratylus* are not etymologies at all. . . . The historical 'falseness' of the majority of these 'etymologies' (120 out of 140, according to Méridier, as cited by Genette) does not tell us very much about their real function."[23] While fully aware of the difference between ancient and modern etymologizing, Cavazza is tempted to measure Plato's dialogue with the yardstick of scientific etymology and to read in some of its statements an *ante litteram* admission of Saussurean arbitrariness. Therefore, Stoic etymologizing would actually be a regression from Platonic positions, because unlike Plato, the Stoics deny "that signifier and signified are independent and thus that the linguistic sign is arbitrary."[24] At least Baxter admits that "modern etymology . . . cannot offer much illumination of Plato's ideal theory"[25] since the one is descriptive and the other prescriptive.

For Gérard Genette, Plato's etymologizing is of a peculiar kind. I am inclined to support Genette's hypothesis that Socrates' etymologies are in fact *eponymies*: they show how a given nickname is well chosen (or correct) by unveiling "the agreement between its designation and its signification." And the *Cratylus* is a study of this very special type of motivation (or *correctness*, ὀρθότης): "given a proper name about which we already know *whom it designates*, [we wonder] about its *meaning*."[26] So, for instance, Astyanax (Ἀστύαναξ) is an effective eponym, because it conveys the quality or state of its bearer: "lord (ἄναξ) of the city." So is Hector (Ἕκτορος), which also means "lord" or "holder" (ἕκτωρ) (392eff.).

To recognize the eponymous quality of etymologies in the *Cratylus* is to pinpoint one of the crucial sources of etymological inquiry in Greek culture. As Jean Lallot showed in his "L'Étymologie en Grèce Ancienne d'Homère aux Grammariens Alexandrines,"[27] Greek poets

23. Genette, *Mimologics*, 13.
24. Cavazza. *Studio su Varrone*, 26.
25. Baxter, *The Cratylus*, 271.
26. Genette, *Mimologics*, 17.
27. In Chambon and Lüdi, *Discours étymologiques*, 135–48.

inherited a mythical tradition that held the names of heroes in high regard because of their undeniable truthfulness. "As a matter of fact, for the poet, the proper name, real or not, was above all inevitably true."[28] And the move from eponymous characters to eponymous names, i.e., names well chosen or veritable, was quick to follow:

To say, in brief, that Polynices (Πολύείκης) "is an eponym" means that his name, once we recognize it as formed by πολύς "numerous, abundant" and νεῖκος "conflict," suits him well insofar as his existence is all placed under the sign of conflict. Then, from the character "eponym," we will easily move on to the eponymous name, a name which "is suitable, truthful." Understood at first in the form of the eponymous relation, the truth of names will also be expressed in a privileged fashion, above all in Aeschylus, with the adjective ἔτυμος (or its variant ἐτήτυμος).[29]

Eponymy accounts for the poetic roots of Greek etymology while it also throws light on the close association, from the earliest times, between etymology and allegory. An eponym is defined in the OED as "a person whose name has given rise (in fact or by repute) to the name of a people, place, institution, etc.," or "a personal name used as a common noun or a noun formed in this way." In other words, an eponymous name works as an allegorical pointer, an umbrella term used to convey a multiplicity of concepts, acts, or events: at once *alieniloquium* (speech about "the Other" or about something else) and *diversiloquium* (speech about a number of diverse elements). Let us think for instance of Hermes (Ἑρμῆς): interpreter (from ἑρμηνεύς), deceptive speaker (from εἴρειν), the god of commerce from whom, for Cratylus, Hermogenes derives his "inappropriate" name (384c). Hence Socrates' analysis of "Hermes":

Well then, this name, "Hermes," seems to me to have to do with speech; he is an interpreter (ἑρμηνεύς) and a messenger, is wily and deceptive in speech, and is oratorical. All this activity is concerned with the power of speech. Now, as I said before, εἴρειν denotes the use of speech; moreover, Homer often uses the word ἐμήσατο which means "contrive." From these two words, then, the lawgiver imposes upon us the name of this god who contrived speech and the

28. Ibid., 136.
29. Ibid.

use of speech—εἴρειν means "speak"—and tells us: "Ye human beings, he who contrived speech (εἴρειν ἐμήσατο) ought to be called Eiremes by you." We, however, have beautified the name, as we imagine, and call him Hermes. (408ab)

What is more important is that behind and beyond questions of style this "allegorization of etymology" has clear epistemological implications: instead of denoting one concept, object, or set of events, a given name accesses allegorically a whole gamut of meanings that are partial but equally true. It is no accident that Jean Lallot should conclude his section on poetic etymology with the remark that "the truthfulness of the proper name which [the use of poetic etymology] entails is that of a pluralistic truth."[30]

My second objection to Cavazza and Baxter rests with their assumption about Plato's notion of "essential truths," a conceptual set that scholars have often found convenient to label "Platonic essentialism" or "Platonic realism." Cavazza grants that Plato's views in the *Cratylus* are provisional and open-ended, but he concludes that the issue of etymology, a practice unable to reach ultimate truths, "is settled in the negative" and is "in conformity with the Platonic conception of universals."[31] Baxter does not hesitate to see the *Cratylus* as a "frontal assault on Greek culture"[32] from an essentialist viewpoint: Plato's target, "the heady mix of allegory, etymology and cosmology" of pre-Socratic philosopher-poets.

Recent shifts in the understanding of Platonic philosophy call arguments like these into question.[33] Plato's "essentialism" has been

---

30. Ibid., 138.   31. Cavazza, *Studio su Varrone*, 24–25.
32. Baxter, *The Cratylus*, 6.

33. Joseph indirectly addresses the issue of Plato's essentialism in dealing with the *physis-nomos* debate and seems willing to acknowledge the complexity of Plato's position: "In its Sophistic form, the *physis-nomos* debate effectively limits to two the possible connections between words and the things they name. Either the connection is material (residing in the shared *physis* of word and thing) or nonexistent (opening it up to free, arbitrary will). Given these two choices, someone with an essentially religious outlook would be inclined to opt for *physis*, since it at least says that language and other human activity connect to something outside themselves. But to someone as deeply (though unconventionally) religious as Plato, the possibilities this dichotomy defines are absurdly limited." Joseph, *Limiting the Arbitrary*, 84.

and is being amply revised on the basis of "unwritten doctrines": doctrines that Plato himself endorses at the end of the *Phaedrus* (278bff.) and that Giovanni Reale, maintaining and extending the work of the Tübingen School, has painstakingly sought to reconstruct.[34] The crucial issue is Plato's distrust of writing in favor of an always self-revising orality: a distrust Socrates is said to vent in his claim that the philosopher never entrusts his most valuable findings to writing (Plato 278cff.). It should be easy to see how a revision of Plato's essentialism in this direction impinges upon our understanding of the *Cratylus* and how it clarifies the relation between allegory and etymology in his work. For a start, if one grants that Plato's dialogues resist final pronouncements, one cannot but question sweeping interpretations like those of Baxter and Cavazza. Should we draw from the *Cratylus* either a peroration on the worth of etymologizing or a curt dismissal of etymology as such, we would greatly betray its dialogic, heuristic thrust. And pitted against the fluid, argumentative mode of orality, even the role of Socratic irony in the *Cratylus* (and in Plato's dialogues generally) ought to be rethought. It is not hard to miscalculate the extent or misrepresent the target of parody in a dialogue where, by Baxter's own admission, "the uncertainty and paucity of evidence . . . means that plausibility is the most one can hope for."[35]

In the end, though, Baxter reads the *Cratylus* as a manifesto against etymology. For him, that "farrago of ingenious word-play and exuberant linguistic speculation" that takes up the central portion of the dialogue serves to expose a faulty epistemological practice: analyzing names on the presumption that they give access to their corresponding essences.[36] After all, Plato's rejection of etymology would be well grounded since it also involves its notorious accomplice, allegory, to be condemned on similar grounds.[37] Both etymology and allegory are

---

34. For a full account of the "paradigm shift" in Platonic studies and complete bibliographic lists including the Tübingen School, see Giovanni Reale, *Per una nuova interpretazione*.

35. Baxter, *The Cratylus*, 45.   36. Ibid., 1–5.

37. Ibid., 117–19.

epistemologically unsound: "[Plato's] two critiques [of allegory and etymology] are very similar, but the critique of etymology is an attack on a series of fallacious assumptions about how names and things are related. In contrast, the critique of allegory opens up no such fundamental philosophical questions."[38] There are at least two reasons why Baxter's anti-allegorical and anti-etymological reading of Plato is unconvincing. The first is that, as seen above, he relies on a narrow interpretation of Platonic essentialism; the second is that the passages he quotes from the *Republic* do not in fact object to allegory (or *hyponoia*) per se, but censure morally objectionable uses of allegory by poets and guardians. As for the passages from the *Phaedrus*, besides the fact that Socrates comments on myths rather than allegory, one should not neglect the philosophical relevance given to mythologizing within the dialogue itself through the famous myth of the soul-charioteer.[39]

How is one to deal then with the indeterminacy of the *Cratylus*? What is one to make of its subtle shifts from irony to seriousness and, above all, of its numerous and "liberal" etymologies? One interesting suggestion comes from the commentary on the *Cratylus* made by the Neo-Platonic philosopher Proclus: the "*scholia Procli*" that I mentioned with regard to *etymegoreia*. First, Proclus sets up the distinction between the thing (the *designatum*) and its appearance (the form, trace, or *denominatum*) and argues that Plato starts his "etymegories" from the former:

Once again in his etymologies [ἐτυμηγορίαις] Plato shows first what the thing (τὸ πρᾶγμα) reveals in and of itself, then what it is similar to, by virtue of the sign contained in the syllables that form its name. For instance, in the case of Orestes, he first mentions his ferine and wild nature [i.e., the way Orestes actually is]; then he adds his being "like a mountaineer" [i.e., the sign is similar to him], as seen in the syllables forming his name. And regarding Agamemnon, he first talks about his being perseverant and tenacious, then

38. Ibid., 119.
39. This point would call for a detailed analysis of both the *Phaedrus* and the *Republic*, which, for the sake of brevity and coherence, I do not undertake in the present study. In support of my arguments, see Giovanni Reale's introduction to his own translation of the *Phaedrus*.

adds these words: "that this man should be admired for his persistence" [is shown by the name 'Αγαμέμνων] and similarly for the names which follow.[40]

In other words, for Proclus, Plato would be "etymegorizing" with an eye on the form (εἶδος) of life,[41] rather than on its material signifier (ὕλης), unlike the *grammatikoi*, who instead "etymologize" by claiming a priority of the signifier over the signified. "Plato, who in his etymologies [ἐτυμηγορίαις] despises matter [ὕλης] and adheres above all to form [εἶδος], says that the name Agamemnon comes from the word ἀγαστός and not from the word ἄγαν. Grammarians, on the other hand, being mostly concerned with the matter and not the form of life, probably etymologize [ἐτυμολογήσουσιν] in reverse."[42] In Romano's words, Proclus's intuition is brilliant because it "shows that the antithesis between φύσει [nature] and θέσει [convention] (and, consequently, the polemic juxtaposition of Cratylus and Hermogenes) is a moot point." Rather than implying "a perfect similarity" between name and thing (Cratylus's thesis), Plato's ὀρθότης τῶν ὀνομάτων refers to a name's "instrumental and functional power to represent the nature or form of the named thing, without consideration for the material (syllabic, formal) aspect of the name itself. What is relevant to the 'correctness' of names is 'form,' or, better, 'the signifying power' [δύναμις], not 'matter.' Semantics is a discourse for philosophers, not for grammarians."[43]

In evaluating Plato's etymologies, one needs to take into account the distance between the discourse of philosophers and the discourse of grammarians: etymegorizing (using etymology with allegorical ends) and etymologizing (using etymology as a grammatical tech-

40. Proclus, Lezioni, 89.
41. The term "form" (εἶδο") in Plato conveys the idea of "ideal form" or "signifying power" and should not be confused with the modern notion of a (superficial) form or signifier opposed to a meaning (or signified). See relevant comments by Francesco Romano in Proclus, Lezioni, xxv.
42. Ibid., 89–90.
43. Ibid., xxvi.

nique to establish word derivations) adopt different strategies and respond to different ends which need not, however, be mutually exclusive. The purpose of my excursion into the *Cratylus* has been to justify a reading of Platonic etymologies that is neither unilaterally scientific nor utterly poetic. I find in this first Western "course of general linguistics" a scientific perception of the multiple linguistic factors involved in naming but also a recognition that names have an allegorical (meta-physical) sense, which it is the duty of the "man of sense" (ἔχοντος ἀνθρώοπος; 440c) to acknowledge and interrogate.

This is what, I think, comes from an analysis of etymologies (or *etymegories*) in Plato's *Cratylus*, to which we now turn for examples. Genette has clearly distinguished between Plato's treatment of later names and of earlier names: the former gives rise to etymologies, the latter to mimologies.[44] This is largely the same distinction made by Baxter between a "semantic" (based on word compounds) and a "mimetic" (based on sounds) etymological method, a distinction that follows Socrates' progression from compounding to phonosymbolism.[45] A study of Plato's phonosymbolism would probably yield clues on allegory, but I choose to deal only with the "semantic" section (the one Genette acknowledges as "etymological") because that is the main thrust of the Western etymologizing, from the Stoics to Giambattista Vico. Also, "semantic" etymology directly engages issues of scientificity that elude phonosymbolism.

Genette contends that most later name etymologies "are, properly speaking, *analyses* of words, the type of 'syntagmatic analyses' (*dix-neuf* = *dix* + *neuf*; *cerisier* = *cerise* + *ier*) that Saussure will make into indices of relative motivation."[46] The example he gives is "*alētheia* (truth) = *alē* + *theia* (divine wondering)." Compounding would appear here as the guiding principle, although Genette must quickly admit that pure compounding is rare and that even "syntagmatic analyses are sometimes

---

44. Genette, *Mimologics*, 13ff.
46. Genette, *Mimologics*, 15.

45. Baxter, *The Cratylus*, 5.

so extended that one hesitates to keep calling them that." "*Agamemnōn* = *agastos epimonē* (admirable for remaining)" and the belabored "*technē* = *echonoē* (the possession of mind)" are good examples. Even more telling are "*sōphrosynē* (self-restraint) = *sōtēria phronēseos* (salvation of thought) or *anthrōpos* = *anathrōn ha opōpe* (he who looks up at what he has seen)." Besides, some etymologies are based on paronymy—or punning—another principle that has nothing to do with analysis, as in the case of *gynē* (woman) = *gonē* (birth).[47] It may suffice, Genette says, to point out the two main features of *analysis* and *paronymy* and explicate specific etymologies by positing "a common feature that sufficiently justifies their presence in a dialogue on the 'correctness' of names: their role in motivation."[48] Important observations on eponymy—which we explored and used earlier—follow.

Genette rightly claims that analysis consists in discovering "the interpretant inside the interpreted term"[49] through a process of decomposition. For instance, it is obvious that the interpretation of ἀλήθεια as "divine wondering" depends on a recognizable parsing of the signifier into ἄλη + θεία, as opposed to the "correct" ἀ (privative) + λήθεια (hiding). Nonetheless, I feel that a purely syntagmatic (or "grammatical") explanation of the selective process at work in Platonic etymologies is unsatisfactory. It fails to do justice to the breadth, the boldness, and even the irony of Socrates' etymologizing because in Socrates' analyses of names, a morphological breakdown of a given word into possible lexical elements goes hand in hand with, and even relies on, an investigation of its meanings. In its final form, etymological analysis does yield one or more interpretants; and these are in fact morphologically contained in or deduced from the interpreted term, as Genette would have it. But I would be wary of taking the resulting homophony as the governing principle of the whole etymological process. Let me explain with examples. Socrates argues that the

47. Ibid., 13.   48. Ibid., 16.
49. Ibid., 14.

proper names Atreus, Pelops, and Tantalus are "correct": Ἀτρεύς alludes to the fact that the character's acts are "damaging and ruinous (ἀτηρά) to his virtue" or that his main features are stubbornness (ἀτειρές) and fearlessness (ἄτρεστον); Πέλοψ epitomizes the character's shortsightedness, his ability to "see only what is near (πέλας)"; and Τάνταλος calls to mind the character's wretched (ταλάντατον) fate—the balancing (ταλαντεία) of the stone above his head in Hades (395bff.). The chain of homophonic affinities is evident. What is perhaps less evident, but certainly present, is the network of semantic correspondences that *tropologically* undergirds this chain.[50]

Socrates' etymological strategy consists in finding a plausible set of meanings (e.g., stubborn, fearless) that simultaneously match the signifying power, the *dynamis*, of a name and its signifier, or form (Atreus). Although Platonic etymologies, like most etymologies in the ancient world, may seem to exhaust themselves in formal wordplay, upon closer scrutiny one finds that semantics plays a much more pervasive role. The gulf between a signifier (Pelops) and its signified (shortsightedness) can only be bridged rhetorically: the etymologist retraces various rhetorical routes that might have led, tropologically, to the condensation of a given meaning into its form. The etymologist's task is to revive possible sets of historical or mythological conditions that make up the *semantic script*[51] of a given name:

SOC: . . . And I think Pelops also has a fitting name; for this name means that he who sees only what is near deserves this designation.
HER: How is that?
SOC: Why it is said of him that in murdering Myrtilus he was quite unable to forecast or foresee the ultimate effects upon his whole race, and all the misery with which it was overwhelmed, because he saw only the near at hand and the immediate—that is to say (near)—in his eagerness to win by all means the hand of Hippodameia. (395d)

---

50. I use *tropological* here in both the OED senses of (1) metaphorical/figurative and (2) applied to a secondary sense or interpretation of Scripture.

51. A structuralist definition of *scripts* and a broad discussion of how they may be said to act as encyclopedic tools can be found in Umberto Eco's *Semiotics and the Philosophy of Language*,

To be sure, in the case of proper names (Astyanax, Agamemnon, Hector, and so on) and the names of gods (Zeus, Eros, Hermes, and so
on) all of which designate rather than signify, the mythological and
rhetorical pattern of motivation is easier to posit: no "received meaning" gets in the way. The very source of Socrates' etymologizing is eponymic, and examples in Plato abound. The gods (θεούς) draw their
name from the "running nature" (θεῖν) of the planets that humans
first worshipped (397d). Zeus is called Zena (Ζῆνα) or Dia (Δία) because he is the author of life (ζῆ'ν), through whom (δι' ὄν) "all living beings have the gift of life" (396b). The word hero (ἥρως) comes
from the god of love Eros (ἔρως) or from the fact that heroes are wise
and clever orators and dialecticians, able to ask questions (ἐρωτᾶν)
(398e). Poseidon (Ποσειδῶν) may owe his name to the fact that his
movements were hindered by the sea, a bond (δεσμός) to his feet
(ποδῶν) or to the fact that he knew (εἰδότος) many things (πολ-
λά). Pluto (Πλούτων) is the giver of wealth (πλοῦτος) (403a). Apollo
(Ἀπόλλω) washes away (ἀπολούων) and delivers (ἀπολύων) from evils
(405b). Artemis (Ἄρτεμις) "appears to get her name from her healthy
(ἀρτεμές) and well-ordered nature . . . or perhaps he who named her
meant that she is learned in virtue (ἀρετή), or, possibly too, that she
hates sexual intercourse (ἄροτπν μισεῖ)" (406b). Hermes (Ἑρμῆς)
is an interpreter (ἐμήνευς) and wise in speech (εἴρειν) (408a). Stars

especially pages 70–72, which includes references to the seminal work of philosopher and lo-
gician Charles Sanders Peirce on argumentation; to the studies of Lakoff and Johnson; and
more widely to artificial intelligence scientists. One telling instance cited by Eco is the sentence John was sleeping when he was suddenly awakened. Somebody was tearing up the pillow. "I imagine," argues Eco, "that a computer fed with dictionary-like information would be able to understand what /to sleep/ and /pillow/ mean, but would be unable to establish what the relation
is between John and the pillow (and which pillow?)." Eco goes on to explain that the notion of
script is linked to the notion of frame: "the addressee (be it a computer or a human being) is
endowed with an enlarged encyclopedic competence which encompasses also a set of frames,
or scripts, among which—for instance—are the frames 'sleeping' and 'bedroom.' By resorting
to this storage of competence, the addressee knows that human beings usually sleep in bedrooms and that bedrooms are furnished with beds, beds with pillows, and so on. By amalga-
mation of two or more frames, the addressee realizes that the pillow just mentioned can only
be the one John was resting his head on." Umberto Eco, Semiotics and the Philosophy of Language,
Advances in Semiotics (Bloomington: Indiana University Press, 1984), 70.

(ἄστρα) "get their name from lightning (ἀστραπή)" or from the fact "that they turn our eyes upward (τὰ ὦπα ἀναστρέφει)" (409c). Air (ἀήρ) is called so "because it raises (αἴρει) things from the earth or because it is always flowing (ἀεὶ ῥεῖ)" (410b).

A similar allegorical pattern is found in common names, names burdened with the weight of dictionary definition. At some point these must have been part of a shared semantic script, later opened up to rhetorical permutations. A good instance is the etymology of human being (ἄνθρωπος), said to derive from the fact that humans remember what they have seen (ἀναθρεῖ ὄπωπε). To this example we can add many others. Wisdom (φρόνησις) etymegorizes as perception (νόη-σις) of motion (φορᾶς) and flowing (ῥοῦ) or benefit (ὄνησις) of motion (φορᾶς). Thought (γνώμη) merges contemplation and generation (γονῆς νώμησις). Intelligence (νόησις) derives from desire (ἔσις) of the new (τοῦ νεοῦ) (411de). Knowledge (ἐπιστήμη) "indicates that the soul which is of any account accompanies (ἕπεται) things in their motion." Courage (ἀνδρεία) indicates an "opposite current or flow (ῥοή)" (413e). Woman (γυνή) is "much the same as" γονή (birth). Evil (κακία) denotes everything moving badly (κακῶς ἰόν) (415b). Soul (ψυχή) has the power to breathe and revive (ἀναψῦχον) the body. Opinion (δόξα) is "derived either from the pursuit (δίωξις) which the soul carries on as it pursues the knowledge of the nature of things, or from the shooting of the bow (τόξον)." Intention (βουλή) comes from shooting (βολή). Eros (ἔρως) is called so because it "flows in (ἐσρεῖ) from without" (420bd).

In all these instances, unifying principles of cosmology and phi-losophy, the ideological scoriae that scientific etymology aims to purge, are not only referred to but are also clearly left open to ques-tion. For each given name, more than one etymological explanation is admitted and deemed appropriate:

Some say [the body] is the tomb (σῆμα) of the soul, their notion being that the soul is buried in the present life; and again, because by its means the soul gives any signs which it gives, it is for this reason also properly called "sign" (σῆμα). But I think it most likely that the Orphic poets gave this name, with the idea that the soul is undergoing punishment for something; they think it has the body as an enclosure to keep it safe, like a prison, and this is, as the name itself denotes, the safe (σῶμα) for the soul, until the penalty is paid, and not even a letter needs to be changed. (400cd)

Ultimately, the name is always an *allegory of its meaning*. It cannot, and it does not, point unequivocally to one "correct" or ideal sense but neither does it utterly fade under the incrustations of time and usage. Names cover the middle ground between nature and convention; they enable human beings to tell a hi(story) and simultaneously to sketch the mimological, motivational patterns that give that hi(story) its variegated senses (this may be Socrates' lesson at the end of the *Cratylus*). Thus the lack, or poverty, of historical perspective in ancient etymologizing—for many an unpardonable sin—may in fact mark one of its forgotten strengths.

Alexandrian Etymologizing

With slight differences, the features of Platonic etymologizing that we have seen so far occur in Alexandrian theorists, above all in the work of Philo. In *Etymology in Early Jewish Interpretation: The Hebrew Names in Philo*, Lester Grabbe identifies and isolates all the Hebrew etymologies in the Philonic corpus, a total of 166 names, and compares these to several *loci classici* of Christian exegesis and Jewish compilations with the intent of assessing the role and the weight of etymologizing in Philo's exegetical work.[52] Grabbe shows that Philo's etymologies almost invariably serve specific interpretative ends, signalled by formulae like χαλεῖται (be called) or the very frequent ἑρμηνεύεται (be interpreted), reserved to Hebrew, not Greek, etymologies: "Philo's use of Hebrew etymologies is in a different category from the paronomasia expected in a Greek writer of this time. He puts more emphasis

---

52. Lester Grabbe, *Etymology in Early Jewish Interpretation: The Hebrew Names in Philo*, Brown Judaic Studies 115 (Atlanta, Ga.: Scholars Press, 1988).

on Hebrew etymologies than he does on his Greek wordplays. Thus Philo's etymologizing of Hebrew names is a well-defined and basically self-contained exegetical device."[53]

Unlike Greek etymologizing, practiced for instance by Pseudo-Heraclitus or Plutarch, Philo's exegesis does not address the "appropriateness of names" and does not entail a theory on the naturalness or conventionality of linguistic signs.[54] Philo, whose apparent ease with Hebrew words may come from an unknown name list from which he taps etymological support for his readings, uses etymology only as "one device among many."[55] For one thing, Philo's etymologies may be said to anticipate the impetus of later Christian exegesis, where language is entirely subordinated to evangelization. But when compared to that of patristic writers, Philo's etymologizing shows a much higher degree of philosophical abstraction and hermeneutical sophistication.

Let us take as an example the etymological pair Ἀβράμ/Ἀβραάμ, which is used to mark the conversion of the Biblical character in Genesis 17:4–5. In the case of Ἀβράμ, Philo proposes an etymology that does not occur in the Septuagint text: "Abram" is derived from the Hebrew 'āb "father" plus rwm "be high." Hence the epithet πατὴρ μετέωρος, "uplifted father" to be found, among others, in Jerome (pater excelsus).[56] As for Ἀβραάμ, Philo seems to disregard the Masoretic etymology of this name as "father of a multitude" ('ā-hāmôn) in favor of a new acronymic parsing ('āb + hāmôn as "echo" + bhr? "choose, elect") that gives "elect father of sound" (πατὴρ ἐχλεχτὸς ἠχούς), later adopted by Ambrose (pater electus soni).[57] In both cases, Philo follows an etymological path that scholars have traced back to the kabbalistic notarikon, where "each letter of a word stands for the whole word, as if the word were itself an acronym."[58] What is more interesting for our purposes, though, is that each of the two names be-

53. Grabbe, Etymology, 44.
55. Ibid., 48.
57. Ibid.

54. Ibid., 4.
56. Ibid., 121.
58. Ibid., 126.

comes the starting point for a long philosophical digression on the properties of mind, speech, and soul. Grabbe reports the passage from *Legum Allegoriae* where Philo offers an allegorical interpretation of "Abram": "For when the mind does not, like a master, frighten the soul . . . but governs it like a father . . . , it soars aloft (meteōropolē) and spends its time in contemplation of the universe." (3.83–84) And the passage from *De mutatione nominum*, which develops the allegorical sense of "Abraham," is equally dense, weaving as it does each of the three elements etymologically derived (father, elect, echo) into a consistent allegorical story where the sound (*hāmôn*), or the uttered word, is fathered by the mind (*'āb*), and reaches its best in the mind of the elect, or the wise (*bhr?*).[59] Philo's etymologies integrate seamlessly into an allegoresis of Scriptures that has repercussions on philosophy, theology, and cosmology. Claude Mondésert rightly notes that Philo's *Legum Allegoriae* presents itself with the depth of a *"histoire morale de l'âme"* and the breadth of a *"cosmologie religeuse,"* a *"doctrine spirituelle ascetique et mystique."*[60] And we cannot fail to see that etymologies provide linguistic cornerstones to these complicated allegories. Philo's allegory of the four rivers of the Garden of Eden[61]—taken as the archetype of virtue—is a good illustration of this point. The first river (Pishon) is said to represent prudence (φρόνησις) because it "spares" (φείδο-μαι) the soul from wrongs. The Hebrew etymology of the next river, the Gihon, signifies "breast" or "butting with horns" and so denotes courage (ἀνδρεία). The Tigris is associated with the virtue of self-control, probably by antithesis to the ferine principle of pleasure (a play on the Greek τίγρϊς). The Euphrates instead symbolizes justice (δικαιοσύνη) via its Greek etymon, "fruitfulness." Philo's etymologizing within the Alexandrian tradition and its indebtedness to onomastics have been attentively analyzed elsewhere and are not covered

59. Ibid.
60. Claude Mondésert, *Legum Allegoriae, Book I–III* (Paris: Éditions du Cerf, 1962), 17.
61. Ibid., 1.63–87.

in this study. My question here is more circumscribed: what are the distinctive features, if any, of Philo's etymologies, and how do these add to our understanding of the practice that we have named "allegorical etymology"? It is hardly surprising that Philonic etymologies should subordinate homophony and analogy to semantic ends: Philo determines the origin of names in accordance with interpretative blueprints warranted by tradition. Let us think, for instance, of Ἀδάμ, derived from the Hebrew 'ǎdmāh (earth) in compliance with the scriptural suggestion.[62] What, however, characterizes Philo's etymologizing is that etyma do not directly explain the meaning of names; they do not consist in plain historical or moral truths that were hidden beneath form and that etymologizing brings to the surface. Rather, etyma themselves become the formal constituents of a further allegorical construction. Thus, Ἀδάμ does not simply etymologize as "perishable earth" with reference to the fate of created beings. Perishability is also symbolical (συμβολικῶς) of an "earthly and perishable mind."[63] Καίν is traditionally linked to the Hebrew qnh (acquire, possess) to mark, historically, Cain's disposition, but is also allegorized as the "self-loving principle" that recognizes the mind as its only master.[64] Via a similar route, as seen above, Ἀβραάμ allegorizes the superior mind of the wise from which sound speech streams forth.[65] I think that the exchangeability of tenor and vehicle that Mondésert notes in his reading of Philo's archetypes—whereby, for instance, the Garden of Eden stands both as God and as Virtue—applies to allegorical etymology. Provided one accepts the classical definition of allegory as a "continua metaphora," after the formula popularized by Quintilian,[66] one sees that Philo's etymologies are two pronged. Not only do

---

62. From Genesis 2:7. Quoted in Grabbe, Etymology, 129.

63. Grabbe, Etymology, 129.

64. Ibid., 177.

65. Most of the examples of Philonic etymologies listed in Grabbe's appendix (part II) seem to follow this model.

66. See chapter 2.

they show the kind of exchangeability of tenor and vehicle inherent in scriptural exegesis, where *littera* and *figura* are endowed with equal meaningfulness, but it also seems that by virtue of an allegorical schema that links tenor and vehicle systematically to each other and to the tenor and vehicle of other terms, the allegorical power of a given etymon is indefinitely extended, or "continued." In other words, an etymon B, which supposedly sums up the tenor of a given vehicle term A, becomes itself the vehicle A1 of a further tenor B1.[67]

> Ἀδάμ ⇆ 'ādāmāh (earth) ⇆ perishable mind
> Vehicle   etymon/tenor B [vehicle A1]   tenor B1

Since it emulates the formal acrobatics of the Jewish kabbala, encompasses the sweeping philosophical horizon of the Greek, and foretells the ordered *gradatio* of fourfold Patristic exegesis, Philo's work bears upon etymological allegory. It is with an eye on Philonic etymologizing that we regain the thread of this chapter and draw at least two general conclusions. First, a given etymology (e.g., 'ādāmāh) could be termed allegorical when it serves to create a tropological lien between a word (Ἀδάμ) and one or more of its arguable semantic attributes (earthly, perishable). It must be stressed that such a lien is not, in any postromantic sense of the word, symbolical (the name "Adam" is not a self-contained icon of "earthly perishability").[68] Rather, it works in context to unveil one or more facets of a wider semantic network, cultural and cognitive (the history of creation and salvation; the sinful state of humankind and so on). To the extent that connections of this kind are

---

67. Possible analogies between this semantic model and the postmodern variants of Charles Sanders Peirce's "unlimited semiosis" will be hinted at in chapter 7. For a discussion of Peirce's theory of unlimited semiosis see, for instance, B. Nordtug, "Subjectivity as an Unlimited Semiosis: Lacan and Peirce," *Studies in Philosophy and Education* 2004, vol. 23, 87-102.

68. The sharp dichotomy between "symbol" and "allegory" is, of course, largely ascribable to Romantic poetics and often proves untenable in the case of ancient and medieval codifications. My juxtaposition of "symbolical" and "allegorical" here is purely operational and relies upon Tzvetan Todorov's discussion in *Theories of the Symbol* of Romantic ideas on symbols in the works of Goethe and Schelling. I am thinking in particular of the distinction between autotelism (a quality of symbols) and heterotelism (a feature of allegory), immediacy and mediation.

systematic in ways that we have already had occasion to discuss, the procedure is allegorical. The second observation proceeds from the first: it has to do with the role that linguistic form plays in allegorical etymology and recalls Ohly's comments about the limits of modern etymology.[69] Twentieth-century linguists who rely on form, be it syntactical, grammatical, or eminently phonological, view pre-1800 etymologies with strong disfavor. But from our reading of the *Cratylus*, from our selection of Stoic etymologies, and from the Philonic examples, it is now clear that linguistic form was *never in itself* taken as the overarching criterion for etymological investigation. Etymologists were indeed aware of morphology, an aspect that was researched, as we shall see shortly, by grammarians like Varro and by medieval scholars of the caliber of Isidore. In some cases, light was even shed on recurrent phonological features. Nevertheless, to most of them form was above all the springboard from which etymology plunged into the pseudo-linguistic depths of semantics and pragmatics, with twists and turns choreographed by broad ideological scripts rather than determined by the localized algorithm of science. By the second century BC, the wisdom of the Stoics had been handed down to the Romans—that dubious concoction of etymology and grammar congealed in a variety of treatises. To the controversies that divide Augustine, Cicero, and Varro over the worth of such treatises, we next turn our attention.

69. See chapter 2. Zamboni deals with the difference between ancient and modern linguistics in these terms: "A given signifier (i.e., the word) is created as a function of the meaning to be expressed (*nomina sunt consequentia rerum*). The latter, which coincides with the idea or the conceptual reality, is the privileged subject of linguistic inquiry, unlike what happens in modern linguistics, where the starting point is form." Zamboni, *L'etimologia*, 16.

CHAPTER 4

QUARTUS GRADUS ETYMOLOGIAE
The Roman Contribution

"AS FAR AS ETYMOLOGY IS CONCERNED, we could say that in Rome there is a pre-Varro and a post-Varro."[1] These are the words Françoise Desbordes uses in her "La Pratique Étymologique Des Poètes Latins à l'Èpoque d'Auguste" to describe Roman etymology. And since it is mainly in light of the Varronian *opus*—particularly the fifth, sixth, and seventh books of his *De Lingua Latina*—that one can make out the scenario of Latin etymologizing, the following analysis focuses on Varro.[2] To be sure, Roman etymologizing is a motley affair. So, to put Varro's achievement in context, I will comment on the forms and fortunes of etymologizing in Rome, and will also spend some time on Cicero and Augustine. Somehow, at the two chronological ends of what we conceive as *Romanitas* and by virtue of an approach to etymology that is neither strictly grammatical nor avowedly mystical, Cicero and Augustine strike a balance that I think also shapes Varro's contribution to *etymegoreia*. Varro's concept of a *quartus gradus etymologiae* marks the supreme degree of etymological inquiry and paves the way to medieval codifications, most prominently to the etymological *summa* of Isidore of Seville. References to relevant works of Augustine, Cicero, and Quintilian occur throughout.

---

1. [En matière d'étymologie, on peut dire qu'à Rome il y a un avant-Varron et un après-Varron.] Françoise Desbordes, "La Pratique Étymologique Des Poètes Latins à l'Èpoque d'Auguste," in Chambon and Lüdi, *Discours étymologiques*, 150.

2. See for instance Jean Collart's *Varron, grammairien latin* Publications de la Faculté des lettres de l'Université de Strasbourg, fasc. 121 (1954); Francesco Della Corte's *Varrone, il terzo gran lume romano* (Florence: La Nuova Italia, 1970); and Robert Schröter's *Studien zur varronischen Etymologie* (Köln: Erster Teil, 1959).

Etymology in Rome

The commonly accepted view is that the Romans brought little innovation to etymologizing. Citing Reitzenstein's monograph on Varro, Paulus Dietrich held that many Latin etymologies were imitations of Greek, and specifically Stoic, ones.[3] For Cavazza, "the Romans, who actively inherited Greek culture in other fields . . . received etymology almost passively," possibly because of its ties with philosophy, at which Romans did not excel.[4] Varro wavered between the Greek term (ἐτυμολογία), its transliteration (etymologia, VII, 109), and the calque origo (V, 3). Cicero proposed veriloquium (Topica, 35) but, as Quintilian remarks, never actually took to it ("ipse Cicero, qui finxit reformidat," Institutio Oratoriae, I, 6.8). Other terms included nota, notatio (Cicero, Topica, 35), originatio, interpretatio verborum (Macrobius), explicatio verborum (Cicero and Quintilian), ratio (Quintilian, I, 6.1), origo verborum, or simply origo (Quintilian, Gellius).[5] There also existed, of course, the ancient tradition of word explication (verborum enodatio), used by annalists, antiquarians, jurists, and poets, but Desbordes rightly notes that those etymologies lacked sustained goals or recognizable methods.[6]

The two main etymological schools handed down from Greece are the Stoic (Cleanthes; Chrysippus) and the Alexandrian (Aristarchus; Aristophanes of Byzantium), somewhat divided, as we have seen, over the issue of physis (nature) versus nomos (convention) and over the parallel controversy between analogía (whereby language is said to develop from regular, recurrent models) and anōmalía (whereby language is the outcome of random irregularity).[7] By Varro's time (70 BC) and af-

---

3. Paulus Dietrich, De Ciceronis ratione etymologica (Jena: Typis G. Nevenhahni, 1911), 33.
4. Cavazza, Studio su Varrone, 37.
5. For a thorough discussion of terms used by Latin grammarians in Varro's time and before, see Cavazza, Studio su Varrone, 20–21, n. 13.
6. Desbordes, "La Pratique," 150.
7. Stoic etymology is discussed in Marcia Colish's Stoic Tradition from Antiquity to the Early Middle Ages: Stoicism in Christian Latin Thought Through the Sixth Century (Leiden: Brill, 1990). See also Zamboni, L'etimologia, 18, and Cavazza, Studio su Varrone, 133ff.

ter sporadic attempts at reconciliation, the two approaches converged into the grammatical and rhetorical studies championed by Aelius Stilo (160 BC) as part of his effort to rationalize etymology. Some critics hold Stilo responsible for incorporating Stoic practices into Roman etymology: Dietrich would have him as the author of an *etymologicon* that translated the Stoic criteria into Latin ("librum etymologicum, quo transtulit rationes Stoicas in Latinum," 32). As Varro's (and Cicero's) master, Aelius Stilo shaped much of Roman etymologizing, even though the supposed existence of a Stilonian glossary that Varro might have pillaged remains unproven.[8]

Cicero and Augustine

Roman etymology plausibly developed under the aegis of Greek scholars in the wake of Stoicism and Alexandrianism. Although it is hard to fit each Latin scholar exactly into either one of the two currents of Stoicism and Alexandrianism, both currents can be traced in their subterranean courses beneath representative etymological theories of the time, as Dietrich did in his classic study *De Ciceronis ratione etymologica*, where he contrasted Cicero, champion of *usus*, and Augustine, supporter of the Stoics. Dietrich compared the etymological rules of the Stoics, taken from Augustine's *De Dialectica* (VI), with those collected from Cicero's works and concluded that differences were significant: "It should be clear from this comparison that Cicero was completely alien to the etymological principles of the Stoa given by Augustine."[9] Several *veriloquia stoica* are scattered in Cicero's work,[10] but these would be mere borrowings that do not do justice to Cicero's etymological insight, attested elsewhere in his concern for the two sensible principles of *derivatio* and *compositio*.

And yet, to read Roman etymologizing solely as the passive rehearsal of a script written by Greeks is to misrepresent its scope. What

8. Desbordes, "La Pratique," 150.   9. Dietrich, *De Ciceronis*, 30.
10. Ibid., 28–29.

is peculiar to Roman etymologizing stands out if one turns to Cicero
and Augustine to see whether behind overt differences there may be
covert similarities. Augustine is often considered as a late devotee of
the Stoic doctrine: a good example of this lies in one anecdote from
his *Confessions* (IX, 12.32), where he admits taking a bath (*balneum*) to
overcome grief over his mother's death. Augustine justifies his act
etymologically "because," he says "I had heard the bath to take its
name from the Greeks, who call it so because it is supposed to drive
sorrows out of the mind" [quod audieram inde *balneis* nomen indi-
tum, quia Graeci βαλανεῖον dixerint, quod anxietatem pellet ex ani-
mo]. βαλανεῖον (to bathe) is derived from βάλλειν ἀνίαν (to banish
pain).[11] But Augustine's official endorsement of Stoic etymologizing
comes from the sixth chapter of the *De Dialectica*, starting with his note
that for the Stoics, "there is no word the origin [ratio] of which cannot
somehow be explained" [nullum esse verbum, cuius non certa ratio
explicari possit, x, 7]. The Stoic principle Augustine states first is onomatopoeia, where a given word sounds like the thing it signifies. Yet,
since examples of onomatopoeia are limited, and we do have words
"which do not sound" [quia sunt res quae non sonant] he moves right
on to observe the effects that harsh or pleasant sounds may have on
our senses. And these phonosymbolic elements—the "*cunabula verborum*" or στοιχεῖα—combine to produce the four broad Stoic categories that will hold sway in the Middle Ages. They are:

(1) *similitudo* (similarity): based on a semantic and formal analogy
between words. It is the case of *crus* (leg), derived from *crux* (cross) because "for length and hardness legs are more similar than other body
members to the wood of the cross" [longitudine ac duritia inter mem-
bra cetera sunt ligno crucis similiora].

(2) *abusio* (improper usage): based on spatial or temporal contigu-
ity, as in the derivation of *piscīnae* (pools) from the fact that pools con-

11. The anecdote is recalled by both Pisani, *L'etimologia*, 26, and Zamboni, *L'etimologia*, 17.

tain water, the element where fish (*pisces*) live ("ubi piscibus vita est"), or from the fact that those swimming in pools become like fish.[12]

(3) *contrarium* (opposition): based on antiphrasis, as in the notorious "*lucus* [forest] *a non lucendo* [without light]" and "*bellum* [war] *quod res bella non sit* [because it is not a pleasant (*bellus*) thing]." Examples of antiphrastic etymology flourished in Varro and were attacked by F. Muller, one of Varro's major detractors.[13]

(4) *vicinitas* (proximity): based on associative strategies of various types:

> *per efficientiam* (cause): *foedus* (pact) from *foeditate porci* (the killing of the pig occurring when pacts are stipulated)
>
> *per effectum* (effect): *puteus* (well) because one drinks (*potat*) from it ("quod eius effectus potatio")
>
> *per id quod continet* (container): *urbs* (city) from the circle (*orbis*) traced around the location where the city will be built.
>
> *per id quod continetur* (contained): *horreum* (barn) from *hordeum* (barley)
>
> *per abusionem a parte totum* (part for the whole): *mucro* (blade-point) used to refer to the whole sword.
>
> *per abusionem a toto pars* (whole for the part): *capillum* (hair) ("quasi capitis pilus")

Augustine's excursus on Stoic etymologies shows that tropology—the kind of interpretation dating back to the Greek *Stoa* and based on secondary, moral senses of words—survived in late Latinity. The practice was mocked or reviled by leading orators (including Cicero) but thrived among Roman grammarians and their compendious *etymologica*. But if Stoicism so clearly runs through the pages of Augustine's *De Dialectica*, does it make sense to talk about "Augustinian" etymologiz-

---

12. Zamboni remarks that this etymology of *piscinae* is "historically accurate" (storicamente reale). Zamboni, *L'etimologia*, 21.

13. F. Muller, *De veterum imprimis Romanorum studis etymologicis* (Utrecht: A. Oosthoek, 1910). "Varronem sensu historico maximopere ac saepissime caruisse," quoted in Cavazza, *Studio su Varrone*, 18, n. 9.

ing? And what do Augustine's etymologies have to share with Cicero?

The two questions are related. I think Augustine's etymologizing is unique because it grafts Stoic doctrines onto a rhetorical agenda. And this rhetorical agenda is, upon closer scrutiny, the one set by Cicero. Augustine takes on Stoic strategies of word explanation but, unlike Philo, he does not primarily aim to devise psychological or cosmological theories (although neither is excluded from his exegesis). Rather, setting up a practice that will gain momentum among medieval exegetes, Augustine uses etymology as a tool for argumentation: to reshape pagan culture in Christian terms and put forward clear historical and ideological claims.[14] And the rhetorical force of Augustine's etymologizing, already present in his De Doctrina Christiana but fully deployed in De Civitate Dei, owes much to Cicero.

Cavazza alludes to Cicero's eclecticism when he cites studies by Gay and Morillon,[15] which frame Cicero as a "timid anomalist" and his work as a middle ground between Stoicism and Alexandrianism. The issue of Cicero's partial adherence to Stoicism (or his utter rejection of it) must be left open for discussion elsewhere. What needs to be said here is that, unlike the Stoics but very much like Augustine later, Cicero favored practical rhetoric over abstract philosophizing. For Cicero, etymology is worthwhile not so much because it grants access to the essence of things but because of its potential for persuasion, because it is a viable way of arguing in every aspect of the social life: in political deliberations, in forensic speeches, in epideictic prose. Cicero's definition of etymology as nota (Topica, 10–35) addresses this question:

Ea est autem, cum ex vi nominis argumentum elicitur; quam Graeci ἐτυμολο-γίαν appellant, id est verbum ex verbo veriloquium; nos autem novitatem ver-

---

14. The "ideological" weight of medieval etymology is mentioned in Philip B. Rollinson, Classical Theories of Allegory and Christian Culture, Duquesne Studies, Language and Literature Series, vol. 3 (Pittsburgh, Pa.: Duquesne University Press, 1981), 48; and in Roswitha Klinck, Die lateinische Etymologie des Mittelalters, Medium aevum; philologische studien, Bd. 17 (Munich: W. Fink, 1970), 138.

15. Cavazza, Studio su Varrone, 112.

bi non satis apti fugientes genus hoc notationem appellamus, quia sunt verba rerum notae. Itaque hoc quidem Aristoteles σύμβολον appellat, quod Latine est nota.

[This is what is used when an argument is developed out of the meaning of a word. The Greeks call this ἐτυμολογία (etymology), and this translated word for word would be in Latin *veriloquium* (veriloquence). But to avoid using a new word that is not very suitable, we call this kind *notatio*, because words are tokens *(notae)* of things. So Aristotle uses σύμβολον (symbolon) for the idea represented by the Latin *nota*.]

Cicero translates etymology as *notatio* to convey the idea that etymology works as a *symbolon*, a gloss that "throws together" (συμβάλλειν) an argumentative line. And this is also the view of etymology held by Augustine. Critical evidence as to the Ciceronianism of Augustine or, for that matter, the Augustinianism of Cicero is plenty: their "case" is relevant to our assessment of Roman etymology since it tells of the Roman answer to the etymological issues and tensions they had borrowed from Greece. For one thing, the Romans carried over and fulfilled the Greek trend towards what we could call a grammaticalization of etymology. As a conscious inheritor of the Greek γραμα-τιστής, a Roman *litterator* (like Priscian) saw and used etymology as a set of rules for word derivation, and no more. Philosophizing of the kind found in the Stoics was shunned. Cavazza suggests:

Once the questions of Greek etymology and of the origin of language converge into Latin culture, the latter will only consider the practical value of language which denominates things. Obviously, there is no trace in the Roman world of the Platonic attempt to connect language to metaphysical forms of knowledge. Language as an instrument of *notitia rerum* is seen only in its pragmatic value. Hence the increasing trend towards grammar, which is precisely a practical tool. Varro himself witnesses this shift, whereby, after the attempts of the first philosophers investigating language, Western culture increasingly abandons the idea that language may give access to ultimate knowledge.[16]

16. [Quando la problematica dell'etimologia greca e dell'origine del linguaggio saranno confluite nella cultura latina, quest'ultima considererà solo il valore pratico della lingua che denomina le cose: nel mondo romano non c'è traccia, ovviamente, del tentativo di aggancio platonico con forme di conoscenza metafisica, mentre la lingua come strumento di *notitia rerum* viene vista solo nel suo valore pragmatico, per cui è logico che si tenda sempre più verso la grammatica che è appunto strumento pratico. Varrone stesso è teste di un simile

Roman grammarians were in fact popularizing a trend already prominent among Aristotelian scholars, at least if one accepts the authenticity of Dionysus Thrax's grammar book Τέχνη Γραμμα-τική.[17] In his work, etymology had de facto become only one of the six parts of grammar, together with "correct pronunciation," "explanation of main poetic tropes," "explanation of glosses," "finding of analogies," and "critical examination of poems."[18] Exact boundaries between different arts in Greek and Roman culture should of course be drawn with caution, particularly given our limited understanding of categories like that of artes liberales.[19] But the general perception in both Greece and Rome seems to have been that etymology could not become an ars,[20] or τέχνη, as long as it failed to achieve the technical perfection of grammar. The often-implied dilettantism of the ἐτυ-μολογικοί[21] only served to highlight the authority and prestige of the γραμματιστής, or, as the Latin calque has it, the litterator.[22]

But Roman rhetoric acted also as a powerful corrective against the technicalities of grammar. It cannot be doubted that for both Cicero and Quintilian a concept like Latinitas and a formula like bene dicendi had pragmatic and moral implications well beyond the scope of syntax, morphology, or style. And this was probably even truer for Augustine, who used etymologizing as an instrument for Christian exegesis. Although its emphasis had shifted from philosophy to praxis, Roman etymology still held on to Stoic assumptions, manifest in Augustine

---

passaggio, che vede dunque la civiltà occidentale tendere, dopo i tentativi dei primi filosofi che esaminarono il linguaggio, sempre più ad abbandonare l'idea che la lingua sia una via di penetrazione verso conoscenze superiori.] Ibid., 32–33.

17. The book is considered by some a pseudoepigraph dating from the fourth century AD. For arguments and counterarguments on this, see Cavazza, Studio su Varrone, 35, n. 41.

18. Zamboni, L'etimologia, 20.

19. See for instance Henri Marrou, Histoire de L'éducation dans L'antiquité (Paris: du Seuil, 1950), 370ff.

20. This point is discussed by Cavazza, Studio su Varrone, 35.

21. The term is used pejoratively in Aulus Gellius, Noctes Atticae, in The Attic Nights of Aulus Gellius, trans. John C. Rolfe, 3 vols, Loeb Classical Library (Cambridge, Mass.: Harvard University Press, 1927), 2, 22, 7.

22. Cavazza, Studio su Varrone, 35.

but present even in Cicero. Cicero was of course skeptical about many of the etymologies in vogue at the time, which he dismissed as *ineptiae*: he could attack the systematizations of grammarians as much as the fabrications of poets.[23] But, by Dietrich's own admission, Cicero did not invariably avoid etymologies of the Stoic (and Augustinian) kind. One finds examples of etymologies by *vicinitas per efficientiam* in *De Divinatione* (*divinatio* from *divis*, I, 1); by *vicinitas per id quod continetur* in the *Tusculana* (*humatus* from *humo*, I, 36.3); by *similitudo* in the *Ad Familias* (*penem* from *penicillus*, IX, 22.2); or by *onomatopoeia* in *De Legibus* (*lessum*; 23, 59). Only etymologies by *contrarium*, Dietrich argues, are absent in Cicero, which means he must have disapproved of this strategy.[24]

What we can draw from this brief comparison between Cicero and Augustine on the subject of etymology is that Roman etymologizing looked more like a composite landscape where Greek and Roman perspectives merged, than a monument already sculpted by Greek hands. And in that landscape, where Romans tried to match the technical rigor of grammar with the persuasive power of rhetoric, *etymegoreia* was to carve its distinctive niche.

Varro's Contribution

Varro's etymologizing took form within the eclectic and volatile culture embraced by Cicero and Augustine, an environment sanctioned in Rome with the arrival of Crates of Mallus (172 or 171 BC), a follower of Chrysippus. Cavazza explains that "Varro is a philologist trained in the Stoic and Alexandrian tradition." Thus, as an etymologist, Varro "devotes himself both to words of 'popular usage' (*consue-*

---

23. Dietrich concludes his study on Ciceronian etymology by emphasizing Cicero's watchful distance from Stoic precepts and their Roman supporters: "Non erat Tullius etymologus neque esse voluit. Respuebat doctrinam Stoicorum ut nimis artificiosam spinosamque atque libentius sequebatur sensum suum, qui ei plerumque viam rectam monstravit. Ea etyma, quae apud eum invenis a verbo explicando sive significatione sive litteris valde distantia . . . suspicor . . . longe ampliore quam ostendi et ostendere poteram propter tenuitatem fragmentorum ex libris antetulliani temporis grammaticis excerptorum." Dietrich, *De Ciceronis*, 151.

24. Ibid., 28–30.

tudo communis, which he thinks more important at least by virtue of their age) and to poetic terms, founded on the *auctoritas* of a writer."[25] In Varro, etymology meets the double purpose of advancing speculation on language—or discovering, in line with fashionable trends, "why and whence words are" [cur et unde sint verba] (V, i, 2)—and of tapping archaeological truths, or reconstructing the *antiquitas*, the history of the ancient Roman world ("In what way names were applied to things in Latin" [quemadmodum vocabula essent imposita rebus in lingua Latina], V, i, 1).

Unfortunately, of the twenty-five books that made up the *De Lingua Latina*, only books 5 to 10 are extant, apart from a few fragments culled from other authors, like Aulus Gellius.[26] The contents of books 2, 3, and 4, where Varro talked about the advantages and disadvantages of "the branch of learning which is called Etymology" (V, 1) must be left to speculation. But conjectures on the scope of Varro's etymologizing can be made by gathering clues from books 5 to 7, where Varro gives us his complex etymological model.

Albeit with variable degrees of appreciation,[27] scholars have pointed out that Varro uses a fourfold scheme: a sort of chart that includes Alexandrian *regulae*, mystic principles borrowed from Pythagoras, and stages of etymological inquiry. At the beginning of book 5, Varro talks about the four pairs of causes (*bis quaternas causas*, V, 6) that bring about changes in the form of a word over time: *litterarum additio* or *demptio* (addition or loss of letters); *litterarum* tra<<ie>>*ctio* or *commutatio* (transposition or change of letters); *syllabarum productio* or *correptio* (lengthening or shortening of syllables); *syllabarum adiectio* or *detrectio* (addition or loss of syllables). He follows conventionalist theories and

25. Cavazza, *Studio su Varrone*, 39.

26. Gellius, *Noctes Atticae* 2, 25, 16,

27. Vivien Law reminds us that "the etymological books are often skimmed over in accounts of Varro's work, for his approach to etymology appears to be quite alien to ours." Vivien Law, *The History of Linguistics in Europe from Plato to 1600* (Cambridge: Cambridge University Press, 2003), 44. On this issue, see also Hellfried Dahlmann, *Varro und die hellenistische Sprachtheorie* (Berlin: Weidmann, 1964), 36ff, and Collart, *Varron*, 37.

takes *vetustas* (antiquity) as a critical factor in linguistic change. But his concept of time also includes the fact that language partakes of the naturalness of the Pythagorean number, the ἀριθμός, which sets up the allegorical *quadripertitio* (fourfold division) of *corpus, locus, tempus, actio* as he states in V, 11, 12:

> Quare fit, ut ideo fere omnia sint quadripertita et ea aeterna, quod neque unquam tempus, quin fuerit motus . . . neque motus, ubi non locus et corpus, . . . neque ubi is agitatus, non actio ibi. Igitur initiorum quadrigae locus et corpus, tempus et actio.

> [Therefore it comes about that for this reason all things, in general, are divided into four phases, and these universal; because there is never time without there being motion . . . nor is there motion where there is not place and body . . . nor where this motion is, does there fail to be action. Therefore place and body, time and action are the four-horse team of the elements.]

Pythagoreanism is central in Varro. And not just by virtue of the numerological set of correspondences behind his fourfold scheme.[28] In its conciliatory approach to the controversy over the nature (*physis*) or convention (*thesis*) of language, Varro's Pythagoreanism takes on principles that we have seen at work in Plato's *Cratylus* and in Proclus's commentary. The Pythagorean number (*arithmos*) is the philosophical analog of that "unity in diversity" that sets *etymegoreia* apart from mere etymologizing. Numerology urges one to find, behind the appreciable diversity of language customs, interpretative patterns that bind these linguistic items together into a coherent (allegorical) picture.[29]

Varro's etymologies in books 5, 6, and 7 are ordered and grouped around rules drawn from Alexandrianism and Stoicism, with their attention to *declinatio* (inflection), *vetustas* and *error*, but also to the mysti-

28. Cavazza devotes a whole section to the architecture and subdivisions of Varro's *De lingua*, to conclude that it is a balanced hybrid of Pythagorean numerology and Stoic philosophy. Cavazza, *Studio su Varrone*, 55–72.

29. In Pythagoras's theory of knowledge, the word has a mystical value, second in importance only to the *arithmos*. It is likely that Pythagoreanism motivated Varro's etymological association of *verbum* (word) and *verum* (truth), an association we find in Augustine's *dialecticae*: "verbum dictum est quasi a verum boando, hoc est verum sonando." Cavazza, *Studio su Varrone*, 22.

TABLE 4-1. Varro's Classification of Etymologies

Degree	Definition	Realm of origin and scope of investigation
Primus gradus (infimus)	The level "to which even the common folk has come" [quo populus etiam venit]	—φύσις (nature) —Derivatives and clear compounds
Secundus gradus	The level "to which old-time grammar has mounted, which shows how the poet has made each word which he has fashioned and derived" [quo grammatica escendit antiqua, quae ostendit, quemadmodum quodque poeta finxerit verbum, quod confinxerit, quod declinarit]	—θέσις (convention) —Lexis (historical research, poetic language) —Figura etymologica
Tertius gradus	The level "to which philosophy ascended, and on arrival began to reveal the nature of those words which are in common use" [quo philosophia ascendens pervenit atque ea quae in consuetudine communi essent aperire coepit]	—θέσις (convention) —Consuetudo communis (common words)
Quartus gradus	The level "where the sanctuary is, and the mysteries of the high priest" [ubi est adytum et initia regis]	—φύσις (nature) —ἀριθμός (access to radix [root])

Source: From Varro, De Lingua Latina, 5, 7–8.

cal, allegorical backdrop of Pythagoreanism.[30] This is clear in the way Varro goes about classifying etymologies. For him, word origin can be studied at four levels of explication ("quattuor explanandi gradus") (V, 7–8), summed up in table 4-1.

Varro's scheme is recursive, because forms at the fourth level make up the natural basis for the forms at the first. Each level carries philosophical assumptions on the origin of language (language as θέσις or φύσις) and entails a specific view of linguistic change (from

30. Varro employs all the Stoic regulae later mentioned by Augustine, and he even cites Aelius Stilo in the notorious contraria: "caleus quod apertum est" and "lucus a non lucendo."

the principle of *analogia*, through *anomalia* and finally all the way back to the mystical, Pythagorean principle of ἀριθμός "number"). Each level zeroes in on one aspect of word origins (popular convention or poetic *auctoritas*); each gives a different account of their development (from the natural phenomenon of *declinatio*, "inflection," through the conventions of *lexis*, "vocabulary," and back to the protoforms of *radix*, "root"). But what may strike a modern reader most is that Varro's *gradatio* is ultimately elusive: the underlying pattern is far from the "clear and distinct" steps of Descartes' method. Its theoretical contours look fuzzy, and scholars struggle to untangle its sources.[31]

The fourfold scheme may best be accounted for as an instance of Varro's eclecticism. He himself acknowledges the mixture of Alexandrian and Stoic sources when he says he studied "not only by the lamp of Aristophanes, but also by that of Cleanthes."[32] Detractors Muller and Murray[33] read Varro's bridging of sources into one etymological model as a symptom of his amateurishness, a sign of methodological unease. But in the eyes of apologists, Varro's strength lies precisely in this conciliatory blending of philosophy (the linguistic mysticism of Neo-Pythagoreans and Stoics), grammar (the lexicographic experiments of Alexandrian scholars), and rhetoric (the Ciceronian canon of *Latinitas*): it is the same "*philosophisch-grammatisch-rhetorischer Synkretismus*" that Dihle[34] detected in Quintilian's work; the syncretism both Quintilian and Varro bring into play whenever tropes—such as onomatopoeia, metaphor, metonymy, and antiphrasis—are used for etymologizing.[35] But eclecticism is only one of the contentious facets of Varro's work. Critics have blamed him for positing a metaphysical

31. Cavazza, among others, finds Varro's work "extremely hard" (*estremamente difficile*) to contextualize. Cavazza, *Studio su Varrone*, 42.

32. [Non solum ad Aristophanis lucernam, sed etiam ad Cleanthis lucubravi.] V, 9.

33. Cited in Cavazza, *Studio su Varrone*, 78, 79ff.

34. A. Dihle, "Analogie und Attizismus," *Hermes* 85 (1957), 203.

35. Dihle is cited by Cavazza in the course of the latter's detailed account of the analogy/anomaly diatribe and the Roman convergence of grammar, philosophy and rhetoric. Cavazza, *Studio su Varrone*, 132ff, particularly note 192. See also Paulus Dietrich who notes that "similis ratio intercedit onter abusionem etymologicam et rhetoricam." Dietrich, *De Ciceronis*, 25.

quartus gradus that, insofar as it remains inaccessible, mars his model and makes it prone to unwarranted speculation.[36] I would rather agree with Della Corte, who ascribed Varro's open-endedness to his awareness of "human impotence in knowing the principles of things."[37]

To deal with the intricacies of language, Varro the etymologist takes on the personae of the philosopher, the grammarian, and the rhetorician. His *De Lingua Latina* is, to use Mikhail Bakhtin's image, a polyphonic text that seeks to unravel in language the "connection between human and divine sciences"[38] rather than confine language to manageable, but inevitably shortsighted, technical models. In its eclecticism, Varro's work sets the conditions for the kind of medieval encyclopedism that runs through Isidore's *Etymologiae*.[39] And I would argue that the "*quartus gradus etymologiae*" is Varro's original contribution in this direction, one that goes beyond Stoic and Alexandrian models, an original synthesis of the rival paradigms of naturalism and conventionalism. The "*quartus gradus etymologiae*" is a form of initiation described in hieratic terms (as *adytum*; as *initia regis*) that go well beyond grammar or rhetoric.

To access the fourth degree of etymological inquiry is to take a truly metalinguistic perspective: not one that reflects on language strictly within the rules (morphological, phonological, grammatical, or even rhetorical) of language itself, but rather one that explores language as *allegory*, as "speaking of the Other(s)," as a meta-physical pointer, as a form that leads (*ad ire*) beyond itself. Certainly, Varro also attends to the systematization of etymology begun by Alexandrian scholars, as is apparent in his coverage of declination and derivation, analogy and

36. See especially Muller, *De Veterum*, and Schröter, *Studien zur varronischen Etymologie*.

37. [Impotenza umana a conoscere i principii delle cose] Filologia 121; cited in Cavazza, *Studio su Varrone*, 58, n. 76.

38. Cavazza, *Studio su Varrone*, 71. For Bakhtin's discussion of polyphony as a feature of narrative, see Mikhail Bakhtin, *Problems of Dostoevsky's Poetics*, ed. and trans. Caryl Emerson (Minneapolis: University of Minnesota Press, 1984).

39. For Cavazza, Varro is "the great mediator towards the medieval tradition: grammar and etymology are vehicles of culture, history, customs, link to other disciplines, harmonization between human and divine sciences." Cavazza, *Studio su Varrone*, 156.

anomaly in books 7 and 8. Much of the criticism leveled against Varronian etymologies has in fact to do with inconsistencies of the phonological or morphological kind found in that part of his work. But we
would hardly do Varro justice by disregarding his mystical-Pythagorean
thrust, his allegorical élan:

> Pythagoras Samius ait omnium rerum initia esse bina ut finitum et infinitum,
> bonum et malum, vitam et mortem, diem et noctem. Quare item duo status
> et motus, <<utrumque quadripertitutm>>. [. . .] Quare quod quattuor genera
> prima rerum, totidem verborum.
>
> > [Pythagoras the Samian says that the primal elements of all things are in
> > pairs, as finite and infinite, good and bad, life and death, day and night.
> > Therefore likewise there are the two fundamentals, station and motion,
> > each divided into four kinds. [. . .] Therefore because the primal classes
> > of things are four in number, so many are the primary classes of words.]
> > (De Lingua, V, 11–13)

The philosophical subtext of the *De lingua Latina*, which repeats the
fourfold model from Pythagoras, cannot be severed from Varro's etymologizing. It would be easy, but pointless and misleading, to divide
Varro's etymologies along modern criteria of etymological correctness, to label them as "wrong" or "false" and to maintain that given
words "are not related," as Roland Kent does in his notes to the English translation of the *De lingua Latina*. If one looks, for example, at
Varro's use of the *radix* (root) metaphor, seen by critics as an anticipa-
tion of later, "reliable" Indo-European studies, one cannot fail to realize its duplicity:

> e quis <<de>> locis et iis rebus quae in his videntur in hoc libro summatim
> ponam. Sed qua cognatio eius erit verbi quae radices egerit extra fines suas,
> persequemur. Saepe enim ad limitem arboris radices sub vicini prodierunt
> segetem. Quare non, cum de locis dicam, si ab agro ad agrarium hominem, ad
> agricola pervenero, aberraro. Multa societas verborum, nec Vinalia sine vino
> expediri nec Curia Calabra sine calatione potest aperiri.
>
> > [From among these (primary classes of words), concerning places and
> > those things that are seen in them, I shall put a summary account in this
> > book; but we shall follow them up wherever the kin of the word under dis-
> > cussion is, even if it has driven its roots beyond its own territory. For of-
> > ten the roots of a tree that is close to the line of the property have gone out

under the neighbor's cornfield. Wherefore, when I speak of places, I shall not have gone astray if, from *ager*, "field," I pass to an *agrarius*, "agrarian" man, and to an *agricola*, "farmer." The partnership of words is one of many members: the Wine Festival cannot be set on its way without wine, nor can the *Curia Calabra*, "Announcement Hall," be opened without the *calatio*, "proclamation."] (*De Lingua*, V, 12–13)[40]

Radix may sound like the modern Indo-European concept of "root" with its neat derivational rules (in this case *ager* >> *agrarius* >> *agricola*). But Varro's idea of "root" has to do with the fact that *multa societas verborum* (words have many associations) and that roots can trespass their derivational limits to enter the territory of rhetoric and semantics (as in *Curia Calabra* [Announcement Hall] << *calatio* [proclamation]). Instances of inverse derivation of the kind

Liba, quod libandi causa fiunt (VII, 44).

[*Liba*, "cakes," so named because they are made *libare*, "to offer," to the gods.]

or

Lacus lacuna magna, ubi aqua contineri potest (V, 26).

[A *lacus*, "lake," is a large *lacuna*, "hollow," where water can be confined.]

are inadmissible to modern scholars but show that, for Varro, etymological routes/roots need not be one-way. Linguistic changes can occur in network-like fashion.[41] A way in which our modern "root" differs from Varro's *radix* is that the former presupposes a bidimensional model (a tree model where roots extend only vertically and/or horizontally from a protoform), whereas the latter is three-dimensional (with roots extending both vertically, horizontally, and deep across semantic borders).

Let us first briefly go over the format of Varro's etymologizing.

40. This "successful" Varronian etymology (Calabra–calatio) is also quoted by Belardi in his chapter on etymology and cultural linguistics. Belardi, *L'etimologia*, 91.

41. Network models and their relevance to current research in artificial intelligence will be dealt with in chapter 8.

As suggested by Wilhelm Pfaffel,[42] Varronian etymologies are usually phrased in one of these two formulae:

> B *ab* (from) A; or B *quod* (because) A

as in

> *ab sedendo* (A) *appellatae sedes* (B) (V, 128)
>
>> [from sedere (sit) were named sedes (seats)]

and in

> *fluius* (B) *quod fluit* (A) (V, 27)
>
>> [fluius (river) is so named because it fluit (flows)].

Their peculiarity has to do with the conflation of the two etymological objectives set by Varro: establishing *cur* (why—*quod*) *et inde* (whence—*ab*) *sunt verba* (words are). Instead of a full explication of the kind

> ** *fluius a "fluendo" "fluius" dictus, quod fluit*[43]

Varro often gives a "shrunken" definition that presupposes either a metalinguistic (the *ab* part; for Pfaffel, *metasprachlicher Gebrauch*) or the denotative (the *quod* part; Pfaffel, *objectsprachlicher Gebrauch*) gloss of the word. Occasionally, the two are laid out neatly, as in

> Iuglans, quod, cum haec nux antequam purgatur, similis glandis, haec glans optima et maxima, a Ioue et glande iuglans est appellata (V, 102).
>
>> [The *iuglans*, "walnut," because while this nut is like an acorn before it is cleansed of its hull, the inner nut, being best and biggest, is called iu-*glans* from Iu-*piter* and *glans*, "acorn."][44]

But most etymological explanation is condensed. The *ab* and *quod* formulae often overlap, as in *hinc etiam, a quo ipsi consortes, sors* (V, 66). [From this (from *serere*), moreover, *sors* (lot), from which the *consortes* (colleagues) themselves are named.]

42. Wilhelm Pfaffel, *Quartus gradus etymologiae: Untersuchungen zur Etymologie Varros in "De lingua Latina,"* Beitrage zur klassischen Philologie Heft 131 (Konigstein: Hain, 1981).

43. Ibid., 11.

44. This apparently spurious etymology is confirmed in Ernout-Meillet's *Dictionnaire étymologique de la langue latine: histoire des mots,* 4th ed. (Paris: Klincksieck, 1967).

Varro's etymologies coalesced derivation (*ab*) and motivation (*quod*), while modern etymology has sanctioned its own scientific nature by excising "motivation" altogether and by establishing historicist rules of formal derivation. In their allegorical layering of morphology and philology, semantics and rhetoric, Varro's etymologies advocate a multidimensional frame for etymological studies; a frame suggested by Isidore and recently hoped for by Yakov Malkiel. See, for instance, Varro's etymology of *ager*, where a Greek derivation is posited along with a parallel historicist motivation:

Ager dictus in quam terram quid agebant, et unde quid agebant fructus causa; ali<<i>> quod id Graeci dicunt ἀγρόν (V 34).

> [*Ager* (field) is the name given to land in which they used *agere* (to drive) something, or from which they used to drive something, for the sake of the produce; but others say that it is because the Greeks call it ἀγρός.]

Or consider the etymologies of *fundus*, *vitis*, and *vinea*, which go against phonological "laws" but bring to the fore plausible semantic interrelations of words in their historical context:

Ager quod videbatur pecudum ac pecuniae esse fundamentum, fundus dictus, aut quod fundit quotquot annis multa. Vineta ac vineae a vite multa. Vitis a vino, id a vi; hinc vindemia, quod est vinidemia aut vitidemia (V 37).

> [Field land, because it seemed to be the *fundamentum* (foundation) of animal flocks and of money, was called *fundus* (estate) or else because it *fundit* (pours out) many things every year. *Vineta* and *vineae* (vineyards) from the many *vites* (grapevines). *Vitis* (grapevine) from *vinum* (wine), this from *vis* (strength); from this, *vindemia* (vintage), because it is *vinidemia* (wine removal) or *vitidemia* (vine removal).]

And again:

Pater, quod patefacit semen: nam tum esse conceptum <<pat>>et, inde cum exit quod oritur (V 66).

> [*Pater* (father) because he *patefacit* (makes evident) the seed; for then it *patet* (is evident) that conception has taken place when that which is born comes out from it.]

Examples like these are countless, and when checked against the bibles of scientific etymology like Ernout-Meillet's *Dictionnaire étymologique de la langue latine* (DEL) or Walde's *Lateinisches Etymologisches Wörterbuch* (LEW),[45] many turn out to be more reasonable than expected. Let us consider, for instance, the etymology of *caelum* (sky, V, 16–18). Varro lists the common interpretations of *caelum* as coming from *caelatum* (carved out),[46] or, by antiphrasis, from *celatum* (hidden), and finally also relates the word to the Latin *cavum* (hollow). Now Kent promptly dismisses Varro's etymologies and invokes a probable (but unspecified) root seen in German *heiter*, "bright."[47] A rapid glance at DEL in fact reveals not only that the etymology of *caelum* remains uncertain but that links with *caelare* and *celare* cannot be excluded. First, we should recall that sky-related words in Latin were a prerogative of augurs and that the sky was seen as a region to be "carved out" (*caelatum*; from *caelare*) or delimited for the purposes of divination.[48] And secondly, one should keep in mind the semantic link indicated in DEL between *caelum* and a *scur* root meaning "sky" from which Latin *obscurus* (obscure, hidden) has come. Analogous cases are *motacilla . . . quod semper movet caudam* ["wagtail" because it is always moving its tail (V, 76)]; *pontufex . . . a ponte* [*pontifex* from *pons* (bridge)(V, 83)]; *mendicus a minus* [beggar from *minus* (V, 92)]; *pecunia a pecu.* [money from flock].

Particularly compelling are etymologies of toponyms, for which LEW and DEL fail to provide conclusive evidence:

Subura<<m>> Iunius scribit ab eo, quod fuerit sub antiqua urbe (V 48)

[Junius writes that Subu̧ra is so named because it was at the foot of the old city *(sub urbe)*.]

Or the etymology of *Saturnus* and *Ops*:

---

45. Alois Walde and Johann B. Hoffman, *Lateinisches Etymologisches Wörterbuch*, 3rd ed. (Heidelberg: Winter, 1939–65).

46. Kent takes *caelatum* as meaning "raised above the surface," perhaps to juxtapose it to the *celatum* (hidden) that follows. I would opt for a straightforward translation from *caelare* (to carve, chisel).

47. Varro, *De lingua Latina*, 17, n. 18.

48. The sense is similar to *templum* (temple; sacred portion of the sky), which may have derived from the Greek verb τέμνω (*temno*; carve, cut out). With reference to *caelum*, DEL uses the expression *ciel découpé* (carved sky).

Quare quod caelum principium, ab satu est dictus Saturnus, et quod ignis, Saturnalibus cerei superioribus mittuntur. Terra Ops, quod hic omne opus et hac opus ad vivendum (V, 64).

> [Wherefore because the Sky is the beginning, Saturn was named from *satus* (sowing); and because fire is beginning, tapers are presented to the patrons at the Saturnalia. *Ops* is the Earth, because in it is every *opus* (work) and there is *opus* (need) of it for living.]

Ultimately, what matters is not whether two words are morphologically related but how they shed light on each other's meaning. We may resist etymologies of the Varronian kind because we have been trained to examine language as a self-sustaining system of formal and semantic features à la Hjelmslev. But this notion has already proven narrow and biased.[49] It fails to account for instances in which the structures of language intersect the institutions of history, in which language models are shaped by the models of rhetoric and philosophy. Hence, in Varro, *ignis a <<g>>nascendo, quod hinc nascitur et omne quod nascitur ignis s<<uc>>cendit* (V, 70). [*Ignis* (fire) is named from *gnasci* (to be born), because from it there is birth, and everything that is born the fire enkindles.][50]

The breadth of Varro's etymologizing can be appreciated in book 7 of the *De lingua Latina*, where he tackles the words of poetry, more difficult than others because further removed from everyday life. Here more than anywhere else, says Varro, etymology cannot hope to explain everything, "praesertim quom dicat etymologice non omnium verborum posse dici causa<<m>>" (VII, 4) [especially since the art of etymology says that we cannot find the motivation of all words]. Its limits must be drawn right away:

49. On this issue, see for instance, Giovanni Bottiroli, *Retorica: L'intelligenza figurale nell'arte e nella filosofia* (Turin: Bollati-Boringhieri, 1993), and Brian Vickers, ed., *Appropriating Shakespeare: Contemporary Critical Quarrels* (New Haven, Conn.: Yale University Press, 1994), especially chapter 1 of the latter.

50. DEL relates Latin *gnasci* to a possible religious root **egnis*, having to do with Sanskrit *Agnih* (god of fire). See also Elisabetta Riganti, *Lessico latino fondamentale* (Bologna: Patron, 1989), v. *ignis*.

Neque si non norim radices arboris, non posse me dicere pirum esse ex ramo, ramum ex arbore, eam ex radicibus quas non video (VII, 4).

[And that if I have no knowledge of the roots of a tree, still I am not prevented from saying that a pear is from a branch, the branch is from a tree, and the tree from roots that I do not see.]

Once these are recognized, however, Varro can proceed to talk about the "words that have been put down by the poets" [de verbis quae a poetis posita sunt (VII, 5)]. And this is where some of the most fascinating word histories can be found. See for instance the allegorical script that maps an intersection between *templum* (temple), *tueri* (gaze), and *extemplo* (at once) (VII, 10–13),[51] or the etymology of *obscaenum*:

Obscaenum dictum ab scaena (VII, 96–97).

[*Obscaenum* (foul) is said from *scaena* (stage).][52]

What is being investigated here are cognitive habits sedimented in language: ways in which we speak, we argue, and we think by setting up short-term metaphorical links between concepts, between levels of awareness, and between words.[53] That is when language works as an allegory, as a continued metaphor of our perceptions. Varro does not disdain insights that may come from the *figurae etymologicae* of poets, as in

a qua vi natis dicat vita et illud a Lucilio:

Vis est vita, vides, vis nos facere omnia cogit (V, 63).

[Those born of this *vis* have what is called *vita* (life), and what was meant by Lucilius:

Life is force, you see, to do everything force compels us.][54]

51. The relation between Latin *templum*, *tueri*, and Greek *temno* is still open to discussion. Kent observes: "In taking the auspices by the flight of birds, the Roman faced south and the Greek faced north; therefore, as the east (where the sun rose) was always the favourable part of the *templum*, the Roman considered the left side favourable and the Greek considered the left unfavourable. Confusion with the Greek method resulted in a double meaning of *sinistra* in Latin." Varro, De lingua Latina, 350.

52. DEL gives this etymology as "uncertain."

53. This issue of whether language should be said to reflect or to construct cognition is a thorny one and is partially addressed in chapter 8.

54. A *vita/vis* connection is not documented in DEL, but since the etymologies of both terms are relatively obscure, one cannot exclude it.

Or in the case of Proserpina, etymologized through Plautus with an eye on its evocative meaning:

Dicta Proserpina, quod haec ut serpens modo in dexteram modo in sinisteram partem late movetur. Serpere et proserpere idem dicebant, ut Plautus quod scribit:

quasi proserpens bestia (V, 68).

> [Proserpina received her name because she, like a *serpens* (creeper) moves widely, now to the right, now to the left. *Serpere* (creep) and *proserpere* (to creep forward) meant the same thing, as Plautus means in what he writes: like a forward-creeping beast.]

If anything, etymologies like these convey the common associative pattern of a Roman speaker, which science may overlook but philology often confirms.[55] But it is to be asked how many among Varro's "popular" etymologies ought to be rethought along the lines of the *caelum* example I gave above. The etymologies that follow, which DEL or LEW cannot fully explain, may be among them:

Sol vel quod ita Sabini, vel <<quod>> solus ita lucet, ut ex eo deo dies sit. Luna, vel quod sola lucet noctu (V, 68).

> [*Sol* (Sun) is so named either because the Sabines called him thus, or because he *solus* (alone) shines in such a way that from this god there is the daylight. *Luna* (Moon) is so named certainly because she alone *lucet* (shines) at night.]

Gladium C in G commutato a clade, quod fit ad hostium cladem gladium (V, 116).

> [*Gladium* (sword), from *clades* (slaughter), with change of C to G, because the *gladium* is made for a slaughter of the enemy.]

Mundus <<ornatus>> muliebris dictus a munditia (V, 129).

> [*Mundus* is a woman's toilet set, named from *munditia* (neatness).]

As we move beyond the Roman heritage, we cannot fail to see Varro's splendid contribution to the *allegorische Deutung* (allegorical interpreta-

---

55. DEL mentions *Proserpina* as a calque of the Greek *Persephone* and labels Varro's explanation as a "popular" (that is, false), if at the time widely attested, etymology.

tion)[56] that pervades the Middle Ages and is at the heart of Isidore's *Etymologiae*. Two concluding remarks must qualify this appreciation. Varro's work is relevant first of all because it resists equally effectively a *tout court* "grammaticalization" or "rhetorization" of etymology. He manages to bring together these competing trends in a model that survives *Latinitas* itself. I agree with Cavazza that Varro had the merit of "reviv[ing] a discipline that at least has a goal in the context of the whole Roman mind-set," because "etymology is a 'Denkenform,' a vehicle of study. It has an etiologic function and is the key to Rome's antiquity . . . There is no joke, or in other words, exegetical exaggeration."[57] To Varro, then, we owe "the felicitous intuition that etymology does not simply go back to the dawn of language, thereby serving only the purpose of grammar and philology, but also to the dawn of culture and serves as an archaeology of a people."[58] Secondly, I am convinced Varro is right to insist that etymology should also have an *adytum* (access) to the other-than-language that it is the duty of the *quartus gradus etymologiae* to ensure. This is the main sense in which Varro's etymology can be said to belong to the allegorical strain. Varro's *quartus gradus* entitles us to examine a number of his etymologies as structurally allegorical, as "Other-arguing" and "arguing-of-the-Other." Allegory is implicit in Varro's understanding of the *quartus gradus* as a way of accessing metaphysical (i.e., not technical) truths. Also, allegoresis in Varro already exhibits the encyclopedic diffusiveness of the medieval mind-set, as witnessed in the analogical layering of the etymological microcosm/macrocosm within the *De Lingua Latina*. These are two aspects of Varro's etymologizing that mirror the two facets of allegory we examined in chapter 2: *allos agoreuein* as "speaking-of-the-Other" or "Other-speaking" and *allos agoreuein* as "speaking-of-the-diverse" or "diverse-speaking." With Isidore of Seville, the subject of my next chapter, the story of allegory in ancient etymology is about to come full circle.

56. Klinck, *Die lateinische Etymologie*, 138.   57. Cavazza, *Studio su Varrone*, 73.
58. Ibid., 161.

CHAPTER 5

ALLEGORICAL ETYMOLOGY AS A DENKFORM

The Middle Ages of Isidore

IT IS HARDLY AN OVERSTATEMENT to say that medieval etymology owes much of its form and its methods to the achievement of one individual. Isidore, bishop of Seville (560–636), author of *Etymologiarum sive originum libri XX*, is invariably cited by critics as one of the most influential figures in the medieval West. For Curtius, the *Etymologiae* or *Origines* of Isidore could well "be called the basic book of the entire Middle Ages."[1] Giulio Lepschy talks about the "enormous popularity" of Isidore's work, which "became the *summa* of an encyclopedic knowledge to whose *auctoritas* it was indispensable to refer in the daily practice of teaching and even of scientific research." For him, Isidore was "the initiator of true medieval culture."[2] And Mark Amsler underlines the importance of Isidore's *Etymologiae* for a standardization of etymology, which was now largely used to interpret Christian and pagan texts within a monastic program of studies.[3]

For our analysis of the relation between etymology and allegory, Isidore's work is crucial, not only as a paradigm of the medieval allegorism masterfully illustrated by Friedrich Ohly and Roswitha Klinck but also as a *summa*, in the double sense of summation and consummation, of the etymologico-allegorical line we have followed in the

1. Curtius, *European Literature*, 496.
2. Giulio Lepschy, *History of Linguistics*, Longman Linguistics Library (London: Longman, 1994), 151–52.
3. Mark Amsler, *Etymology and Grammatical Discourse in Late Antiquity and the Early Middle Ages* (Amsterdam: Benjamins, 1989), 133–34.

preceding chapters. With this in mind, we are going to sketch the layout of the Etymologiae and place it in the context of Christian exegesis and of the medieval artes liberales. We will then focus on Isidore's definition of etymology and on his use of etymologizing as a tool for interpretation, a genus interpretationis, based on the allegorical cast of mind. The theoretical and methodological tensions that lead to the reformulation of etymegoreia in the Late Middle Ages and the early Renaissance are also discussed here.

The Etymologiae and the Seven Liberal Arts

The mold of Isidore's Etymologiae is that of the seven liberal arts: the trivium of grammar, rhetoric, and dialectic, and the Boethian quadrivium of arithmetic, geometry, music, and astronomy. Book 1 deals with grammar, book 2 with rhetoric and dialectics, and book 3 covers the artes of the quadrivium. The remaining seventeen books relate to the seven major arts and cover most of the secular disciplines, among which are medicine (book 4), law (book 5), zoology (book 12), and architecture (book 15). Three specific books on language are book 8 (on sacred onomastics), book 9 (on languages and institutions), and book 10 (an alphabetized compilation of glosses, or vocabuli). The encyclopedic scope of the Etymologiae met two objectives: one more theoretical—that of drawing a compendium of human knowledge in light of a broad theological schema; and one more practical—that of offering a handy primer for readers who approached the scriptures and pagan texts.

Competing views have been expressed on the significance of Isidore's encyclopedism as shaped by the seven liberal arts. Assuming that in the Middle Ages etymological grammar functioned as a "universal discursive practice," Amsler claims that the Etymologiae is authoritative because "it says clearly and succinctly what is sayable within the discursive space of early medieval science."[4] He endorses the

4. Ibid., 147.

views that Isidore brings about a Christianization of the pagan encyclopedia[5] and that his encyclopedia rests on the essentialist axiom
whereby words give access to the nature of things.[6] He concludes,
however, that Isidore's ontological *parti pris* in the end leads him to as-
sert language over things:

Isidore articulated and helped codify a theory of language dependent on the
mythographic perception of language as a verbal construction motivated by
extraverbal reality. The goal may have been to transform language from an end
into a means to a higher truth, but the result was that language, language in
texts, became the primary focus of monastic pedagogy and intellectual activity. The *ars grammatica* was the master discipline and the fruit of the new mo-
nasticism.[7]

The *Etymologiae* would then be an "an etymological account of both
the world and language, of the world as language."[8]

The merit of Amsler's analysis is that it gives a detailed linguistic
account of Isidore's work within the broader background of grammatical studies in late antiquity: he is—as we shall see—especially good
at pinpointing the metalinguistic strategies Isidore adopts to seal together the multiple discourses of his age into a commanding whole.
Also, he is attentive to the ways in which Isidore's work perpetuates or
alters the linguistic habits of its immediate sources, namely of Jerome,
Fulgentius, and Augustine. Nevertheless, there are two points in his
analysis that call at the very least for a qualification. One is his insistence on language as the all-embracing measure of reality, an article
of postmodern faith that staunchly equates Isidore's encyclopedism
with "a non-distinction between what is seen and what is read, [. . .]
an immediate dissociation of all language, duplicated, without any as-

5. Amsler quotes Curtius's claim that "Isidore's 'poetics' integrates the doctrines of pagan late Antiquity into the systematized *didascalium* of the Western church." Ibid., 171.
6. "[Isidore] writes the knowledge of things into the knowledge of words and thus
shrinks the universe into a one-volume library, conveniently located on the monastic shelf. But
as we shall see, the formalization of science as discourse does not close off discourse and thus
science. Rather, by formalizing the grammatical model for producing scientific discourse,
Isidore sets the stage for the dispersion and even the rejection of his own text." Ibid., 134–35.
7. Ibid.
8. Ibid., 145.

signable term, by the constant reiteration of commentary."[9] In this postmodern reading, the allegorism of Isidore's etymologies is the by-product of a formal device, a rhetorical scheme that strives in vain to bridge its distance from an unattainable transcendence only to trigger a disruptive—and allegedly liberating—drift into language. I would say rather that Isidore's allegorism, coupled with etymology, carries cognitive value and has heuristic force. I would read it as an instance of that "figural intelligence" whereby, for Giovanni Bottiroli, our conscious and unconscious cognitive mapping of the world occurs.[10]

My second misgiving is linked to the first and has to do with Amsler's conclusion that "by formalizing the grammatical model for producing scientific discourse, Isidore sets the stage for the dispersion and even the rejection of his own text."[11] This statement holds insofar as it points to the technicalization of etymology, a historical process that was championed by the thirteenth-century scholars known as *modistae* and that saw the progressive detachment of etymology from allegorical (or "spiritual") pursuits.[12] The *modistae* aimed to substitute rigorous, discrete accounts based on rational measure (*modus*) for the intuitive, holistic *formulae spiritalis intelligentiae* (formulae of spiritual insight) applied by early Church Fathers.[13] What may mislead is the almost causal link that Amsler sets up between Isidore's work and etymology's technicalization. The problem lies, I think, with conceiving the *Etymologiae* as a "formalization" or—which is the same—as a blunt redefinition of the *artes liberales* in grammatical terms. Once appointed as the master discourse of the liberal arts, grammar will deviously undercut appeals to "extraverbal reality," as Amsler ironically sug-

9. Ibid., 135, quoting Foucault.

10. Bottiroli, *Retorica*.

11. Amsler, *Etymology and Grammatical Discourse*, 135.

12. In the OED definition, *modistae* is "the collective name given to a number of medieval grammarians who developed and expounded a system of Latin grammar wherein Priscian's word classes and categories were integrated into the framework of scholastic philosophy."

13. Most of the allegorical dictionaries mentioned by Latin Father Petrus Pictaviensis rely on this *formula spiritalis intelligentiae*, codified by Eucherius of Lyons (fifth century AD) and notably exemplified by the *Clavis* of Meliton of Sardes.

gests: "Socrates's dream of a static, extraverbal reality which justifies language and origins was paradoxically realized most fully in Isidore's grammatical discourse. As with Patristic predecessors, Isidore reaches the *numen* through the *nomen* but his paradigm is more sharply outlined than any before him."[14] One cannot of course deny the prestige attached to grammatical studies in the Latin Middle Ages at Isidore's time and beyond. However, these studies ought to be understood as a part of a broader epistemology where the study of *voces*, of verbal signs, goes hand in hand with the study of *res*, of objects and phenomena, that are framed in language but exist beyond it.[15] This is one of the tenets of medieval hermeneutics. Ohly's analysis hinges on it. In "On the spiritual meaning of the word in the Middle Ages," he explained that "disciplines connected with philology and dealing with words [*voces*] served as an introduction to the disciplines of the quadrivium, which focused on things [*res*] with the intent of uncovering their spiritual meanings."[16] The medieval scholar was faced with two central tasks: one was to refine the philological tools of the trivium, normally applied to pagan texts but now used to interpret the literal sense of the Scripture. This is the aspect of medieval philology that Amsler favors and that upholds his claim about the overwhelming ascendancy of grammar. But there is also another, more challenging, task that consisted in unveiling the "spiritual" meaning hidden beneath the "letter [that] killeth."[17] The whole gamut of created things, expressed in words, had to be studied through the quadrivium and subjected to allegorical reading. The famous adage, "non solum voces, sed et res significativae sunt,"[18] expresses a rooted conviction that reverberates in innumerable medieval texts. Think for instance of Alan de Lille's "Omnis

14. Amsler, *Etymology and Grammatical Discours*, 171.

15. In chapter 8 of the *Speculum ecclesiae*, we read that "trivium vocum, quadrivium physicarum rerum administrat notitia." Quoted in Ohly, *Geometria e Memoria*, 255.

16. Ohly, *Geometria e Memoria*, 255.

17. On the historical senses of the term "spiritual" see Ohly, *Geometria e Memoria*, 251–52.

18. Richard of St. Victor, *Excerptiones*, Patrologiae cursus completes, series Latina, ed. J. P. Migne, II, 3, cited in Ohly, *Geometria e Memoria*, 253.

creatura significans," or of Hugh of St. Victor's "Omnis natura Deum loquitur."[19] It is especially in regard to this second, allegorical aspect of medieval philology that I find Amsler confusing: he seems to imply that allegorism is mainly a byproduct of the enhanced linguistic awareness promoted in Late Antiquity and the Middle Ages by advances in grammatical studies. If it were so, then Isidore's *Etymologiae* would justly represent the manifesto of an epistemology that—albeit involuntarily—brings everything down to language, a "stunning instance of science as a discursive practice" carrying out a large-scale "formalization" of "what can be said."[20] Allegory and etymology would figure here only as two, although the most important, of the compositional devices used by the philologist to maintain this sweeping grammatical view. But statements like these are open to question.

First of all, one needs to recall the basic medieval perception that the language of human beings and the language of things created by God differ.[21] Human *voces* signify reality in a "literal" fashion, not so much in the sense that they reproduce it faithfully, but because they are *litterae*, signs, forms, and vestiges of the real. One word conveys concepts that, as Amsler would say, "formalize" the corresponding thing. The language mechanisms that regulate such correspondences in their several historical manifestations are studied in the *trivium*, focused—to use a Saussurean term—on the signifier. But the things created by God and signified through these words have a different language, codified by the natural and formal properties (*proprietates*) with which each *res* was endowed. Klinck rightly notes that "one of the prerequisites for probing the meaning of a thing was the exact knowledge of its properties, and these were often warranted by etymology."[22] Yet, unlike a word, an object was perceived as inherently polysemous and could have as many meanings as exterior or interior qualities (its *visibi-*

19. Ohly, *Geometria e Memoria*, 253–55.
20. Amsler, *Etymology and Grammatical Discourse*, 135.
21. Ohly, *Geometria e Memoria*, 250.
22. Klinck, *Die lateinische Etymologie*, 139. All translations from Klinck are mine.

lis *forma* or its *invisibilis natura*), all of which were catalogued and studied by the quadrivium.[23] Ohly gives the example of snow, which means
something because of its form (its whiteness) and something else because of its nature (its coldness).[24] And Klinck also notes that in medieval treatises, "the derivations of animal or plant names are preferably
interpreted from an allegorical viewpoint. They are often invested with
divine or human properties, with the conduct of saints or that of the
devil, of heretics and traitors, of the church and the sacred Scripture.
At times etymologies also take on theological concepts."[25] Thus, the
same object can take on negative or positive connotations. To name
but two of its possible meanings, the lion can signify Christ the Savior
in *bonam partem* or a blood-thirsty devil in *malam partem*, in accordance
with an exegetical practice that runs through "the entire encyclopedia
of the Middle Ages": bestiaries, herbaria, lapidaria, the *Physiologus*.[26]

Amsler's semiotic study blurs the dividing line set up in medieval
epistemology between *voces* and *res*. And I argue that this *limen* ought
to be reasserted, not because it can be drawn neatly and conclusively,
but because substantial documentation, of the kind adduced by Ohly,
bears witness to its fine, continuous trace. One can conflate *res* with
voces, as Amsler does from his postmodern viewpoint, only by assuming that the *voces* are the ruling factor and that the naturalistic forays
of the quadrivium were solely extensions of its linguistic foundation,
the trivium. Not only is this view historically biased—if one considers
for instance that mathematics and physics, not grammar or dialectic,
were close allies to medieval theology—it is also theoretically neglect-
ful of the enormous debt that modern linguistics and hermeneutics
owe to medieval speculations.[27]

23. Peter of Poitiers explains this concept in these terms: "Quaelibet enim res, quot habet
proprietates tot habet linguas aliquid spirituale nobis et invisibile insinuantes, pro quarum di-
versitate et ipsius nominis acceptio variatur." Peter of Poitiers. *Allegoriae super tabernaculum Moysi*, eds. Philip S. Moore and James A. Corbett (Notre Dame, Ind.: University of Notre Dame,
1938), 254.

24. Ohly, *Geometria e Memoria*, 254.   25. Klinck, *Die lateinische Etimologie*, 139.
26. Ohly, *Geometria e Memoria*, 255.
27. "We, as run-of-the-mill philologists, have no awareness . . . of the extent to which

Semiologists sympathize with the Middle Ages, and particularly with the group of late medieval scholastics called *modistae*, whom they use to validate their claims.[28] But their readings of Augustine or Isidore are almost always inscribed and described in Saussurean terms that call for critical caution. In the Middle Ages, Christian exegesis did not merely amount to extending linguistic tools from texts to *realia*. The metaphor of "the book of nature" presupposed a close study of reality, and reality obviously can only be known through language, but that did not mean that reality was coterminous with language. Rather, language was *allegorical*, the visible form of invisible meanings: "litterae autem sunt indices rerum, signa verborum, quibus tanta vis est, ut nobis dicta absentium sine voce loquantur" [letters are the indices of things, the signs of words—there is so much potency in them, that what is said to us speaks to us of things that are absent].[29] And etymology was allegory's handmaiden, because it retraced these innumerable paths, seamlessly connecting the *res*, the *voces*, and their multifaceted essence. As Klinck explains, "etymology is once again the link between the literal meaning and the allegorical interpretation. Through its intervention, the two levels of interpretation are not separated in the eyes of the reader but flow into each other without breaks. It is in fact easier for the exegete to show how the allegorical meaning is one with the literal meaning within the form of letters."[30]

Medieval and Isidorian epistemology is certainly complex. One need not be reminded of the wealth of studies on this and on related aspects of medieval culture to own to one's critical and historical shortcomings. I have ventured the remarks above with two purposes in mind:

---

our interpretative art is indebted to Patristic and medieval exegesis." Ohly, *Geometria e Memoria*, 250.

28. Umberto Eco's work is steeped in scholastic philosophy. See for instance *Semiotics*, and *The Search for the Perfect Language: The Making of Europe*, trans. James Fentress (Cambridge, Mass.: Blackwell, 1995).

29. Isidore, *Etymologiae*, I, ii, iii.

30. Klinck, *Die lateinische Etymologie,*, 165. In Richard of St. Victor's words, "omnes itaque artes subserviunt divinae sapientiae et inferior scientia recte ordinata ad superiorem conducit." Richard of St. Victor, *Excerptiones*.

those of placing Isidore's *Etymologiae* in the context of the medieval arts and of arguing that his work and its context cannot and should not be explicated solely as a function of grammar. In both cases, I have availed myself of Ohly's study on spiritual meaning in the Middle Ages, which, I believe, strikes a sensible balance between the sweeping dictates of contemporary linguistics and a remarkable, if to some old-fashioned, sensitivity to the shifting nuances of cultural history. Thanks to Ohly, we can view Isidore's work as a landmark in the line that starts with the *Formulae spiritualis intelligentiae* of Eucherius of Lyons (fifth century), is enhanced in Rabanus Maurus' *De Universo* and Pseudo-Meliton's *Clavis* (ninth century), threads its way through the many allegorical dictionaries and *distinctiones*, and survives under changed forms and with diverse intents in exegetical and scholarly literature up to the eighteenth century.[31] Following our discussion in previous chapters, we could in fact extend this line all the way back to Plato and Origen and see Isidore's *Etymologiae* as the Christian summation of a *sensus spiritualis* at the crossroads between *allegoria* and *etymologia*, which Greek and Roman scholars had erratically adumbrated.

The phrase *sensus spiritualis* recurs in medieval treatises and is obviously tied to a multilayered view of the Scriptures and of the world, as condensed in the popular distich on the four senses (literal, allegorical, anagogical, moral), which are the keys to the medieval episteme.[32] Surely, the main interpretative effort behind medieval etymology was directed to the Bible as the ultimate repository of truths. But Christian exegetes also found in allegorical etymology a convenient instrument for appropriating and adapting pagan culture. As noted by Klinck, "a different etymological explanation of a given word was not the only possibility [Christian exegetes] had to counter the pagan ex-

31. Ohly, *Geometria e Memoria*, 267.
32. For a detailed account of medieval exegetical practices, see for instance Beryl Smalley's "Some Latin Commentaries on the Sapiential Books in the Late Thirteenth and Early Fourteenth Centuries," *Archives d'histoire doctrinale et littéraire du moyen âge*, vols. 25–26 (Paris: J. Vrin, 1950–51), 103–28, as well as Robert Holkot's *English Friars and Antiquity in the Early Fourteenth Century* (Oxford: Oxford University Press, 1960), 133–202.

planation of that word. One could also weaken or modify the sense of an ancient derivation by interpreting it allegorically. This artifice could serve a double purpose: pagan etymology could be adopted into Christian literature without danger and therefore become an acceptable basis for Christian allegoresis."[33] Christian typology differed from Stoic allegorism in at least one important aspect: its starting claim was stubbornly historical. The various *formulae spiritalis intelligentiae* that Patristic scholars used to read the Bible allegorically were rooted in, and nourished on, historical convictions, in that *figural* climate where, in Erich Auerbach's words, "the two poles of the *figurae* are separate in time, but both are ... within time, within the stream of historical life."[34] As a complement to the *allegoria in verbis* of exegetes like Philo, scholars like Ambrose, Augustine, Bede, and Hugh of St.Victor add the *allegoria in factis*, which becomes the privileged channel of Christian propaganda.[35] And Klinck herself warns us that "unlike Greek allegorists, who used myths to symbolize cosmic forces, ethical values or historical events, medieval scholars believed that each thing had a specific symbolical content [*Zeichengehalt*] that could be unveiled through interpretation."[36] Medieval, and above all Isidorian, etymologizing should be seen against this elaborate background.

Isidore's Definition of Etymology

Isidore defines etymology in these terms:

Etymologia est origo vocabulorum, cum vis verbi vel nominis per interpretationem colligitur. Hanc Aristoteles σύμβολον, Cicero adnotationem nominavit, quia nomina et verba rerum nota facit exemplo posito; ut puta "flumen,"

---

33. Klinck, *Die lateinische Etimologie*, 138.

34. Erich Auerbach, *Scenes from the Drama of European Literature*, Theory and History of Literature, vol. 9 (Minneapolis: University of Minnesota Press, 1984), 49.

35. On these two types of "allegoria," see Pépin, *Mythe et allégorie*; Henri de Lubac, *Exégèse médiévale: les quatres sens de l'écriture* (Paris: Aubier, 1959); R. Hanson, *Allegory and Event: A Study of the Source and Significance of Origen's Interpretation of Scripture* (London: S.C.M. Press, 1959); Rollinson, *Classical Theories*; and Ohly, *Geometria e Memoria*.

36. Klinck, *Die lateinische Etimologie*, 139.

quia fluendo crevit, a fluendo dictum. Cuius cognitio saepe usum necessarium habet in interpretatione sua. Nam dum videris unde ortum est nomen, citius vim eius intellegis. Omnis enim rei inspectio etymologia cognita planior est. Non autem omnia nomina a veteribus secundum naturam imposita sunt, sed quaedam et secundum placitum, sicut et nos servis et possessionibus interdum secundum quod placet nostrae voluntati nomina damus. Hinc est quod omnium nominum etymologiae non reperiuntur, quia quaedam non secundum qualitatem, qua genita sunt, sed iuxta arbitrium humanae voluntatis vocabula acceperunt.

> [Etymology is the origin of words, when the force of a word or name is determined through interpretation. This Aristotle called *symbolon* and Cicero *adnotatio*, because it explains (provides a gloss for) names and words of things in a certain fashion; for example *flumen* (river) is said to arise from *fluendo*, because it arose from flowing. The knowledge of etymology is often necessary in (its?) interpretation. When you see the origin of a name, you will understand its force more swiftly. For the examination of each thing is clearer with a knowledge of its etymology. However not all names were imposed by the ancients according to nature, but some also arbitrarily, just as we occasionally give names to our slaves or our estates according to what appeals to our will. Thus the etymologies of some names cannot be found, since some received their names not according to the quality through which they were born, but according to the arbitrary will of human beings.][37]

I quote the passage in full because it includes the main points of Isidore's theory of etymology and because it is the section frequently cited and variously translated by critics. Lepschy and Irvine quote it in their studies. Amsler also mentions Wolfang Schweickard's 1985 analysis of previous translations to show how complex Isidore's work is.[38] We can follow Amsler's thematic subdivision of the text, which is very clear: first comes a definition of etymology (*Etymologia est . . .*); secondly an account of etymology's function in exegesis (*Cuius cognitio . . .*); lastly, we have an acknowledgment of etymology's limits (138).

The phrasing of Isidore's definition is important: etymology consists in recollecting or inferring (*colligere*) the *vis* (force) of a word or name (*verbi vel nominis*) through a process of interpretation (*per interpre-*

37. Isidore, *Etymologiae*, I, xxix, 1–10.

38. See Lepschy, *History of Linguistics*; Martin Irvine, *The Making of Textual Culture: 'Grammatica' and Literary Theory, 350–1100*, Cambridge Studies in Medieval Literature 19 (Cambridge: Cambridge University Press, 1994); and Amsler, *Etymology and Grammatical Discourse*.

tationem). The verb *colligo* emphasizes the relational nature of etymology, a feature noted by Zumthor, Bloch, and Schweickard, and restated by Amsler. Quite appropriately, Klinck described Thomas Cistercensis's etymology as a "bundle of *notae*": "Etymology deciphers meanings of words that are signalled in the sequences of letters or letter clusters. Thomas suggests to his reader that a word is not tied to a one-way meaning. It is, rather a bundle of notes (*notae*) that can be unravelled in various ways."[39]

Here I would add that *colligere* is analogous in meaning to that "gathering together into one" that we mentioned with regard to allegory as *allos agoreuein* (chapter 2). What is being collected or recollected is the *vis* of a word, a term on which translators fail to agree[40] but which one can triangulate around the semantic coordinates of "essence," "actual force," and "potency."[41] Amsler compares Augustine's rhetorical idea of *vis*,[42] with Isidore's legal and grammatical uses ("vis est virtus potestatis," 5.26.4), and despite its wordiness, his final paraphrase of the term as "essential potency/semantic motivation" makes sense. The etymologist uses interpretation to collect not only the morphological or phonological features of a word (here, the fact that *flumen* derives from *fluendo*), but also the word's various actual or potential semantic scripts (e.g., the fact that *flumen* arose from flowing). These scripts build up a dynamic network of meanings (of the kind found in the medieval *distinctiones*), which are indexes, tokens, or allegories of the things nominated. Hence the relevance of the Aristotelian concept of etymology as *symbolon*—which Isidore recalls in the very next sentence—as a sign bridging (*syn* [together] + *ballein* [throw]) the depths of semantics, the surface of contingent forms, and the essences that they designate. Hence also the appropriateness of mentioning Cicero's rhetorical

---

39. Klinck, *Die lateinische Etimologie*, 164.
40. Amsler, *Etymology and Grammatical Discourse*, 138.
41. These senses of *vis* are confirmed by Ernout-Meillet, *Dictionnaire étymologique*, v. *vis*.
42. "Vis verbi est, qua cognoscitur quantum valeat. Valet autem tantum quantum movere audientem potest." (*De Dialectica*, 7).

theory of *adnotatio*,[43] whereby etymology exemplifies (*nota facit exemplo posito*) the names of things (*nomina et verba rerum*).[44] It should be clear from this that the Isidorian idea of *origo* does not assume one-way derivation. Rather, it takes into account multiple (at times, we shall see, even contradictory) routes to disclose the *vis*, the rhetorical and cognitive potential, of a given word. In this sense, as Klinck observes, medieval etymology coincides with interpretation: "Etymology does not have to trace the origin (*origo*) of a word. As later expressed by Petrus Helie, etymology is an interpretation (*expositio*); its task is to lead from the literal to the spiritual meaning, whereby the allegorical meaning is unlocked from the form of the word."[45] Isidore's etymological model is similar to the three-dimensional schema we found in Varro. This model brackets "the grammatical-temporal plane" and "the historical-chronological plane," thereby yielding at the same time diachronic etymologies confirmed by scientific research and nonscientific explanations, which make sense as "attempts at synchronic motivation of the sign in the linguistic consciousness of the speaker, on the plane of the mental processes of paronomastic association and verbal puzzles."[46] But to these two directions of etymological research, still roughly with-

43. "Tum notatio, cum ex vi verbi argumentum aliquid elicitur" and "multa etiam ex notatione sumuntur. Ea est autem, cum ex vi nominis argumentum elicitut: quam Graeci etymologian appellant, id est verbum e verbo, veriloquium." Cicero, *Topica*, Loeb Classical Library (Cambridge, Mass.: Harvard University Press, 1976), ii.10, and x.35, respectively. Compare to Quintilian, *Institutiones oratoriae*, in *The Institutionio oratoria of Quintilian*, trans. H. E. Butler, 4 vols. (Cambridge: Cambridge University Press, 1933–36), I, 6, 28.

44. Both Amsler's and Lepschy's translations of the crucial passage "quia nomina et verba rerum nota facit exemplo posito" are unconvincing. Amsler ignores the "exemplo posito" ablative and condenses the Latin sentence into "because it explains the names and words of things." Amsler, *Etymology and Grammatical Discourse*, 138. Lepschy takes "nomina et verba" instrumentally "since it produces a sign by the names and words of things in a given pattern." Lepschy, *History of Linguistics*, 222. The notion of sign as an allegory of meaning is left by both to fade into the background. Lepschy notes that Cicero's definition is found in the *Topica* and complies with the widespread classical view of words (*verba*) as signs (*notae*) of things. The Latin noun *nota* involves a range of concepts that goes from the negativity of stigma to the suggestiveness of the musical notes. Isidore must of course have had in mind the technical use of *nota* as popularized by the Imperial grammarians, but it is likely that within a highly charged allegorical context such as that of Christian exegesis, the term took on much wider epistemological implications.

45. Klinck, *Die lateinische Etimologie*, 62.   46. Lepschy, *History of Linguistics*, 153.

in the limits of linguistic orthodoxy, one must add, I believe, a third
dimension, which uses the first two as bridges to other conceptual-
izations: it is the dimension of allegory, borrowed from rhetoric and
expressed in the philosophical and exegetical practice of medieval typology. In terms that should be familiar to us, Isidore echoes Cicero's
and Quintilian's definitions of allegory in the technical section *De tro-
pis* of the first book of the *Etymologiae*:

Allegoria est alieniloquium. Aliud enim sonat, et aliud intellegitur.

> [Allegory is Other-speaking. It has the sound of one thing, and it is under-
> stood as another.][47]

There follows a list of the seven main allegorical tropes, which consists of *ironia, antiphrasis, aenigma, charientismos, paroemia, sarcasmos,*
and *astysmos*. Like allegory, all these function as meta- or extralinguistic pointers. As species of the genus allegory, they differ according to their degrees of obscurity and with reference to specific rhetorical situations. Thus, for instance, "allegory and enigma differ because
the efficacy of allegory is double: it signifies something figuratively
by something else. The sense of an enigma, instead, is indeed much
more obscure, and it is adumbrated by certain images" [inter allego-
riam autem et aenigma hoc interest, quod allegoriae vis gemina est et
sub res alias aliud figuraliter indicat; aenigma vero sensus tantum obscurus est, et per quasdam imagines adumbratus].[48]

As the key figure of typological thinking in the Middle Ages, allegory finds in etymology its ally and its complement. At a lexical level, etymologies open up interpretative routes that allegory follows and
ratifies at higher discursive levels. De facto, etymologies function as
the linguistic pillars on which allegory builds its interpretative edifice.
To a certain extent, medieval etymologizing develops the implications
of Stoic etymologizing, according to which "poetry is a sign of deep-
er structures in the nature of things" and allegory provides through

47. Isidore, *Etymologiae*, I, xxxvii, 22.
48. Ibid., 26.

etymology "the key to systematically hidden meaning in a text."[49] Although the claims of medieval (and specifically patristic) etymologists seem just as farfetched, by Isidore's time the Stoic tradition had been rethought not only in light of Roman grammar and rhetoric—via the contributions of Cicero and Varro—but also under the lens of Christian exegetes like Origen, Ambrose, and Augustine. In the hands of Stoic scholars etymologizing worked mainly on the level of lexis, which Irvine paraphrases as the level of "connected verbal expression,"[50] and was limited to poetic texts, seen as repositories of immanent philosophical truths. In its naturalistic outline, the Stoic theory of language was "similar to that defended by Cratylus in Plato's dialogue."[51] By the late Middle Ages, etymologizing had simultaneously opened up to the claims of faith and the demands of history, in a common ground that solved dynamically the conflict between naturalist and conventionalist views on language. The result was a multifaceted discipline keenly aware of its limits but also sufficiently eclectic to incorporate criteria from grammar and rhetoric:

Sunt autem etymologiae nominum aut ex causa datae, ut "reges" a [regendo et] recte agendo, aut ex origine, ut "homo," quia sit ex humo. Aut ex contrariis ut a lavando "lutum," dum lutum non sit mundum, et "lucus," quia umbra opacus parum luceat. Quaedam etiam facta sunt ex nominum derivatione, ut a prudentia "prudens"; quaedam etiam ex vocibus, ut a garrulitate "garrulus"; quaedam ex Graeca etymologia orta et declinata sunt in Latinum, ut "silva," "domus." Alia quoque ex nominibus locorum, urbium, [vel] fluminum traxerunt vocabula. Multa etiam ex diversarum gentium sermone vocantur. Unde et origo eorum vix cernitur.

[The etymologies of words can be of several kinds. Some depend on motivation (ex causa), as in reges (kings) from their just behavior (recte agendo); on historical origin (ex origine) as in homo (man) coming from humo (earth); on antiphrasis (ex contrariis) as in lutum (mud) from lavando (washing), since mud is unclean, or in lucus (sacred woods) because, being darkened by shadows, the place has very little light. Some etymologies result from word derivatives (ex nominum derivatione), as in prudens (wary) from pruden-

49. Irvine, The Making of Textual Culture, 37.
50. Ibid., 36.
51. Ibid., 37.

tia (caution); from sounds (ex vocibus) as in garrulus (talkative) from garrulitate (talkativeness). Some come from the Greek (ex Graeca etymologia) and
are inflected into Latin, as in the case of silva (forest) or domus (house);
others proceed from place names, from names of cities or rivers (ex nominibus locorum, urbium, fluminum). And many are also borrowed from the
languages of various peoples (ex diversarum gentium sermone) and their origin is hard to make out.][52]

Isidore's Etymologiae encompasses the above criteria and combines
morphology with allegorical interpretations that involve extralinguistic motives. At the beginning of book X (De vocabulis), Isidore does set
up a distinction between etymologies per denominationem—which on
grammatical and philosophical grounds draw homo (man) from humanitas (humanity) or sapiens (the wise) from sapientia (wisdom)—and
those special (specialis) etymologies based on derivatio—which explore
origins and draw homo (man) from humo (earth). The former are introduced by formulae of morphological derivation (a, ab, "from"; ex,
e, "out of"), as in auctor ab augendo [auctor (author) is from augere (to
increase)]; or alumno ab alere [alumno (pupil) from alendo (to nour-
ish)] (Etym X, i, 2). The latter are signposted by complementizers like
quod, quia, or quasi used to invoke, as Amsler notes, "extrasystemic
criteria."[53] It is the case of animosus [(undaunted) because it is full of
courage and force = quod sit animis et viribus plenus] or of amicus [amicus
(friend) almost like animi custos (guardian of the soul)],[54] both of which
sound more like definitions than derivations. Yet, it is clear from the
start that Isidore draws this distinction mainly for ease of analysis: etymology to him is an encyclopedic project that straddles disciplines
and defies strict categorization. So, for instance, while he uses gram-

52. Isidore, Etymologiae, I, xxix, 5–10.
53. Amsler has valuable comments on Isidore's tendency to join concepts like causa, origo, and ratio, derivatio. He rightly notes that the many types of etymologies listed by Isidore in
his definition (ex causa, ex origine, ex contrariis, ex derivatione) are "not so much separate kinds of
etymological explanations as aspects of causa." Unlike Amsler, though, I do not read Isidore's
conflation as a further "confounding of word and thing" but as a detechnicization of grammatical discourse in light of compelling allegorical ends. Allegorical etymologizing is the
strategy that allows analysis within a synthetic view of meaning (one-in-many, many-in-one).
Amsler, Etymology and Grammatical Discourse, 141ff.
54. Isidore, Etymologiae, X, i, 4–7.

mar, he refuses to base his etymologies solely on grammatical tools. And that applies also to the first kind of etymologies seen above (the ones founded on denomination) which, to the dismay of linguists, do not discriminate between a root word and its derivatives. *Homo* (man) is derived from *humanitas* (humanity) and *sapiens* (sage) from *sapientia* (wisdom) because, Isidore argues, the two abstract concepts (humanity and wisdom) must philosophically precede their historical embodiments (the human or wise individual, X, i, 1). And later on,[55] Isidore also gives a wider definition of *sapiens* in relation to its possible senses: *sapiens* is connected to the savoring of food because, just as taste allows one to make out different flavors, so *sapientia* allows one to discriminate among things and concepts [sapiens a sapore; quia sicut gustus aptus est ad discretionem saporis ciborum, sic sapiens ad dinoscentiam rerum atque causarum].[56] In his multifaceted etymological model, Isidore uses grammar, semantics, and rhetoric to chart word histories and weave them into an allegorical hi(story) of the world. Numerous examples of this type are found throughout the *Etymologiae*.

We noted above that one of Isidore's introductory formulae is the complementizer, *quasi*, used in Latin to set up a hypothetical comparison. One can translate *quasi* as "as though," "as if," or "somewhat like," "nearly," "not far from."[57] *Quasi* figured in the kind of construction I explained in chapter 2, when I discussed allegorical etymology as a link of approximation (⇌) between a given word and its supposed meaning(s). The example I cited there was that of *amicus . . . quasi animi custos* (friend . . . as though a guardian of the soul), but many more of these etymologies are present throughout the *Etymologiae*. We can cite for instance *beatus* (blessed), *quasi bene auctus* (as if endowed with good, X, i, 22); *candidus* (candid, unblemished), *quasi candor datus* (as

55. Ibid., X, i, 240.

56. The link between *sapiens* and *sapor* is well documented and supported among others in Ernout-Meillet, *Dictionnaire étymologique*, v. *sapio*.

57. Isidore's *quasi* is analogous to the marker promoted in the field of "fuzzy logic," which introduces in logical statements the notion of approximation. See for instance Bart Kosko's *Fuzzy Thinking: The New Science of Fuzzy Logic* (New York: Hyperion, 1993), or Zhang Qiao's *Fuzzy Linguistics* (Dalian Shi: Dalian ch' ban she, 1998).

if devoted to splendor); or *piger* (sluggish), *quasi pedibus aeger* (almost like feeble-footed, X, i, 212). Isidore refers to etymologies of this kind whenever he wants to indicate a "bundle" of rhetorical, historical, or semantic factors that might have led to one of the senses of a given word. He is not establishing a linear, chronological link between words, and his use of the *quasi* formula should make it evident. He is, in fact, adopting an etymological approach of the kind hoped for by Malkiel and based on cross-referenced conjectures. Isidore undoubtedly grafts his etymologizing onto a Christian view of the world, but perhaps unlike later etymologists, his ideological stance is clear-cut. To him language is not a neutral descriptor of "what is or has been out there," but it is a creative and interpretative tool, *omen* and *consequentia rerum*. And one may be surprised to find how many of Isidore's etymologies, even among those one would at first sight discard as pure nonsense, are in fact negotiable when checked against the "authoritative" pronouncements of etymological science.

An outstanding example is the notorious *lucus a non lucendo* (sacred wood from the fact that there is no light, I, xxxvii, 24; XIV, viii, 30; XVII, 6, 7). This etymology is often cited as the outrageous illustration of that nonsensical attitude that led premodern scholars to etymologize by antiphrasis. *Lucus*, some etymologists would now argue, "has nothing to do with" light. And even if it had, serious etymologies cannot possibly be based on antiphrasis. But a closer look at some of the Latin sources on *lucus* challenges this scientistic view. First of all, the link between *lucus* and *lux* (light) is not all that farfetched. In her etymological account of Latin lexis, largely based on LEW and DEL, Elisabetta Riganti (v. *lucus*) mentions a reconstructed root *leuk* to which Latin *lucus*, *lux* and Germanic *lichtung* in all probability refer.[58] To this one should add Seneca's comments on *lucus* as denoting an especially thick forest and not, as in the case of Latin *nemus* (sacred woods), a clearing in the forest:

58. Riganti, *Lessico latino fondamentale*.

Si tibi occurrerit vetustis arboribus et solitam altitudinem egressis frequens lucus et conspectum caeli [densitate] ramorum aliorum alios protegentium summovens, illas proceritas silvae et secretum loci et admiratio umbrae in aperto tam densae atque continuae fidem tibi numinis faciet (*Epistulae ad Lucilium* 41, 3).

> [Should you come across a forest of old trees, taller than usual, whose thick branches, mutually intertwined, bar the view of the sky, then the sight of that forest, the mystery of the place, and the striking scene of such dense and continuous shade amidst the open countryside, will make you aware of the presence of a god.][59]

It is a definition very similar to the one Isidore himself provides in book 14, viii, 30. "*Lucus* is a place guarded by thick trees, which block sunlight" [lucus est locus densis arboribus septus, solo lucem detrahens]. I am not saying that the modern explanation of *lucus* is wrong. A relation with an Indo-European root *lougas* with the meaning of "section of a forest cut down for religious purposes" might well exist. What I am arguing is that a linear approach of that kind, tracing back the Latin *lucus* to a hypothetical root, may in fact overlook plausible historical senses that the word evoked to a Latin speaker. As in the case of *fermer* mentioned in chapter 1, here we could be dealing with an "irresponsible" popular etymology that is in fact more accurate, semantically and morphologically, than its scientific counterpart. Philological evidence—we saw above—seems to substantiate this guess.

To revalue the *lucus* etymology is particularly important because it means to grant some credibility to etymology *ex contrariis*, the laughingstock of modern etymologists. It means to acknowledge that antiphrasis may have something to contribute to our understanding of old and new etymologies. After all, if one accepts that rhetorical strategies like metaphor and metonymy can influence the formation of words and the changes in their meaning(s) over time, then I do not see why antiphrasis cannot.

One concluding example that comes to mind is the famous ety-

---

59. Similar characterizations of *lucus* can be found in Tacitus's *De Germania* (ix), and in Vergil's *Aeneid* (viii, 345 ff.).

mology of *bellum* (war) as something *non bellus* (not pleasant). In book XVIII, i, 9, Isidore mentions this together with the currently accepted derivation from *duellum* (struggle):

Bellum antea duellum vocatum eo quod duae sint partes dimicantium, vel quod alterum faciat victorem, alterum victum. Postea mutata et detracta littera dictum [est] duellum. Alii per antiphrasin putant dictum (eo quod sit horridum; unde illud [Verg. Aen. 6, 86]: Bella horrida bella, cum bellum contra sit pessimum).

> [*Bellum* comes from *duellum*, because in it there are two parties of fighters, a winner and a loser, so to say. Later *duellum* became *bellum* with the change and the suppression of one letter. Others think that *bellum* derives from antiphrasis (that which is horrible, as in Bella horrida bella [wars horrible wars], when on the contrary war is wretched).]

The quote from Virgil makes one ponder over the recurrent use in Roman poetry of the *figura etymologica*, whose influence on actual Latin coinages might be subtler than we expect. Then again, closer philological analysis could suggest that the link between *bellum* (with its attested etymology *duellum*) and the popular form *bellus* (supposedly derived from *bonulus* by analogy with a reconstructed **dwenolos*) does not simply depend on poetic wordplay. While certainly rigorous and well documented, the etymologies of *bellum* and *bellus* given in LEW and Riganti are still within the realm of conjecture. And the same holds true for a conspicuous number of etymological entries, like *littera* (letter), *obscaenum* (obscene), *segnis* (sluggish), *sanus* (healthy), *castus* (chaste), which LEW labels as *inconnue* and which Isidore diligently enumerates.

And what most sets an esteemed comparatist dictionary like LEW apart from the *Etymologiae* if not allegory? Allegory, a disposition to read and to interpret disparate anecdotes of language as pieces of "another," wider pattern. Allegory, a rhetorical figure of synthesis that builds up a holistic narration, a *historia* of institutions signified through and as language. Allegory, a dynamic, multifaceted *Denkform* that relies on intuition (Eucherius's *spiritalis intelligentiae*) rather than on systematic discrimination. One of the striking features of

Isidore's *Etymologiae*, and something that serves to epitomize the gist of my research, is, finally, the "cohesive openness" of his allegorico-etymological model: a thick mail of rhetorical, philological, historical, and cosmological conjectures through which he sifts the sediments of language. The breaks caused in that mail by the emerging, anti-allegorical thrust of the late Middle Ages and the beginning of the Renaissance are the subject of our next chapter.

CHAPTER 6

EMITHOLOGIA

Etymology's Riddles from 1500 to 1700

THE PRACTICE OF ETYMOLOGIZING underwent subtle, continual changes towards the end of the Middle Ages and throughout the period commonly known as the Renaissance. It may be true, as some have argued, that such changes were more in emphasis than in content and that "the new was bound to the old by ultimate faith in the power of etymology."[1] But, in the large-scale rearrangement of the semiotic landscape that charted the gradual collapse of medieval culture, the fact that etymologizing came to be conceived more and more as matter of technique seems highly consequential.[2] Some hu-

1. Frank Borchardt, "Etymology in Tradition and in the Northern Renaissance," *Journal of the History of Ideas* 29, no. 3 (1968), 416. Notable late medieval examples of the etymegorizing mode may be found in Giovanni Boccaccio's shaky etymologies in *Filostrato* (the title itself erroneously etymologized as "the man vanquished and struck down by love") and *Filocolo*. Perhaps the most notorious instance comes from Boccaccio's *Genealogie deorum gentilium libri*, ed. Vincenzo Romano (Bari: Laterza, 1951), I, 1, 13–15), where the ancient deity, Demogorgon, is presented as the founder of a whole progeny of gods by way of a faulty derivation, conflating Latin *daemon* (demon) and Greek *demos* (people). For a discussion of this "grammatical error, become god" see Jean Seznec's *The Survival of the Pagan Gods: The Mythological Tradition and Its Place in Renaissance Humanism and Art*, trans. Barbara F. Sessions (Princeton, N.J.: Princeton University Press, 1995), especially pages 220 and following. In most cases, late medieval and early Renaissance etymologizing follows the patterns of Isidore or Balbus, as in the case of *laborinthus*, fancifully derived from the "labour" of "entering" a maze. As Thomson notes, Chaucer may have had this etymology in mind. N. S. Thomson, *Chaucer, Boccaccio and the Debate of Love* (Oxford: Oxford University Press, 1999), 24. On the close interaction between mythography, rhetoric, and grammar see Jane Chance's *Medieval Mythography*, vol. 1 (Gainesville: University Press of Florida, 1994).

2. From a semiotic viewpoint, the Renaissance may be generally said to mark a process of a "syntagmatization," whereby language is exhausted on the level of the "signifier," along word chains (syntagms), rather than explored as a paradigmatic pointer to transcendence. This ironically precipitates the rationalistic turn of the seventeenth century when we witness, in Bottiroli's words, a broader "war waged by literalism against figuralism" of the kind extensively explored by Michel Foucault. Bottiroli, *Jacques Lacan*, 169. See Michel Foucault, *The Order*

manists invested rhetoric and etymology with unprecedented prestige, but while they kept the medieval curriculum of *studia humanitatis*
alive around the core disciplines of trivium and quadrivium, their rigorous efforts were directed to poring over texts in their original sources, which must imply some acceptance of the very formalistic logic
they had set out to discard.[3] Of course, humanism resists sweeping
generalizations. Charles Trinkhaus reminds us that "Plato and Aristotle were not at odds in humanist ideals" and that we should declare a
truce between the two. He thinks "we forget that the humanists were
in many cases readers if not hearers of rhetoric and famous as critics
and interpreters of texts. They viewed the rhetorical relationship certainly as much from the viewpoint of the recipient as of the deliverer,
both in their actuality as living citizens and theoretically as critics and
analyzers of eloquence."[4]

Also, humanism looks somewhat suspended between medieval
scholasticism and modern science. Nancy Struever gives an indication
of this when she says that Lorenzo Valla's discursive practice was "no
longer bound by the communicative and role conventions of the medieval university with its formalized disputations, theological institutions of *docere*; but its teaching roles and communicative modes do not
yet possess the professional resonances of early modernity; the peda-

of Things: An Archaeology of the Human Sciences (London: Routledge, 2002). See also Juri Lotman,
Universe of the Mind: A Semiotic Theory of Culture, trans. A. Shukman (Bloomington: Indiana Uni-
versity Press, 1990); and Juri Lotman, "On the Metalanguage of a Typological Description of
Culture," *Semiotica* 3 (1975), 101–25.

    3. Etymology's technicalization during the fifteenth, sixteenth, and seventeenth centuries
is discussed at length by Paul Zumthor in *Langue, texte, énigme* (Paris: Éditions du Seuil, 1975).
See especially pages 150–53, where he gives an account of the restriction in meaning that "etymologia" had faced ever since medieval scholasticism. I would call this "syntagmatization,"
because it tended to exhaust research in the chain of words (syntagms) rather than to see language as an extrasystemic pointer (paradigms). In her essay on "Effort and Achievement in
17th Century British Linguistics," Vivian Salmon talks about a "movement towards concen-
tration on 'etymology' in the sense of word-formation." Vivian Salmon, *Language and Society in
Early Modern England: Selected Essays 1981–1994* (Amsterdam: Benjamins, 1996), 19.

    4. Charles Trinkhaus, "The Question of Truth in Renaissance Rhetoric and Anthropol-
ogy," in James J. Murphy, ed., *Renaissance Eloquence: Studies in the Theory and Practice of Renaissance
Rhetoric* (Berkeley: University of California Press, 1983), 209.

gogic and research institutions described in Ramism, Protestant scholasticism, Jesuit reform, encyclopedism, are not yet in place."[5]

Etymologizing in the Renaissance was popular. Yet, in the wake of
philology, etymology's (and rhetoric's) scopes would be progressively
restricted: their resources curtailed, their aims secularized, and their
results for the most part divested of heuristic value. According to Paul
Zumthor, already by the fourteenth century the term *etymology* applied
almost exclusively to the technical field of grammar.[6] And although
technicism had always been, as we saw, a part of etymological inquiry,
starting with the thirteenth-century Aristotelian *modistae*, it had turned
into a subtle reaction against allegorical etymologies in Greek and Latin poetry and against the medieval *formula spiritalis intelligentiae* of Eucherius of Lyons and Isidore of Seville. Renaissance technicism developed
the exhilarating notion "that words are in some way autonomous and
constitute a 'word-world,'"[7] to be quite legitimately explored without
special provisions for political rhetoric, philosophy, or metaphysics.

At the same time, paradoxically, this keen awareness of the technical workings of language—of the potential for unrestrained manipulation—provided fuel for new, acrobatic feats in the heavily
allegorized and secretive realms of hermeneutics and divination, Neo-
platonic practices which technique and method were expected to en-
hance.[8] Thus, sixteenth- and seventeenth-century Western etymolo-

5. Nancy Struever, "Vico, Valla, and the Logic of Humanistic Inquiry," in *Giambattista Vi-
co's Science of Humanity*, ed. Giorgio Tagliacozzo and Donald Philip Verene, 173–85 (Baltimore:
Johns Hopkins University Press, 1976), 83. See also Lisa Jardine and Anthony Grafton, *From
Humanism to the Humanities: Education and the Liberal Arts in Fifteenth- and Sixteenth-Century Europe*
(Cambridge, Mass: Harvard University Press, 1986).

6. Zumthor, *Langue, texte, énigme*, 153–55. The years between 1550 and 1650 marked the
definitive shift of etymology to the Renaissance technical use. As far as allegory is concerned,
see Don Cameron Allen's thorough discussion of the process he describes as the "rationaliza-
tion of myth and the end of allegory" in Renaissance culture. Don Cameron Allen, *Mysteriously
Meant: The Rediscovery of Pagan Symbolism and Allegorical Interpretation in the Renaissance* (Baltimore:
Johns Hopkins University Press, 1970), 309ff.

7. Although wordplay is common enough in medieval literature, the idea that "words
are in some way autonomous and constitute a 'word-world' was a Renaissance discovery." K.
Ruthven, "The Poet as Etymologist," *Critical Quarterly* (1978), 11.

8. See Allen, *Mysteriously Meant*, and also Heinrich Plett's recent *Rhetoric and Renaissance
Culture* (Berlin: de Gruyter, 2004).

gizing is found to straddle incipient science and ancient magic, and its elaborate word histories come to us, intertwined, from philological commentaries and scientific textbooks, from the guarded language of hermetic tomes and the hazy formulas of alchemical manuals.[9] We are left with a puzzling tangle that even experts of Renaissance language theory are admittedly ill equipped to unravel.[10]

My purpose here must be simply to get a general sense of how allegory and etymology fared during the sixteenth and seventeenth centuries, by looking at how they were defined in English rhetoric manuals.[11] I zero in on this very limited area of Renaissance studies following a suggestion from Brian Vickers, who maintains that "the English Renaissance both domesticated and energized the tropes and figures more intensely than any other European literature."[12] As a matter of fact, one of the first things English writers and rhetoricians of the time seem eager to acknowledge when dealing with allegory is that we should not take it too seriously. Allegory is quite simply a pleasant form of embellishment: a "color," a stylistic "device,"

9. Interestingly, the OED notes that the term *alchemy* itself may have resulted from etymological blending between the Greek word for the ancient "land of Egypt" and another similar-sounding Greek word meaning "infusion or pouring."

10. A comprehensive treatment of British linguistics and its theoretical shortcomings in the seventeenth century may be found in Vivian Salmon's essays, *Language and Society*. For Brian Vickers, "most modern critics have yet to acquire the basic knowledge of rhetoric that would allow them to identify the verbal devices used by Renaissance poets, the necessary first stage in evaluating how they have been used, according to the coherent rationale given by rhetoricians like Puttenham or Peacham ('for a figure is ever used to some purpose'). It is a rather striking demonstration of how the post-Romantic dismissal of rhetoric has conditioned readers not to notice rhetorical devices, that no editor of Shakespeare's sonnets and very few critics have observed that they use many common figures and tropes, hundreds of times over." Brian Vickers, *English Renaissance Literary Criticism* (Oxford: Oxford University Press, 1999), 22.

11. An analysis of allegorical etymology in scientific, alchemical, or Hermetic texts requires a separate book. The same applies to the convoluted aspects of Italian Renaissance rhetoricians (Bruni, Salutati, Landino, Petrarch) and their close ties to late medieval scholasticism. Among the many possible references on these subjects, see T. H. Stahel's "Cristoforo Landino's Allegorization of the *Aeneid*: Books iii and iv of the *Camaldolese Disputations*," (Ph.D. diss., Johns Hopkins University, 1986); Giuseppe Mazzotta's *Cosmopoiesis: The Renaissance Experiment* (Toronto: University of Toronto Press, 2001); Ann Moss's *Renaissance Truth and the Latin Language Turn* (Oxford: Oxford University Press, 2003); and Simon Gilson's *Dante and Renaissance Florence* (Cambridge: Cambridge University Press, 2005).

12. Vickers, *English Renaissance*, 20.

a figure of speech that draws its charm from hiding behind a "dark" veil precepts that one could have stated—if not so effectively—in plain language. This is the apologetic view Spenser voices in his "Letter to Sir Walter Ralegh," prefixed to the 1596 edition of *Faerie Queene*:

Sir, knowing how doubtfully all allegories may be construed, and this book of mine, which I have entitled The Faerie Queene, being a continued allegory, or dark conceit, I have thought good as well for avoiding of jealous opinions and misconstructions, as also for your better light in reading thereof (being so by you commanded), to discover unto you the general intention and meaning which in the whole course thereof I have fashioned. [. . .] The general end therefore of all the book is to fashion a gentleman or noble person in virtuous or gentle discipline. Which, for that I conceived should be most plausible and pleasing, being coloured with an historical fiction, the which the most part of men delight to read, rather for variety of matter than for profit of the example. [. . .] To some, I know, this method will seem displeasant, which had rather have good discipline delivered plainly in way of precepts, or sermoned at large, as they use, than thus cloudily enwrapped in allegorical devices. But such, me seems, should be satisfied with the use of these days, seeing all things accounted by their shows, and nothing esteemed of that is not delightful and pleasing to common sense.[13]

The underlying idea, whereby doctrine should be made "more profitable and gracious . . . by example than by rule,"[14] belongs to classical rhetoric. But what comes to the fore is the passion for appearance and "shows," which Spenser says is common among his contemporaries. That he should find it necessary to apologize for the obscurity of his conceit and make clear its intent is significant: behind this popular Renaissance taste for "pleasing" forms, it tells of a growing bias—in an entrepreneurial, bourgeois milieu where clarity and efficiency count—against pronouncements of rhetoric and poetry that go beyond the limits of enjoyable aesthetics. Later in the passage, Spenser tries to vindicate both poetry's worth and the heuristic value of rhetoric's pleasurable language. He explains that, unlike a historiographer, who is expected to tell events in orderly fashion and in a logical sequence, a poet "thrusts into the midst [. . .] recoursing to the things

13. Edmund Spenser, "Allegory and the Chivalric Epic," in Vickers, *English Renaissance*, 297.
14. Ibid.

for past, and divining of things to come" with the intent of making
"a pleasing analysis of all." But the idea is only hinted at, and his final claim is that his "dark conceit" is meant to avoid "tedious" exposition.[15] As rhetorician Thomas Wilson bluntly puts it in his 1560
manual, "the mystical wise men and poetical clerks will speak nothing but quaint proverbs and blind allegories, delighting much in their
own darkness, especially when none can tell what they do say."[16] In
his *Garden of Eloquence*, Henry Peacham did praise allegory as a "figure
compounded of many stars [. . .] which we may call a constillation."[17]
And there are of course literary critics who, like George Puttenham,
acknowledge allegory's power as "the chief ringleader and captain of
all other figures, either in the poetical or oratory science." But in an
academic environment that calls more and more for plainness of language, allegory's "blindness" and "darkness" also spell duplicity and
dissimulation suited to Machiavellian politics:

> The courtly figure *allegoria*, which is when we speak one thing and think anoth-
> er, [so] that our words and our meanings meet not. The use of this figure is so
> large, and his virtue of so great efficacy, as it is supposed no man can pleasantly
> utter and persuade without it, but in effect is used never or very seldom to thrive
> and prosper in the world that cannot skilfully put in use. [. . .] Qui nescit dissim-
> ulare nescit regnare. Of this figure therefore, which for his duplicity we call the
> figure of "false semblant" or "dissimulation," we will speak first.[18]

And since allegory relies on "doubleness," Puttenham goes on, it may
well serve to mask questionable ends with "guileful and abusing"
speech:

> As figures be the instrument of ornament in every language, so be they also
> in a sort abuses or rather trespasses in speech, because they pass the ordinary
> limit of common utterance, and be occupied of purpose to deceive the ear and
> also the mind, drawing it from plainness and simplicity to a certain double-
> ness, whereby our talk is the more guileful and abusing. For what else is your

---

15. Ibid.
16. Thomas Wilson, *An English Rhetoric Book III on Elocution*, cited in Vickers, *English Renaissance*.
17. Cited in Marjorie Donker, *Dictionary of Literary-Rhetorical Conventions of the English Renaissance* (Westport, Conn.: Greenwood Press, 1982), v. *allegory*.
18. George Puttenham, "English Poetics and Rhetoric," in Vickers, *English Renaissance*, 232.

metaphor but an inversion of sense by transport; your *allegory* but a duplicity of meaning or dissimulation under covert and dark intendments; . . .[19]

This ambiguous attitude, coming from an authoritative source, whereby allegory is at once to be extolled and distrusted, may give us a hint as to how English scholars were expected to view and to use rhetorical figures.[20] And the fact that allegory was often featured *sub nomine agentis* as "courtier or figure of faire semblant"[21] confirms Vicker's idea that scholarly English pronouncements on language and rhetoric were closely tied up with courtly politics.[22] When, in his 1667 *History of the Royal Society of London, for the Improving of Natural Knowledge,* Thomas Sprat protested against the "many mists and uncertainties" that "specious Tropes and Figures [had] brought on [. . .] knowledge,"[23] he was probably defending both his own academic position against colleagues and the supposedly plain language of the English against the outlandish prose of popish humanists and rhetoricians. A statement like Sprat's may well be taken to epitomize the strain of monarchic and northern humanism that, between 1500 and 1700, strived to distance itself, stylistically and politically, from the civic and Ciceronian eloquence of Italian humanists.[24]

A few English poets were perhaps less afraid to recognize and em-

19. Ibid.
20. Which is not, of course, to say that English scholars in fact subscribed to that view. Francis Bacon, for one, is said to have valued "rhetoric as a serious art and a great responsibility," for "it brings knowledge into play in the world. It links morality with reason," which "is not sufficient in and of itself to enforce ethical behaviour." Quoted in Murphy, *Renaissance Eloquence,* 624.
21. Ibid., 370.
22. Vickers argues that dismissal of rhetoric on the part of Royal Society writers should not be taken at face value but is a rhetorical strategy to attack political opponents. So most of the issues discussed are actually more political than rhetorical. Brian Vickers, "The Royal Society and English Prose Style: A Reassessment," in *Rhetoric and the Pursuit of Truth: Language Change in the Seventeenth and Eighteenth Century,* Papers read at a Clark Library Seminar, March 8, 1980. James Murphy notes that in the Renaissance there was "a close parallelism between rhetorical and poetical theory, and a good deal of mutual influence between the two." Murphy, *Renaissance Eloquence,* 16.
23. Quoted in Murphy, *Renaissance Eloquence,* 112.
24. On this and other aspects of Renaissance humanism, see Heinrich Plett, "The Place and Function of Style," in Murphy, *Renaissance Eloquence,* 356–75.

brace the ontological claims traditionally attached to some figures of speech (and above all to metaphor and allegory). And they may have been more willing to accept the patristic view of allegory's darkness as guarding secret (and possibly transcendental) truth.[25] Sir John Harington says that "the ancient poets have indeed wrapped as it were in their writings diverse and sundry meanings, which they call the senses or mysteries thereof" and "these same senses that comprehend so excellent knowledge we call the allegory."[26] Sir Philip Sidney apparently restates this belief in his Defense of Poesie: "It pleased the heavenly deity . . . under the veil of fables, to give us all knowledge, logic, rhetoric, philosophy natural and moral. [. . .] Believe, with me, that there are many mysteries contained in poetry, which of purpose were written darkly, lest by profane wits it should be abused."[27] Sidney's appreciation for the didactic usefulness of what he calls "pretty allegories"[28] typifies the courtly-aesthetic mélange of English poetry, where pragmatic *sprezzatura* combines with medieval and classical exegesis. This also comes through, I think, in John Hoskyns's comment on Sidney's *Arcadia*, when he held that "a metaphor is pleasant because it enricheth our knowledge with two things at one, with the truth and with similitude."[29]

For cultural and political reasons, etymology never quite paralleled allegory's fortune in the English Renaissance, although in some form it did make its appearance in allegorical literature.[30] On the one hand,

25. See the examples cited under the entry "Allegory" in Marjorie Donker's *Dictionary of Literary-Rhetorical Conventions*.

26. John Harington, "An Apology for Ariosto: Poetry, Epic, Morality," in Vickers, *English Renaissance*, 302.

27. Vickers, *English Renaissance*, 390.

28. "For conclusion, I say the philosopher teacheth, but he teacheth obscurely, so as the learned can only understand him; that is to say, he teacheth them that are already taught. But the poet is the food for the tenderest stomachs, the poet is indeed the right popular philosopher, whereof Aesop's tales give good proof; whose pretty allegories, stealing under the formal tales of beasts, make many, more beastly than beasts, begin to hear the sound of virtue from these dumb speakers." Ibid., 353.

29. Ibid., 401.

30. Etymology in Milton, Spenser, Sidney, and Shakespeare has of course been variously approached, if primarily as punning and wordplay. One fascinating contribution comes from

etymology had been by that time largely incorporated into grammar: English rhetoric manuals only mentioned it in passing under the inconsistent names of *adnominatio, traductio,* or *polyptoton,* which meant the repetition of the same word variously throughout a sentence or thought, as in John of Gaunt's "with eager feeding food doth choke the feeder" from Shakespeare's *Richard II,* 2.1.37.[31]

Etymology as *interpretatio* or *notatio* survived sporadically, in law tracts and devotional books, which at times gave a vernacular translation of Quintilian's or Isidore's definition. This is what we find, for instance, in Abraham Fraunce's *The lavviers logike:* "Notation or Etymologie, is the interpretation of the woord. For woords bée notes of thinges, and of all woords eyther deriuatiue or compound, you may yéelde some reason fet from the first arguments, if the notation bée well made. It is called Originatio, quod originem verborum explicet: and Etymologia, id est, veriloquium."[32] And yet *etymologie* figures in Fraunce's *Arcadian rhetorike* only indirectly in his definition of *polyptoton,* the "falling or declining of one word, [. . .] when as words of one ofspring haue diuers fallings or terminations."[33] Again, in Francis Roberts's *Mysterium & Medulla Bibliorum (the Mysterie and Marrow of the Bible)* we find passages that are formally similar to Isidorian etymologizing. "The English word Sincere, is from the Latine Syncerum, or Sincerum: Of which some give the Etymon thus, Sincerum, as it were Sine-cera, without wax; An allusion to pure honey perfectly segregated

---

Marvin Spevack's, "Etymology in Shakespeare." Vestiges of *etymegoreia* in Renaissance literature are yet to be investigated in full and call for separate treatment.

31. This is apparently the chief sense given in the manuals of Sherry (1550), Peacham (1577), Fraunce (1588), and Day (1599), although Sherry also has a direct reference to "etymologie or shewyng the reason of the name." See also Miriam Joseph, C.S.C., *Shakespeare's Use of the Arts of Language* (New York: Columbia University Press, 1947), 162–63, v. *notation.*

32. Abraham Fraunce, "The Lavviers Logike Exemplifying the Praecepts of Logike by the Practise of the Common Lawe" (London: Imprinted by William How, for Thomas Gubbin, and T. Newman, 1588). Another instance of Isidorian definition is found in Richard Mulcaster's *Elementarie,* cited in Jane Donawerth, *Shakespeare and the Sixteenth-Century Study of Language* (Urbana: University of Illinois Press, 1984).

33. Abraham Fraunce, *Arcadian Rhetorike* (London: Imprinted by William How, for Thomas Gubbin and T. Newman, 1588), 25.

and clarified from the wax and dross; Others thus, Syncerum, that is, [. . .], with the wax, both honey and wax, the whole and entire profit of the Bee."[34] But later on Roberts shows what he means by etymology when he rejects it as a practice of "Grammatical Teachers" and complains: "Herein these Grammatical, rather then Theological Teachers do much err, that they derive the signification of words rather from Etymologie, then from the Common use of Scriptures and good Authors. He will fetch the sense of words from Etymologies when they will serve his turn: but when they make against him, he will reject them."[35] Etymology seems overall to have lost much of its heuristic and interpretive edge, possibly also because—even in the unruly and reckless experimenting of Hermeticists—etymologizing was too close to Latinate exegesis and popish indoctrination.[36]

The picture gets hazier if we try to place sixteenth-century English views on etymology in the broader context of the continental Renaissance, so much so that it makes sense, I think, to try to bring it into focus by refurbishing an old—and now partly dismissed—perspective. I would say it helps to look at Renaissance texts as records of a painstaking and ultimately unresolved negotiation—within the study of language—between the competing and complementary modes of

34. Francis Roberts, *Mysterium & Medulla Bibliorum the Mysterie and Marrow of the Bible, viz. God's Covenant with Man in the First Adam before the Fall, and in the Last Adam, Iesvs Christ, after the Fall, from the Beginning to the End of the World: Unfolded & Illustrated in Positive Aphorisms & Their Explanation* (London: Printed by R. W. for George Calvert, 1657).

35. Ibid.

36. One notable exception could be John Johnson's *Academy of Love*, where the crafts of women are analyzed and exposed in terms of rhetorical and grammatical ruses. There, "etymologie" figures as one of the techniques shrewdly employed by "the girls" to ensnare their suitors:

> But the women are expert both in tropes and figures; tropes to delude their adorers, who suppose their reall words to bee full or reall meaning, when as they onely commit a few complements more to enflame their simplitians heartes, and to feed their owne toyish fancy, then any reality; for they abhorre it worse then the poxe. We practice also in Topickes, and first we beginne with Notatio, sive Etymologia, which is both according to us and Cicero, defined, *Indagatio originis*: and by this we search out the true primitive of our courtiers, and provide his place correspondently. John Johnson, *The Academy of Love Describing the Folly of Young Men and the Fallacie of Women*, (London: Printed for H. Blunden, 1641).

rhetoric (grounded on persuasion) and dialectic (based on demon-stration),[37] a negotiation historically complicated by the need to as-sert national and individual esteem while simultaneously going back to "classical prototypes."[38] As they interacted, the two modes were bound to engender their own extremes, which at times paradoxical-ly overlapped: rhetoric would invoke dialectical "methods" to justify Hermetic forays, and dialectic would turn to rhetorical "distinctions" to uphold a pervasive discourse on truth that would eventually lead to Peter Ramus and to Descartes.[39] And to recognize these baffling inter-actions is also to see the Renaissance as the fertile—and still relative-ly unexplored—ground where classical and medieval suggestions on language as a polysemic and "modal" thinking tool are pushed to the limits, tested out, and dramatized.[40]

One of the Renaissance fields that best exemplifies rhetorical and dialectical wordplay is that of emblems,[41] or *impresas*, which play upon the split between an image and its accompanying epigram, or motto, and thus shed light on fifteenth- and sixteenth-century notions of *et-ymegoreia*.[42] As Carlo Innocenti explains, in Renaissance and Baroque impresas, image and caption functioned respectively as the body (out-

37. Hugh Davidson sees the two discursive trends at work in Pascal's "Art of Persuasion." Murphy, *Renaissance Eloquence*, 28off.

38. See Helmut Schanze, "Problems and Trends in the History of German Rhetoric to 1500," in Murphy, *Renaissance Eloquence*, 12off.

39. I am thinking here of the method of exploring arguments through contraries (or *dissoi logoi*), used also by Erasmus and Ramus. Interestingly, Frances Yates has linked Ramist dichot-omies to the Hermetic tradition, where the spatial arrangement of symbols is a way of control-ling the order of the world. Frances Amelia Yates, *The Art of Memory* (London: Pimlico, 1992). The bifurcated tree diagrams that Peter Ramus used to organize his rhetorical material can be said to anticipate the tree diagrams of nineteenth century etymologizing.

40. This is along the line of the "modal" approach to meaning and truth suggested by Jacques Lacan and brilliantly discussed by Bottiroli, *Jacques Lacan*, 139–40.

41. The suggestion comes from Walter Ong's *Rhetoric, Romance, and Technology* (Ithaca, N.Y.: Cornell University Press, 1971, 1980, 1990), and is supported by Dominic Larusso in her account of rhetoric in the Italian Renaissance in Vickers, *Renaissance Eloquence*, 51ff.

42. In the OED definition, an emblem is "a drawing or picture expressing a moral fable or allegory; a fable or allegory such as might be expressed pictorially." Thomas Blount in his "Art of Making Devices" (1646) defines the emblem as "A sweet and morall Symbole, which con-sists of picture and words, by which some weighty sentence is declared." Cited in Donker, *Dic-tionary of Literary-Rhetorical Conventions*, v. emblem.

FIGURE 1. Sumitur *et aby-citur* from Ferro's *Teatro d'Imprese* (1623). Repro-duced with permission of Bib-lioteca Civica Angelo Mai.

er form) and the soul (inner meaning) of an opaque message, suppos-edly decipherable but always elusive.[43]

One can recall for instance the impresa cited by Giovanni Ferro in his *Teatro d'Imprese*, showing a mask with the motto *sumitur et abycitur* (it hides and it shows; figure 1). Or one can look at the esoteric motto of the Italian "*Accademici Occulti*" (figure 2), which reads *intus non extras* (inside not outside).[44]

Ironically, the Hermetic and esoteric emphasis on the essential and the ineffable (what is inside, hidden behind the form) results in a "dissociation of each object from its form, of each signifier from its

43. Carlo Innocenti, *L'immagine significante: studio sull'emblematica cinquecentesca* (Padua: Livi-ana, 1981), 155.

44. Similar assumptions underlie the even more obscure form of rebuses, ever since the satirical pieces of sixteenth-century Picardy.

FIGURE 2. Frontispiece of *Rime degli Accademici Occulti con le loro imprese e discorsi* (1568). Notice the motto *Intus non Extra*. Reproduced with permission of Biblioteca Civica Angelo Mai.

signified,"[45] so that what comes to the fore is, in the end, form itself. It is on form, hieroglyph, *simulacrum*, or mask of an unattainable meaning that most Renaissance scholars focus their attention. It is to form, and to its countless analogical echoes and allusions, that they devote their energies.[46] So, for instance, Ericius Puteanus noted that the letters of the verse written by the Jesuit poet Bernardu Bauhusius—*Tot tibi sunt dotes, Virgo, quot sidera caelo* (Yours are as many gifts, o Virgin, as there are stars in heaven)—could be combined in 1,022 different ways, which was the number of known stars at the time. This meant that the sky "was a perfect emblem of the Virgin's virtues."[47]

The fortune of allegory and etymology in Hermetic texts throughout the Renaissance must be seen to coincide with a far-reaching redefinition of their roles. The medieval mind-set was, we have seen, primarily paradigmatic. Language could give oblique access to metaphysical truths, and *etymegoreia*—whereby form became the allegory of meaning—served to explore those truths. Renaissance Hermeticists inherited this mystic knowledge but overstressed the split, or gap, between form and meaning and eventually recast both of them as masks (surface image plus fragmentary caption) of an otherwise inaccessible, vague core.

Let us look for instance at the visual sonnet of the sixteenth-century Roman poet Giovambattista Palatino, *Dove son gli occhi e la serena forma* (Where are the eyes and the serene form).[48] Cast in the popular form of the rebus, this sonnet "relies on the relationship and the exchange of words and images"[49] and involves homophonic etymological play:

45. "Dissociazione di ogni cosa dalla propria forma, di ogni significante dal proprio significato." G. Agamben, *Stanze. La parola e il fantasma nella cultura occidentale* (Turin: Einaudi, 1977), 169. Cited in Innocenti, *L'immagine*, 156.

46. Emphasis on form is evident in the numerous mottos that rely on various kinds of homophonic play, as in the example given in Innocenti: INFESTUS INFESTIS, FLECTIMUR NON FRANGIMUR, COMINUS ET EMINUS. Innocenti, *L'immagine*, 160.

47. This example is given in Mario Praz, *Studi sul concettismo* (Florence: Sansoni, 1946).

48. Giovambattista Palatino, *Sonetto Figurato*, in *Libro di M. G. B. Palatino cittadino romano nel quale s'insegna a scrivere ogni sorta di lettera Antica e Moderna di qualunque nazione, con le sue regole e misure e essempio et con un breve discorso et util de le cifre* (Rome: Blado, 1547).

49. Innocenti, *L'immagine*, 165.

Where are the eyes, and the serene form
of the sacred, joyful, and loving look
Where is the ivory hand and beautiful breast
the thought of which turns me into a fountain.

Where is the trace of that serene foot,
dancing gaily and delightfully
where is the sweet singing, and the intellect
which was clear norm to each virtue.

Where is the mouth and the golden violets,
the vague dress, and blond tresses
which shine like another Sun on her forehead.

Alas, that not much soil hides her now
The world does not find her and Love aches
that I should every hour burn and call who does not answer.[50]

As is evident from figure 3, the attributes of the absent mistress (*occhi*, eyes; *mano*, hand; *petto*, breast; *bocca*, mouth; *trecce bionde*, blond tresses; *fronte*, forehead) are fragmented and disseminated along the chain of words/images that make up the sonnet. So *occhi*, for instance, appears in verse one with reference to the mistress's eyes and returns in the homophonic pun *io chiami* "I call out" (made up of "the eyes I love"— *i occhi ami*) of the final verse.[51] Allegory is present here only under its new semblance: a sort of *metonymia continuata*: "The repeated use of metonymy (or synecdoche) in this rebus highlights the fragment, the fetish, the dead 'piece.' Through this mosaic of pieces metonymy attempts to reconstruct, within the very structure of the sonnet, the contour of the human body, the ghostly, absent image."[52]

Allegorical etymology is thus reduced to metonymic, analogical

---

50. [Dove' son gli occhi, et la serena forma, / del santo alegro, et amoroso aspetto? / dov'è la man eburnea ov e'l petto, / ch'appensarvi hor' in fonte' mi transforma? / Dov'è del fermo pie' quella sant'orma / col ballar pellegrin pien di diletto? / dov'è 'l soave' canto, et l'intelletto, che' fu d'ogni valor prestante norma? / Dou'è la bocca è' l'auree vìole, / l'abito vago. Et l'alme treccie bionde, / che' facean nel fronte' un nuovo sole? / Lasso che' poca terra hoggi l'asconde' / non la retruova l'mondo amor si duole / ch'ardendo io chiami ohn'hor chi no risponde.] Ibid., 166.

51. Ibid., 165.

52. Ibid., 168.

FIGURE 3. Sonetto *Figurato di Palatino, Dove son gli occhi.* Reproduced with permission of Biblioteca Civica Angelo Mai.

wordplay. The figure used in Palatino's sonnet can be compared to the table taken from Rabanus Maurus's *De Laudibus S. Crucis* (figure 4).

Against the backdrop of words on a page, Rabanus draws an ideal bas-relief of the name "Adam," which contains within itself the allegorical "etymology" of the first human being (*protoplastus*). While the sense of Palatino's message is inscribed *within* the sequence of rebuslike words that make up the sonnet, in Rabanus the chain of words (in itself a valid exposition of Adam's plight) is the basis for a wider (i.e., allegorical) interpretation that the shape ADAM covers and signifies.

To be sure, playful etymologizing is not a Renaissance invention. It is, after all, quite possible to trace similarities between Hermetic and classical uses of etymology. The difference is, I think, both a difference of proportions and of quality: to most Renaissance scholars, allusiveness became the mode of etymological inquiry. It was used to warrant a new dogma of ineffability, whereby etyma are unfathomable, and allegory, which uses them, shortsighted with respect to their *origines*. In the sonnet above, the recurrent *ubi sunt* topos (*Dove son gli occhi, Dov'è la bocca*) reinforces the melancholic motif of loss, which the sixteenth-century rebus form so vividly renders.

One way to think about the exemplarity of Palatino's sonnet is to see it as a Renaissance solution to the tension between nominalism and essentialism: a tension played out in Plato's *Cratylus*, but inherent in allegorical etymology ever since its appearance. It is as if the line of allegorical etymology that we followed up to this point breaks off in two separate directions. Allegorical etymology of the kind observed in Isidore survives as the weaker branch. It is found mainly in the forensic tradition, when not heavily curtailed by formal concerns, and it evolves into the humanist construct of the locus *ab etymologia*. By and large, though, the Renaissance marks the beginning of a drift along the chain of words. Allegory's edifice collapses into a sprawling, mazelike structure. Etymology suffers an analogous destiny. The "etymological furor" of the time has been read by critics simply as a resurgence of Cratylism, of quaint Stoic views to which newborn sciences

FIGURE 4. *De nomine Adam protoplasti*, from Rabanus Maurus's *Laudibus S. Crucis*.
Reproduced with permission of Biblioteca Civica Angelo Mai.

are indebted but which they finally seek to dissipate.[53] But I would submit that this etymological enthusiasm was much unlike its predecessors, for while its aim was often that of asserting the primacy of Hebrew, from which all languages were postulated to derive,[54] its very core was shaped by technicistic views on language and its pseudoscientific proceedings validated through formalistic models.[55] This is evident in the massive comparative effort of Konrad Gessner's *Mithridates*, of 1555, as well as in 1613 in the monumental *Trésor de l'histoire des langues de cet univers* of Claude Duret. It reappears in the 1667 *Alphabeti veri naturalis Hebraici brevissima delineatio*, written by Mercurius van Helmont, and undergirds the anthropological scope of Athanasius Kircher's *Turris Babel*, of 1679.[56] Against all these overreaching and ambitious projects, it comes as no surprise that more and more scholars should, by the end of the seventeenth century, unabashedly reject allegory as stilted and etymology as futile.

53. This is Eco's view in *The Search for the Perfect Language*.
54. As in *L'harmonie étymologique des langues* of Estienne Guichard (1606) cited by Eco in *The Search*.
55. Ibid.   56. Ibid.

CHAPTER 7

REDEFINING DIFFERENCE
Allegorical Etymology in de Man, Derrida, and Vico

THIS SURVEY on allegorical etymology could very well have ended with the Middle Ages. If it is true, as Ohly suggests, that allegorical etymologizing waned with the decline of Latin and has appeared only sporadically in the national languages ever since, it would have made more sense to focus on Isidore, give his work ampler coverage, and provide an in-depth analysis of his contribution to the medieval debate on language.[1] Nonetheless, this chapter is, I think, consistent with the premises of my research and complementary to its findings. When I set out to trace *etymegoreia*, I did so not only with an eye to its paradigmatic medieval embodiment but also with the conviction that different ways of reading, writing, and thinking in an etymologico-allegorical fashion survive to this day and above all that their scope need not be restricted to the "unscientific" milieu of poetry or the "trifles" of wordplay.

It is for these reasons that, having talked about the change that allegorical etymology underwent with the demise of the Roman Middle Ages and the onset of the Renaissance, I turn to compare texts that reach analogous, yet subtly divergent, conclusions on the meaning and function of *etymegoreia*: Paul de Man's "The Rhetoric of Temporality," Jacques Derrida's "Plato's Pharmacy," and Giambattista Vico's *The New Science of Giambattista Vico*. I bring these distant voices into the same arena because I feel that they shape in remarkable ways—if obviously with unequal ascendancy—post-Cartesian ideas on etymol-

1. Ohly, *Geometria e Memoria*, 264.

ogy and allegory. Vico on one side, and Derrida and de Man on the other can be taken respectively as representatives of two main lines of allegorical etymologizing.[2] For Vico, allegorical etymology retains a strong argumentative potency, borrowed from the Renaissance jurist tradition. As I have argued elsewhere,[3] Vichian etymologies are hermeneutic tools: they trace cognitive networks that map history also through the "spiritual" projections of desire. Derrida's etymologizing has a similar heuristic vigor, but its light and shade values are reversed: it rests on a deconstructive celebration of allegory, sanctioned by Paul de Man, and relies on the self-effacing, vertiginous effect of unlimited wordplay.

This chapter defies chronology to highlight Vico's contribution to an understanding of allegorical etymology. I begin with a brief exposition of de Man's pronouncements on allegory, relate them to Derrida's etymologies, and finally move back in time and compare these to the ideas of Vico. It is clear that, by engaging Derrida and de Man, I encroach upon territories that are under the insignia of poststructuralism. And in such territories, "allegory has been used to describe and to register the dislocations that constitute our modernity," as Deborah Madsen puts it from her "post-essentialist" perspective.[4] Let me say from the start that I welcome Madsen's conclusion whereby "allegory articulates itself as both an agent and a record of cultural change,"[5] as well as her suggestion that "allegory offers at least a paradigm for the way in which generic discourses seek to engage with cultural values, establishing relationships that are of the greatest significance for the way we live our lives."[6] I resist, however, her implicit claims that allegory (and hence for us allegorical etymology) rests only on discursive

2. I contrast Vico with Derrida and de Man only for the sake of analysis. Such a stark opposition is just as arbitrary and arguable as my unproblematic coupling of de Man and Derrida on the same deconstructive side of the allegorico-etymological rivalry.

3. Davide Del Bello, "Forgotten Paths: The Making of Vico's Etymology," *Semiotica* 113 (1997), 171–88.

4. Madsen, *Rereading Allegory*, 27.   5. Ibid., 133.

6. Ibid., 147.

play and that allegory as "Other speaking" or "speaking of the Other" must be discarded as "essentialist" because it is not "sensitive to the shifting nature of temporality."[7] An "essentialist"/"nominalist" dichotomy of the kind Madsen sets up not only reasserts the very Western, logo-centric framework it professes to debunk but also masks a ideological tactics that recent criticism has, I think, rightfully exposed.[8]

In the pages that follow I am going to argue that *etymegoreia* can be thought of as an approach that is both referential and relational, "essentialist" and phenomenological.

Allegory and *Chronos* in Paul de Man

Earlier we noted that one of the subcomponents of *allēgoria*, the noun αγορά, was used both in reference to the marketplace—the supplies of trade, as in ἀγορας περικόπτειν (to cut off supplies)—and as a chronological marker, for instance in the expression αγορά πλήθουσα (the forenoon). These two senses inform Paul de Man's brilliant discussion of allegory in "The Rhetoric of Temporality," as well as the pace-setting deconstructionist élan of his *Allegories of Reading* and *The Resistance to Theory*. In these works, de Man associates allegory with death, namely with the spiraling chronological dizziness of organic decay and the lifeless materiality of writing. According to Jan Rosiek, allegory as de Man conceived it in the 1960s anticipated a term that became "the very *symbolon* of deconstructionists" in the 1970s and 1980s.[9] Under the influence of Walter Benjamin, de Man was drawn to allegory as an "experience of silence," a way "of reaching the limits of language," of "keeping alive the idea of *reine Sprache* [pure language]."[10]

7. Ibid., 133.

8. See for instance the chapter on deconstruction in Vicker's *Appropriating Shakespeare*.

9. Jan Rosiek, "Apocalyptic and Secular Allegory, or How to Avoid Getting Excited—Walter Benjamin and Paul de Man," *Orbis Litterarum* 48 (1993), 146.

10. Ibid., 10.

This is the idea expressed in the posthumous *The Resistance to Theory*, together with an acknowledgment of indebtedness to Benjamin: "Everyone has always known that allegory, like the commodity and unlike aesthetic delight, is, as Hegel puts it, 'icy and barren.' 'Allegory,' however, is a loaded term that can have different implications. . . . In his treatment of allegory . . . for him [Benjamin] allegory is best compared to a commodity; it has, as he puts it in a term taken from Marx, *Warencharakter*, 'matter that is death in a double sense and that is anorganic.'"[11] Allegory is "anorganic" in the sense that it is purely intralinguistic: it does not point to an ontological meaning but "repeatedly" decrees its own "vertiginous" digression from it. "The commodity is anorganic because it exists as a mere piece of paper, as an inscription or a notation on a certificate. The opposition is not between nature and consciousness (or subject) but between what exists as language and what does not. . . . Allegory names the rhetorical process by which the literary text moves from a phenomenal, world-oriented, to a grammatical, language-oriented direction."[12] In "The Rhetoric of Temporality" de Man explores the alternation of irony and "secularized" allegory in the late eighteenth-century writings of Hölderlin, Rousseau, and Wordsworth, to conclude that "the two modes . . . are the two faces of the same fundamental experience of time."[13] Allegory endlessly "impl[ies]" an unreachable anteriority,"[14] a pre-existing meaning that is not present: it "engend[ers] duration as the illusion of a continuity that it knows to be illusionary."[15] In this self-conscious process, allegory uncovers a "void" that defeats symbolic hopes of transcendence as well as the "mimetic mode of representation in which fiction and reality coincide."[16]

11. Paul de Man, *The Resistance to Theory* (Minneapolis: University of Minnesota Press, 1986), 68.

12. Ibid.

13. Paul de Man, "The Rhetoric of Temporality," in *Interpretation: Theory and Practice*, ed. Charles S Singleton, 173–209 (Baltimore: Johns Hopkins University Press, 1969), 207.

14. Ibid., 203.   15. Ibid., 207.

16. "Whereas the symbol postulates the possibility of an identity or identification, allegory designates primarily a distance in relation to its own origin, and, renouncing the nostalgia and the desire to coincide, it establishes the void of this temporal difference." Ibid., 204.

Recent criticism has thrown light upon some of the contradictions embedded in de Man's text: his inconsistent distinction between "allegory" and "metaphor," his ambiguous use of words like "literal" and "essential" in a reading practice that proclaims the inescapable figurality of all language, and above all his problematic view of history. Niranjana Tejaswini, for instance, argues that "de Man's notion of allegory performs a valuable critique of representation" but lacks "a rich conception of history or historicity." More specifically, de Man's readings "cannot account for either the historical construction of a text or its specific deployments in different historical situations."[17] I sidestep the thorny issue of history here because my intent is to see de Man's use of "allegory." In fact, I feel that one of the issues to be addressed is precisely de Man's "valuable critique of representation," which Tejaswini welcomes. One passage from "The Rhetoric of Temporality" seems particularly worth citing in this respect:

> The terms [allegory and irony] are rarely used as a means to reach a sharper definition, which . . . is greatly needed. It obviously does not suffice to refer back to the descriptive rhetorical tradition which, from Aristotle to the eighteenth century, defines irony as "saying one thing and meaning another" . . . This definition points to a structure shared by irony and allegory in that, in both cases, the relationship between sign and meaning is discontinuous. . . . *The sign points to something that differs from its literal meaning and has for its function the thematization of this difference.*[18]

De Man was looking for a "sharper definition" of the rhetorical qualities of allegory and irony. He was hindered by a canonical definition that he claimed "lack[ed] discriminatory precision" and applied equally to both. After a painstaking analysis of "the structure of the trope itself" through pre-Romantic texts supposedly "demystified and, to large extent, themselves ironical,"[19] de Man concluded, as we have seen, that allegory and irony are "linked in their common dis-

---

17. Niranjana Tejaswini, "Deconstructing Allegory: Reading Paul de Man," *Indian Journal of American Studies* 19 (1989), 98.
18. de Man, "Rhetoric of Temporality," 192 (emphasis added).
19. Ibid., 194.

covery of a truly temporal predicament."[20] They both strive to demystify symbolic or mimetic representations. At least two comments can be made at this point. First, de Man's search for "sharper definition" and "discriminatory precision" sets epistemological standards that sound vaguely Cartesian—one can reach for truth through clear and distinct perceptions—and calls for a linguistic model that is markedly Saussurean—a sign is a discrete unit, and meaning arises in the tension between a *signifier* and its corresponding *signified*. Besides, de Man's notion of temporality relies on a linear analog that, in order to make sense, presupposes referentiality ("pure anteriority"), and therefore contradicts the possibility of a purely intralinguistic experience: "This relationship between signs necessarily contains a constitutive temporal element; it remains necessary, if there is to be allegory, that the allegorical sign refer to another sign that precedes it. The meaning constituted by the allegorical sign can then consist only in the *repetition* . . . of a previous sign with which it can never coincide, since it is the essence of this previous sign to be pure anteriority."[21] What these Cartesian and Saussurean grids filter out is the possibility of an alternative model of signification: a model where fiction and reality need not clash at all times and may, in fact, overlap while maintaining a difference—not a Derridian *différance*, but, as Walter Benjamin calls it, a constellation, or "condensed diversity." In retrospect, de Man may be overlooking salient clues in Walter Benjamin's *Origin of The German Tragic Theater*, not least of all Benjamin's deliberate indecisiveness between a "secular" and an "apocalyptic" perspective on allegory. We can conclude by citing the very beginning of Benjamin's chapter "Allegory and Trauerspiel": "It is by virtue of a strange combination of nature and history that the allegorical mode of expression is born. Karl Giehlow devoted his life to shedding light on this origin. [In] his monumental study, *Die Hieroglyphenkunde des Humanismus in der Allegorie der*

20. Ibid., 203.
21. Ibid., 190.

Renaissance [he] discovered the impulse for [allegory's] development in the efforts of the humanist scholars to decipher hieroglyphs."[22]

Derrida's Pharmakon

Digression, drift, vertiginous playfulness, and writing as death are all images that become familiar to readers of de Man. But these themes are above all tied to the controversial achievement of Jacques Derrida: from his ground-breaking De la Grammatologie, through his lecture-manifesto on différance, to Dissémination, and the puzzle-like montage of Glas. Whether one should think of de Man and Derrida as belonging to one definite school to be labeled "deconstruction" must be left for discussion elsewhere.[23] Here, I am interested in Derrida as "an author so excruciatingly aware of the minutest linguistic différance,"[24] one who "always writes with close attention to the resonances and the punning humour of etymology."[25] And I compare him to de Man because they seem to share views on what allegory together with etymology can do (or undo).

As noted above in the quote from Barbara Johnson, Derrida had frequent recourse to etymology in all his works. Ever since his pivotal 1968 lecture on différance,[26] it is clear that Derrida employs etymology for its punning, subversive potential: rather than trace the etymon of a given word, etymologizing serves to unveil the innumerable "cor-

22. Walter Benjamin, The Origin of German Tragic Drama (London: Verso, 1985), 168–69.

23. Until his death in 1983, de Man certainly contributed to spreading Derrida's views in U.S. literary academia. The series of conferences held in 1984 at the University of California, Irvine, by Derrida in memory of Paul de Man, attests to their theoretical affinity, as does Derrida's article "La guerre de Paul de Man," published in the French edition of the conferences under the title Mémoires (1988).

24. Barbara Johnson, The Critical Difference: Essays in the Contemporary Rhetoric of Reading (Baltimore: Johns Hopkins University Press, 1981), xviii.

25. Ibid., xiv.

26. This famous coinage is derived from the punning mix of the verbs to differ and to défer, upon which Derrida builds his deconstructive conception of writing and reading. For a discussion of différance, see Alan Bass's introduction to his translation of Writing and Difference. Alan Bass, "Introduction," in Jacques Derrida, Writing and Difference, trans. Alan Bass (London: Routledge, 1978).

ridors of meaning"[27] that words build up in a text with or without the complicity of its author.[28] Etymology is, in fact, the central mechanism of deconstructive reading and writing: it does not strive for interpretative unity, but for a "dissemination" that "subverts all . . . recuperative gestures of mastery" found in "the Book, the Preface, and the Encyclopedia," seen as "structures of unification and totalization."[29]

"Plato's Pharmacy," written in 1968 and published in French in 1972 in the volume *Dissémination*,[30] is an outstanding example of this kind of etymologizing. We are going to look for the gist of Derrida's discourse, although that necessarily means violating its rhetorical integrity, its pervasive allusions, and the sustained play of multiple perspectives. Derrida rereads Plato's *Phaedrus* on the central question of written versus spoken language. His analysis centers on the polysemous word *pharmakon*, which comes up at supposedly critical points of the dialogue, is used to qualify written words (*logoi en bibliois*), and can be taken to mean, among other things, "drug," "remedy," "poison," "perfume," "color," and "scapegoat." The chains of signification built up by all these senses, which cooperate and conflict in unpredictable ways within the text, serve to "deconstruct" the *Phaedrus*. The result: a "stammering buzz of voices,"[31] which undermines the unity of the message and averts final interpretative closure. The etymological mesh on the final page of "Plato's Pharmacy" makes translation hardly possible:

In this stammering buzz of voices, as some philological sequence or other floats by, one can sort of make this out, but it is hard to hear: *logos* beds itself [*le logos s'aime lui-même* = logos loves itself; *s'aime* is a homonym for *sème* to sow as

27. Johnson, *Critical Difference*, xvii.
28. This comment is from a stark metalinguistic section at the beginning of section 4 of the "Pharmacy": "Finely regulated communications are established, through the play of language, among diverse functions of the word and, within it, among diverse strata or regions of culture. These communications or corridors of meaning can sometimes be declared or clarified by Plato when he plays upon them 'voluntarily.'" Jacques Derrida, "Plato's Pharmacy," in *Dissémination*, trans. Barbara Johnson (Chicago: Chicago University Press, 1981), 95.
29. Johnson, *Critical Difference*, xxxii.   30. Derrida, "Pharmacy," 63–171.
31. Ibid., 170.

in a flower bed.—Trans.] . . . *pharmakon* means *coup* . . . "so that *pharmakon* will have meant: that which pertains to an attack of demoniac possession [*un coup démoniaque*] or is used as a curative *against* such an attack" . . . an armed enforcement of order [*un coup de force*] . . . a shot fired [*un coup tiré*] . . . a planned overthrow [*un coup monté*] . . . but to no avail [*un coup pour rien*] . . . like cutting through water [*un coup dans l'eau*] . . . *en udati grapsei* . . . and a stroke of fate [*un coup du sort*] . . . Theuth who invented writing . . . the calendar . . . dice . . . *kube-ia* . . . the calendar trick [*le coup du calendrier*] . . . the unexpected dramatic effect [*le coup de théâtre*] . . . the writing trick [*le coup de l'écriture*] . . . the dice-throw [*le coup de dés*] . . . two in one blow [*le coup double*] . . . *kolaphos* . . . *gluph* . . . *col-pus* . . . *coup* . . . glyph . . . scalpel . . . scalp . . . *krusos* . . . *crhysolite* . . . *chrysology* . . . Plato gags his ears [*Platon se bouche les oreilles; boucher* = to plug up; *bouche* = mouth.—Trans.] the better to hear-himself-speak, the better to see, the better to analyze. He listens, means to distinguish, between two repetitions.[32]

Derrida himself informs us that, metalinguistically, we are dealing with a "process of substitution, which . . . functions as a pure play of traces or supplements or, again, operates within the order of the pure signifier which no reality, no absolutely external reference, no transcendental signified, can come to limit, bound, or control."[33] It is here that the link between allegory and etymology, deconstructively conceived, comes to the fore: Derrida's etymological play, his etymological *jouissance* draws its strength from the reversal of traditional allegory, which relied on a distinction between a material signifier and a transcendental signified. As de Man would say, allegory keeps pointing beyond itself, but rather than being a "continued metaphor" of what transcends language, it is simply a "continued metonymy" of language itself. The search for word origins does not yield transcendental patterns;[34] it simply leads to an analogical drift of the kind noted with Hermeticism. In the case of Derrida and de Man, the phrase

32. Ibid.

33. Ibid., 89.

34. The word "transcendental" is of course problematic. Here I use it provisionally in the Aristotelian sense of "extending beyond the bounds of any single category" (OED) and thus as a partial synonym of "metaphysical," "spiritual." In psychoanalysis terms like these may be used with reference to the unfulfilled plans or projections of desire. For a discussion of unexpected links between transcendentalism and deconstruction see Richard Rorty's "Is Derrida a Transcendental Philosopher?" in *Essays on Heidegger and Others*, Philosophical Papers, vol. 2 (Cambridge: Cambridge University Press, 1991), 119–28.

"allegorical etymology" must ultimately be taken to signify an indefinite deferral of meaning, a "play of differences" within the linguistic chain that we, as readers or writers, are never allowed to exceed.

"Plato's Pharmacy" is intriguing also for another reason. To support his deconstructive reading of Plato, Derrida devotes pages to an analysis of the myth of Theuth, or Egyptian Thoth, the god of writing that Plato cites in the *Phaedrus*.[35] The story goes like this. Theuth is said to have been admitted before King Thamus and to have presented to him the invention of writing: a *pharmakon* (remedy or poison) that would make the Egyptians wiser and would improve their memories (*sophoterous kai mnemonikoterous*). But the King objects that the effects of writing will not be beneficial. Writing will only engender forgetfulness and make people believe they are wise, while they are in fact only opinion-bearers (*doxosofoi*). Theuth has only invented a *pharmakon* for recalling to memory (*hypomnesis*), not one for active remembering (*mneme*).

For Derrida, Plato's "meshing of the mythological and the philosophical points to some more deeply buried necessity."[36] This myth presents a "hierarchical opposition between son and father, subject and king, death and life, writing and speech"[37] and then destroys oppositions altogether through the cunning intervention of Theuth:

No doubt the god Thoth had several faces, belonged to several eras, lived in several homes. The discordant tangle of mythological accounts in which he is caught should not be neglected. Nevertheless, certain constants can be distinguished throughout, drawn in broad letters with firm strokes. One would be tempted to say that these constitute the permanent identity of the god in the pantheon, if his function, as we shall see, were not precisely to work as a subversive dislocation of identity in general, starting with that of theological regality.[38]

In Theuth, or Thoth, Derrida sees the mythological personification of that semantic drift alluded to in the polysemy of the *pharmakon*: a ma-

35. Plato, *Phaedrus*, 274c–275b.   36. Derrida, "Pharmacy," 86.
37. Ibid., 92.   38. Ibid., 86.

lignant sort of *coincidentia oppositorum* that works only "by metonymic substitution, by historical displacement, and sometimes by violent subversion."[39] "This messenger-god is truly a god of the absolute passage between opposites. If he had any identity—but he is precisely the god of nonidentity—he would be that *coincidentia oppositorum* to which we will soon have recourse again."[40] And again: "The god of writing is thus at once his father, his son, and himself. He cannot be assigned a fixed spot in the play of differences. Sly, slippery, and masked, an intriguer and a card, like Hermes, he is neither king nor jack, but rather a sort of joker, a floating signifier, one who puts play into play."[41] Let us finally fix our eyes on this Hermes, the Greek counterpart of Thoth never mentioned by Plato in the *Phaedrus* but evoked by Derrida in his etymological pharmacy. Hermes, unidentifiable messenger of an ever-absent "Other" but also "floating signifier" that annuls all oppositions, should linger in our memory as a symbol of the allegorical etymologizing embraced by Derrida and contemplated by de Man. And let us call this Hermes to mind as we move on to consider his role and his allegorical status in the thought of our third interlocutor: Giambattista Vico.

Hermes Thrice-Greatest

In *The Origin of the German Tragic Theater*, cited above as the main source of de Man's discourse on allegory, Walter Benjamin deals with the mix of Egyptian, Greek, and Christian pictorial languages in the scholarly allegories of the high Baroque. He concludes that the Baroque rediscovery of medieval allegory consisted in a hieratic "making present" of "the tension between immanence and transcendence."[42] Structural, stylistic, and thematic features mark the work of the Italian philosopher Giambattista Vico (1668–1744) as a continuation—in an

---

39. Ibid., 89.
41. Ibid.

40. Ibid., 93.
42. Benjamin, *The Origin*, 183.

increasingly enlightened milieu—of issues that haunted the Baroque mind. Allegory and etymology figure prominently among them and must be seen as part of Vico's broader philosophical-philological concern for the origin of language and social institutions.[43]

In section 1, book 1 of *The New Science*, dealing with the establishment of general principles, Vico devotes a whole axiomatic paragraph, or *degnità*, to the Greek-Egyptian god, "the Hermes who, on the authority of Cicero, *On the Nature of the Gods*, was called by the Egyptians [Thoth or] Theuth (from which the Greek are said to have derived theos), and who brought the Egyptians letters and laws."[44] Trismegistus, messenger of the gods, founder of the occult sciences and alchemy, god of commerce, of eloquence, and, more generally, of the arts of life, is cited many times throughout the book and comes up in a key paragraph on poetry and the primitive cast of mind: "A truly golden passage is that of Iamblichus in *On the Mysteries of the Egyptians* to the effect that the Egyptians attributed to Thrice-Great Hermes all discoveries useful or necessary to human life."[45] Clearly, the champion joker of Derrida's text is here invested with a "constructive" role. He is adduced as a striking instance of the allegorical thinking common among the first peoples of the human race: namely, the conflation of multiple perceptions of social usefulness or good to a single ideal paradigm.[46] For Vico, Hermes Thrice-Greatest personifies the initial

---

43. For an analysis of the far-reaching implications of Vico's "philosophical-philological method" see John Schaeffer's *Sensus communis: Vico, Rhetoric, and the Limits of Relativism* (Durham, N.C.: Duke University Press, 1990), 82; Giuseppe Mazzotta's *The New Map of the World: The Poetic Philosophy of Giambattista Vico* (Princeton, N.J.: Princeton University Press, 1998), especially page 101; and Jurgen Trabant's *Vico's New Science of Ancient Signs*, trans. Sean Ward (London: Routledge, 2004), 8ff.

44. Giambattista Vico, *The New Science of Giambattista Vico*, trans. Thomas Goddard Bergin and Max Harold Fisch (Ithaca, N.Y.: Cornell University Press, 1976), 66.

45. "E' un luogo d'oro di quel di Giamblico, *De mysteriis Aegyptiorum*, che gli egizi tutti i ritrovati utili o necessari alla vita umana richiamavano a Mercurio Trimegisto." Vico, *New Science*, 207.

46. "I primi uomini, [. . .] non essendo capaci di formar i generi intelligibili delle cose, ebbero naturale necessità di fingersi i caratteri poetici, che sono generi o universali fantastici, da ridurvi come a certi modelli, o pure ritratti ideali, tutte le spezie particolari a ciascun genere somiglianti." Ibid., 207–9.

FIGURE 5. Hermes *Trismegistus* (Latin Mercury) with his common attributes: a *caduceus*, or divining rod; a purse symbolizing trade; and the *petasus*, or winged cap, which characterizes the Messenger of the Gods. Reproduced with permission of Biblioteca Civica Angelo Mai.

mode of a three-phased evolution in human language: that of a *hieroglyphic* language.[47] He is also an allegory—that is to say a condensed mythical utterance—of the intersection between the temporal and the prelapsarian histories of humankind (figure 5):

[Hermes] must therefore have been, not an individual man rich in esoteric wisdom who was subsequently made a god, but a poetic character of the first men of Egypt who were wise in vulgar wisdom and who founded there first

47. The three phases are (1) hieroglyphic or divine language, based on religion; (2) heroic language, linked to blazonings; and (3) vulgar language, or articulated speech "used by all nations today." Ibid., 928ff.

the families and then the peoples that first composed that great nation. From this same passage just cited from Iamblichus it follows that, if the Egyptian division stands of the three of gods, heroes and men, and this Thrice-Great was their god, then the life of this Hermes must embrace the entire Egyptian age of the gods.[48]

Hermes recalls the very first human activity: a process of assemblage, arrangement, or, as Vico notes, a "poetic" mode[49] that humans use to establish mnemonic, synthetic paragons (heroes, gods) of diverse perceptions or emotions ("men, deeds, things": uomini, fatti, cose), resulting in dependable cognitive patterns:

So the Egyptians reduced to the genus "civil sage" all their inventions useful or necessary to the human race which are particular effects of civil wisdom, and because they could not abstract the intelligible genus "civil sage," much less the form of the civil wisdom in which these Egyptians were sages, they imaged it forth as Thrice-great Hermes. . . [This was one of the] true poetic allegories [which] gave the fables univocal, not analogical, meanings for various particulars comprised under their poetic genera. They were therefore called diversiloquia; that is, expressions comprising in one general concept various species of men, deeds, or things.[50]

At first, their poetic mode comes with the awestruck apprehension of divinity, ciphered in hieroglyphs. Eventually, the poetic imagination sets up a mental language centered on three main social prescriptions: religions, matrimony, and burial (religioni, matrimoni e seppolture).[51] In

48. "Egli dee essere stato, non un particolare uomo ricco di sapienza riposta che fu poi consacrato dio, ma un carattere poetico de' primi uomini dell'Egitto sapienti di sapienza volgare, che vi fondarono prima le famiglie e poi i popoli che finalmente composero quella gran nazione. E per questo stesso luogo arrecato testé di Giamblico, perché gli egizi costino con la loro divisione delle tre età degli dèi, degli eroi e degli uomini, e questo Trimegisto fu loro dio, perciò nella vita di tal Mercurio dee correre tutta l'età degli dèi degli egizi." Ibid., 68.

49. Etymology restores the relevance of the term: the verb poieo meant, in Greek "to create / to assemble / to put together," and in Sanskrit, "to heap up."

50. "Appunto come gli egizi tutti i loro ritrovati utili o necessari al gener umano, che sono particolari effetti di sapienza civile, riducevano al genere del 'sappiente civile,' da essi fantasticato Mercurio Trimegisto, perché non sapevano astrarre il gener intelligibile di 'sapiente civile,' e molto meno la forma di civile sapienza della quale furono sappienti cotal'egizi. [. . .] E quest'ultima degnità, in séguito dell'antecedenti, è 'l principio delle vere allegorie poetiche, che alle favole davano significati univoci, non analogi, di diversi particolari compresi sotto i loro generi poetici: le quali perciò si dissero 'diversiloquia,' cioè parlari comprendenti in un general concetto diverse spezie di uomini o fatti o cose." Vico, New Science, 209–10.

51. Ibid., 281.

very general terms, Vico's theory takes each cultural system as a specific, historicized model of a universal mental vocabulary. This model is set up as individuals, in accordance with epochal or geographical standards, privilege certain aspects of their common mental vocabulary and anesthetize others: "There must in the nature of human institutions be a mental language common to all nations, which uniformly grasps the substance of things feasible in human social life and expresses it with as many diverse modifications as the same things may have diverse aspects."[52]

Metaphor and its counterpart allegory (which is *metaphora continuata*) are among the poetic tools humans use to frame a culture. Vico would describe them as time-bound embodiments (birth, nature = *nascita, natura*) of universal schemas. Hence the importance of poetic language in human history, the master discovery of Vico's *New Science*: "We find that the principle of these origins both of languages and of letters lies in the fact that the first gentile peoples, by a demonstrated necessity of nature, were poets who spoke in poetic characters. This discovery, which is the master key of this Science, has cost us the persistent research of almost all our literary life."[53] Language is not so much the byproduct of fortuitous biological or social conjunctures, but coexists with biological and social evolution. And myth, Vico remarks, bears witness to the relevance that "letters" have had since the very first forms of human intercourse. Letters do not evolve after language; they are an integral part of it. "We here bring to light the beginnings not only of languages but also of letters, which philology has hitherto despaired of finding. . . . [W]e shall observe that the unhappy cause of this effect is that philologists have believed that among

52. "E' necessario che vi sia nella natura delle cose umane una lingua mentale comune a tutte le nazioni, la quale uniformemente intenda la sostanza delle cose agibili nell'umana vita socievole, e la spieghi con tante diverse modificazioni per quanti diversi aspetti possan avere esse cose." Ibid., 161.

53. "Principio di tal'origini e di lingue e di lettere si truova esser stato ch'i primi popoli della gentilità, [. . .] furon poeti [. . .]; la qual discoverta, ch'è la chiave maestra di questa Scienza, ci ha costo la ricerca ostinata di quasi tutta la nostra vita letteraria . . ." Ibid., 34.

the nations languages first came into being and then letters; whereas
(to give her a brief indication of what will be proved in this volume)
letters and languages were born twins and proceeded apace though
all their three stages."[54] Vico forms his concept of allegory within this
Baroque theory of language, a theory that harks back to classical rhetoric but grows in the daylight of the Enlightenment. We find a full definition of allegory in the second book of the *New Science*, entitled "Poetic Logic":

Allegory is defined as *diversiloquium* insofar as, by identity not of proportion
but (to speak scholastically) of predicability, allegories signify the diverse species or the diverse individuals comprised under these genera so that they must
have a univocal signification connoting a quality common to all their species
and individuals (as Achilles connotes an idea of valour common to all strong
men, or Ulysses an idea of prudence common to all wise men); such that these
allegories must be the etymologies of the poetic languages, which would make
their origins all univocal, whereas those of the vulgar languages are more often analogical. We also have the definition of the word "etymology" itself as
meaning *veriloquium*, just as fable was defined as *vera narratio*.[55]

Here emphasis is placed on "diversity," not "difference" or "reference." Unlike de Man, Vico views allegory as an instance or a process of poetic condensation: a *diversiloquium* historically exemplified
in hieroglyphical enigmas and reminiscent of Baroque emblemat-
ics. De Man probed eighteenth-century poetics to expose allegory as
a self-alienating, "liberating" scheme that negates transcendence, ori-

54. "Però qui si dánno gli schiariti princìpi come delle lingue così delle lettere, d'intorno
alle quali ha finora la filologia disperato, e se ne darà un saggio delle stravaganti e mostruose
oppenioni che se ne sono finor avuto. L'infelice cagione di tal effetto si osserverà ch'i filologi
han creduto nelle nazioni esser nate prima le lingue, dappoi le lettere; quando (com'abbiamo
qui leggiermente accennato e pienamente si pruoverà in questi libri) nacquero esse gemelle e
caminarono del pari, in tutte e tre le loro spezie, le lettere con le lingue." Ibid., 33.
55. "Il qual nome [allegoria] come si è nelle Degnità osservato, ci venne diffinito 'diversiloquium,' in quanto, con identità non di proporzione ma, per dirla alla scolastica, di predi-
cabilità, esse significano le diverse spezie o i diversi individui compresi sotto essi generi: tanto
che devon avere una significazione univoca, comprendere una ragion comune alle loro spezie
o individui (come d'Achille, un'idea di valore comune a tutti i forti; come d'Ulisse, un'idea di
prudenza comune a tutti i saggi); talché si fatte allegorie debbon essere l'etimologie de' parlari
poetici, che ne dassero le loro origini tutte univoche, come quelle de' parlari volgari lo sono
più spesso analoghe. E ce ne giunse pure la diffinizione d'essa voce 'etimologia,' che suona lo
stesso che 'veriloquium,' siccome essa favola ci fu diffinita 'vera narratio.'" Ibid., 403.

gin, and reference in favor of an overwhelming temporality. Vico re-furbished Quintilian's *diversiloquium* to suggest that allegory actively shapes human history, while it also points to cognitive patterns that are not altogether coterminous with historical language. Again, de Man was sensitive to the temporality inherent in the allegorical mode and showed rents in the texture of human signs. He was also, howev-er, impervious to allegory's diverse oracles, to the polyphony of histor-ical meanings and rhetorical utterances that allegory *impersonates*—or voices through. Peter Carravetta has used these words to summarize Vico's enticing epistemological perspective:

[Vico's allegory] is equiprimordial to the instancing itself of human language. For Vico allegory is that *diversiloquium* which alone can speak of myth—as *vera narratio*. Allegory is what gives poetic diction its human temporality, for fables are always told by someone; moreover allegory, as *other-speaking*, is what per-mits one to speak of that about which one cannot speak, either because the words for it are not available—as in the case of the *bestioni* and the *famuli* in the forests—or because it is not known what something is in a concrete rational way, but is somehow sensed or felt or divined. Allegory tells of that real, social world out there, transcending the single individual yet requiring that he/she be there to tell and/or to listen.[56]

Hence to Vico the value of a myth like Hermes's: the god's attributes—his petasus, his caduceus, his purse—are the visual analogs of multi-ple, intersecting, communal discourses that the god condenses alle-gorically.[57] One may be unable to pinpoint the meaning of the figure of Hermes, but within the intricate texture of its myth, one is made sub-tly aware of the holistic patterning that gives transcendent unity to the contingency of separate historical utterances.

Given these premises, it is not by chance that allegory and etymol-ogy should figure within the same passage of Vico's science: "Allego-

56. Peter Carravetta, *Prefaces to the Diaphora: Rhetorics, Allegory, and the Interpretation of Post-modernity* (West Lafayette, Ind.: Purdue University Press, 1991), 251.

57. In his article on Vico's syncretic allegory, Angus Fletcher pithily concludes: "Perhaps the simplest of all approaches to allegory is to understand that symbolic mode as the narrative or dramatic emplotment of a set of ideas presented initially in a static, diagrammatic, or picto-rial form." Angus Fletcher, *Allegory: The Theory of a Symbolic Mode* (Ithaca, N.Y.: Cornell Univer-sity Press, 1964), 30.

ries must be the etymologies of the poetic languages, which would make their origins all univocal, whereas those of the vulgar languages are more often analogical. We also have the definition of the word "etymology" itself as meaning *veriloquium*, just as fable was defined as *vera narratio*."[58]

The ancients, Vico argued, built up an allegorical image like Hermes by using "poetic logic": a cognitive model not based on analytical reasoning but on imaginative, i.e., mythopeotic, frameworks.[59] Within the realm of "poetic logic," allegory and etymology coincide, because the historical institution of language coincides with the creation of myths. Also, both allegory and etymology are true (*vere*), not only as reliable records ("true and trustworthy histories") of the ways in which poetic logic was used at given historical times, but also as cognitive modes at work in the human mind beside discrete, analytical reasoning.[60]

Etymegoreia is relevant to Vico: principles of etymological inquiry are "abundantly illustrated throughout [t]his work"[61] and have been variously acknowledged. But a thorough investigation of Vico's etymologizing has yet to be done.[62] For one, Vico stood up against those among his contemporaries who supported the fashionable hypothesis of linguistic monogenesis, "those recent etymologists who attempt[ed] to trace all the languages of the world back to the origins of the eastern tongues." But he also attacked the ante-litteram Saussureanism of philologists "who have all accepted with an excess of

---

58. Vico, *New Science*, 403; original in note above.

59. "We find that the principle of these origins both of languages and of letters lies in the fact that the first gentile peoples, by a demonstrated necessity of nature, were poets who spoke in poetic characters." Ibid., 34.

60. Ibid., 7.

61. Ibid., 14.

62. See Andrea Battistini, "Vico e l'etimologia mitopoietica," Lingua e Stile 9 (1974), 31–66; Nancy Struever, "Vico"; Donald Verene, *Vico's Science of Imagination* (Ithaca, N.Y.: Cornell University Press, 1981); Michael Mooney, *Vico and the Tradition of Rhetoric* (Princeton, N.J.: Princeton University Press, 1985); John Schaeffer, *Sensus communis*; Marcel Danesi, *Vico, Metaphor, and the Origin of Language*, Advances in Semiotics (Bloomington: Indiana University Press, 1993). I addressed this and other issues in my article "Forgotten Paths."

good faith the view that in the vulgar languages meanings were fixed by convention." Meanings, Vico argues, had "natural origins" and as such "they must have had natural signification."[63] Etymologizing for Vico made clear first of all the native history of the peoples who spoke the language. He set apart "native etymologies," which are "histories of institutions signified by the words in the natural order of ideas," and "foreign etymologies," which, "on the other hand, are mere stories of words taken by one language from another."[64] Therefore,

the order of ideas must follow the order of institutions. This was the order of human institutions: first the forests, after that the huts, next the cities, and finally the academies. This axiom is a great principle of etymology, for this sequence of human institutions sets the pattern for the histories of words in the various native languages. Thus we observe in the Latin language that almost the whole corpus of its words had sylvan or rustic origins. For example, lex. First it must have meant a collection of acorns. Thence we believe is derived ilex, as it were illex, the oak (as certainly aquilex means collection of waters); for the oak produces the acorns by which the swine are drawn together. Lex was next a collection of vegetables, from which the latter were called legumina. Later on, at a time when the vulgar letters had not yet been invented for writing down the laws, lex by a necessity of civil nature must have meant a collection of citizens, or the public parliament; so that the presence of the people was the lex, or "law," that solemnized the wills that were made calatis comitiis, in the presence of the assembled comitiis. Finally, collecting letters, and making, as it were, a sheaf of them for each word, was called legere, reading.[65]

63. Vico, New Science, 444. The adjective "natural" is used in the Vichian sense specified above of "historically born." Natura, nature, is derived from nascimento, birth.

64. Ibid., 22.

65. "L'ordine dell'idee dee procedere secondo l'ordine delle cose. L'ordine delle cose umane procedette: che prima furono le selve, dopo i tuguri, quindi i villaggi, appresso le città, finalmente l'accademie. Questa degnità è un gran principio d'etimologia: che secondo questa serie di cose umane si debbano narrare le storie delle voci delle lingue natie, come osserviamo nella lingua latina quasi tutto il corpo delle sue voci aver origini selvagge e contadinesche. Come, per cagion d'esempio, lex, che dapprima dovett'essere 'raccolta di ghiande,' da cui crediamo detta ilex, quasi illex, l'elce (come certamente aquilex è 'l raccoglitore dell'acque), perché l'elce produce la ghianda, alla quale s'uniscon i porci. Dappoi 'lex' fu 'raccolta di legumi,' dalla quale questi furon detti legumina. Appresso, nel tempo che le lettere volgari non si eran ancor truovate con le quali fussero scritte le leggi, per necessità di natura civile lex dovett'essere 'raccolta di cittadini,' o sia il pubblico parlamento; onde la presenza del popolo era la legge che solennizzava i testamenti che si facevano calatis comitiis. Finalmente il raccoglier lettere e farne com'un fascio in ciascuna parola fu detto legere." Ibid., 238–40.

If we check Vico's etymology of *lex* against the pronouncements of an etymological dictionary like Ernout-Meillet's DEL, we realize that Vico's hypothesis cannot be easily refuted. The etymology of *lex* figures, in fact, among the many words that scientific etymology has been unable to unravel and has written off as "obscure." Vico's agrarian origin, linking *lex* (law) to *ilex* (acorn), cannot be that farfetched if we consider that DEL supports the etymology of *stipulare* (to stipulate) as coming from the Latin word *stipula* (blade that clothes the grain).[66]

The ultimate issue is that Vico the etymologist does not query language with the intent of tracing systematic, irreversible derivations between words. His purpose is, rather, to take heed of partial glimpses, trace possible interconnections, and make out, in the turmoil of historical events, an overarching allegorical pattern, a "design of an ideal eternal history traversed in time by the histories of all nations."[67] Thus,

[Human ideas] began with divine ideas by way of contemplation of the heavens with the bodily eyes. Thus in their science of augury the Romans used the verb *contemplari* for observing the parts of the sky whence the auguries came or the auspices were taken. These regions, marked out by the augurs with their wands, were called temples of the sky (*templa coeli*), whence must have come to the Greeks their first *theoremata* and *mathemata*, things divine or sublime to contemplate, which eventuated in metaphysical and mathematical abstractions.[68]

66. The agrarian etymology of *stipulare* is mentioned also by Vico, together with other intriguing etymologies (*urbs, adorare, pagus, logos*) that I analyzed in my article "Forgotten Paths." Vico, *New Science*, 550.

67. Vico, *New Science*, 7. It is not my purpose here to talk about the philosophical implications of Vico's position or to establish whether or not Vico's etymologizing can be written off as the by-product of a now dubious pre-Romantic idealism. I think that Vico's etymologizing is relevant, independently of the fact that it can be historically ascribed to a now more or less unfashionable philosophical milieu.

68. "[Idee umane] come testé si è veduto, incominciarono da idee divine con la contemplazione del cielo fatta con gli occhi del corpo: siccome nella scienza augurale si disse da' romani *contemplari* l'osservare le parti del cielo donde venissero gli augùri o si osservassero gli auspìci, le quali regioni, descritte dagli àuguri co' loro litui, si dicevano *templa coeli*, onde dovettero venir a' greci i primi τεωρήματα e μαθήματα, 'divine o sublimi cose da contemplarsi,' che terminarono nelle cose astratte metafisiche e mattematiche." Ibid., 391.

My purpose in this chapter was to discuss two of the central senses that I think "allegorical etymology" took on after the Renaissance. I associated the first of these with the dazzling deconstructionist suggestions of Paul de Man and Jacques Derrida and opposed it to the second model, set up by one distant, but now increasingly important, interlocutor: Giambattista Vico. On the one hand, these two senses betray a common origin: they revive intimations of ancient and medieval scholars, who saw *etymegoreia* at work in the treacherous and inspiring quests of grammar, philosophy, and rhetoric. It is clear, on the other hand, that these carry different implications. As part of their attack against "logocentrism," Derrida and de Man favor allegory's power for disruption and redefinition.[69] Vico sees allegorical etymology not much as a Nietzschean *loculus*—the tomb of ontological meaning[70]— but as a Ciceronian *locus*, the seat, place, or reservoir of memory where historical institutions intersect broader, transcendental designs. Derrida weaves the diaphanous etymological maze of his texts, mainly to bewail the absence of foundations in the Western edifice of meaning. But the brilliance of his work should not obscure the trails that Vico blazes as he makes for hermeneutical strongholds, however hazy their contours may appear.

69. The issue is obviously too complex to be addressed here. I think it could be argued, in fact, that de Man's and Derrida's approach is in some respects still logocentric. In furtive compliance with the post-Saussurean model of language, some of their passages promote a hermeneutical style that is *logo-rrhoeic* (as evidenced in Derridian passages above) and a philosophical stance that is *logo-latric*.

70. "Science unceasingly works on this columbarium of concepts, the graveyard of perceptions." Friedrich Nietzsche, "On Truth and Lies in the Extramoral Sense," in *Philosophy and Truth: Selections from Nietzsche's Notebooks of the Early 1870s*, ed. and trans. Daniel Breazeale, 77–97 (Atlantic Highlands, N.J.: Humanities Press, 1979), 88.

CHAPTER 8

ALTERNATIVE ROUTES

THIS BOOK has taken a bird's-eye view of etymological practices from Greek antiquity to the present day, with the intent of showing how these can be used to redraw the boundaries of etymological inquiry. From the start, I was not interested in gathering literary specimens that constitute a genre, like "poetic etymology": that has been done in the past, in fuller and sharper detail than I could hope to cover here.[1] Nor did I want to restate the truism that literary etymologizing is an independent endeavor, valid with respect to "serious" etymology only under the implicit provision that one should take its pronouncements with a generous dose of scientific skepticism. What I was intrigued by was the erratic overlay of rhetoric and "science" found in premodern etymologies, and the idea that their "nonrigorous" approach might point to alternative ways of thinking about cognition: very old (but in a sense very new) ways of coming to terms with the disputed relation between thought, language, knowledge and institutions. My first step was to look for features that could account for the word "spiritual," used by some scholars to label premodern etymologizing.[2] And amidst the bulk of critical material at my disposal, I zeroed in on the interaction between etymology and allegory, "handmaidens" of the premodern literary tradition that science has taken pains to separate. Using etymology to explain the "spiritual" aspect of allegory, and allegory to reclaim the cognitive scope of etymology, I reached the con-

1. Besides Genette's *Mimologics* or Curtius's famous excursus on etymology, *European Literature and the Latin Middle Ages*, one can think of K. Ruthven's article "The Poet as Etymologist."
2. Expressions like *"geistige Etymolgie,"* *"étymologie spirituelle,"* or *"étymologie méta-physique"* are used by Austrian linguist Leo Spitzer (1887–1960) and are mentioned by Baldinger, *L'étymologie*, 44.

clusion that they are complementary modes of thought: allegorical etymology, or, Proclus's term, *etymegoreia*, entails a holistic model of language that brackets science and poetics as one. First, I argued, we need to counter the view of allegory as a stale literary "device" that sets up more or less intelligible (but quite predictable) links between levels of meaning: etymology proposes that we read allegory (*diversiloquium*) as the rhetorical analogue of a cognitive process whereby a person bundles or blends together several (diverse) aspects of experience into one model, script, or story.[3] At that point, we may start to appreciate the acuity of premodern etymologizing, where allegory plays its insightful role. Premodern etymologies are allegorical because they break down *etyma*, not simply according to a linear model of chronological descent but with an eye on wider conceptual framework where the historical narratives of ideology and the cognitive and volitional patternings of language cross refer.[4]

Looking back at the chapters of this study, we can of course draw some sort of chronological chart of allegorical *etymegoreia* from ancient times to the present. But the resulting timeline is thin and dis-

3. An important suggestion along these lines comes from Ruthven: "The point of using etymological information is to get the reader to entertain *more than one idea at a time*." K. Ruthven, *The Poet as Etymologist*, 19 (my emphasis). Another technical way of thinking about scripts, within the Lacanian research line proposed by Bottiroli, would be to see them as "thick descriptions" of the multiple types of articulations whereby—both synchronically and diachronically—a signifier cuts through both the amorphous Saussurean planes of sound and meaning. Bottiroli, *Jacques Lacan*. The analysis of the synchronic aspect of etymology is linked above all to the work of Joseph Vendryes. See "Pour une Étymologie Statique," *Bulletin de la Société de Linguistique de Paris* 49 (1953): 1–19, where Vendryes defines synchronic etymology as a static (nonhistorical) way of viewing linguistic changes, first associated with the Indian etymological practice of *Mimasma*.

4. Fredric Jameson's *The Political Unconscious* seems to me a remarkable contribution in this direction. Jameson revaluates medieval exegesis as "an essentially allegorical act which consists in rewriting a given text in terms of a particular interpretive master code" and proposes an analogous approach to the study of culture in Marxian terms. His argument is too complex to be summarized here, but his concepts of "metacommentary" and "political unconscious" could be fruitfully related to the present research. Fredric Jameson, *The Political Unconscious: Narrative as a Socially Symbolic Act* (Ithaca, N.Y.: Cornell University Press, 1981), 10. Equally intriguing suggestions in the field of theological studies come from Ian Ramsey's *Models and Mystery* (London: Oxford University Press, 1964), and *Religion and Science: Conflict and Synthesis, Some Philosophical Reflections* (London: S.P.C.K., 1964), both of which would be well worth investigating for our purposes.

continuous. More research is needed to bridge gaps and reenact the historical and discursive contexts that used and shaped allegorical etymology. Conversely, we can see each chapter as one among the many facets that make up the synthetic model of etymologizing I sketched above. Each chapter serves, synchronically, to highlight this or that aspect of allegorical etymologizing.

Chapter 1 confronts modern etymology to show some of its fissures. The ensuing portrait is that of a hazy discipline, a cluster of conjectures more than a system of reliable rules. Chapter 2 reclaims the concept of *etymegoreia* from Proclus's commentary on Plato: a given etymology is allegorical if it exceeds the technicalities of grammar and is shaped as a *diversiloquium*, a "bundle" or "blend" of interwoven meanings. Chapter 3 samples Greek and Alexandrian etymologizing as a paradigm of the allegorical mindset, which uses etymologies to set up and merge multiple semantic scenarios. Chapter 4 follows the Pythagorean implications of Varro's *Quartus gradus etymologiae*. From Varro's hierarchical model, we infer the three-dimensional, network-like structure of allegorical etymologizing, at once synchronic and diachronic. Chapter 5 makes a foray into Isidore's *Etymologiae* to probe allegorical etymology as an epistemic mode: a strategy for knowing and structuring the world encyclopedically. Certainly, the interpretative freedom of *etymegoreia* carried along with itself a strong potential for sheer manipulation or disruption: a strain which came vigorously to the fore in the syncretic, "syntagmatic" milieu of the Renaissance, when etymology, mixed and vied with "the sciences" and dabbled in the occult. And manipulation can range widely from unchecked, esoteric wordplay, of the kind often indulged in by Hermeticists (chapter 6), to forceful political or philosophical debunking, of the kind resorted to with varying degrees of success by some deconstructionists (chapter 7).[5]

---

5. In fact, Hermetic and deconstructionist etymologizing may be said to share features, although their "ends" diverge. Heightened awareness of language and vertiginous wordplay

It is now time to consider how all these facets of *etymegoreia* find corroboration in heuristic models like the ones envisaged, among others, by metaphorologist Eve Sweetser or, more recently, by cognitivists Mark Turner and Gilles Fauconnier. And then we will comment on the influence allegorical etymology extends over two regions that we glimpsed in our initial survey of allegory but that the present study must be content to touch upon only in passing: memory and volition.

Sweetser's *From Etymology to Pragmatics* deals with issues that are particularly relevant to an understanding of the allegorico-etymological model we have outlined: traditional comparativist theories, she claims, trace morphological roots of a supposed protolanguage, but the semantic definitions they come up with are vague. Scholars who call for an objectivist semantic theory whereby words and objects systematically match, try to describe meaning by using discrete connotational tags (e.g., *bachelor* = + *adult* + *male* + *unmarried*) that are chosen arbitrarily. Rather than focusing on an "understanding of the *lexical meaning per se*," feature-based semanticists are concerned with an "economical representation of relevant contrasts":[6] "But it is scarcely surprising that to many linguists, the nonphonological side of etymology appears inherently nonscientific. Synchronic as well as diachronic linguistics has found sound a more accessible domain for study than meaning."[7]

Semantic features employed by linguists are "analogues of phonological-distinctive features" of the kind used by Saussure,[8] and as such they fail to convey the complex cognitive mapping that languages perform, above all in cases of homonymy and polysemy. If we reconstruct an alleged protomeaning or "lowest possible denominator" solely by virtue of a loss or addition of semantic features, we reach the unreal-

---

occur in both, but Hermeticism is pervaded by a "syndrome of the secret" backed by metaphysical and essentialist claims that a deconstructionist gaze is directed to expose and dismantle. Eco, *The Search*, 38.

6. Sweetser, *From Etymology to Pragmatics*, 2.

7. Ibid., 23.

8. Ibid., 24.

istic level of abstraction of Proto-Indo-European monographs.[9] To get
around this, we should turn to glottogenetics and cognitive science
and take up on their suggestion that language and cognition "operate
metaphorically."[10] Accordingly, Sweetser argues for a new etymological approach "grounded in speakers' understanding of the world"[11]
and more attentive to the metaphorical connections that speakers establish as they build upon their knowledge of the world: "What we
would like to have is a motivated account of the relationships between
senses of a single morpheme or word, and of the relationships between historically earlier and later senses of a morpheme or word. By
'motivated' I mean an account which appeals to something beyond
the linguist's intuition that these senses are related, or that these two
senses are more closely related than either is to a third sense."[12]

Sweetser advocates a cognitive-semantic perspective, neither objectivist nor subjectivist. As she puts it: "I assume that the real world
exists, but our only access to it is through our experience, both physical and cultural."[13] Her primary aim is to refocus the efforts of etymologists on processes that are not confined to phono-linguistics but
flexibly tap the resources of cognitive sciences. Her basic claim is that
metaphorical—hence, for us also allegorical—mappings play a greater role than has been so far acknowledged: "What I am arguing is not,
or not yet, that any specific proposed etymologies or reconstructed
proto-senses of morphemes are wrong. My point is that the semantic side of the whole corpus of received etymological research is subject to question, because we have little or no idea of what constitutes
a reasonable semantic reconstruction."[14] By laying emphasis on how
words are related, and by assessing metaphor beyond pure morphology, Sweetser admits a reading of ancient etymologizing that deflates

9. In chapter 1, I provide an example of abstract etymologizing in my discussion of Meyer-Lübke's etymology of *ferrum*.
10. Sweetser, *From Etymology to Pragmatics*, 8.
11. Ibid., 25.   12. Ibid., 3.
13. Ibid., 13.   14. Ibid., 26.

positivistic objections. Once we are made aware of the limits of current etymologizing, we are urged to reenact the bizarre analogies premodern etymologists pursued, and we are invited to see whether the conjectural routes they mark are, at all, viable. A recent study in the field of cognition by Turner and Fauconnier would seem to indicate that at least some of them are.[15]

In cognitivist terms, the act of "putting together multiple things into one bundle or blend"—which we assigned to allegorical etymology—would be an instance of "conceptual blending," a mental operation that, they claim, is highly imaginative but "crucial to even the simplest kind of thought."[16] Blending is vital to creative thinking and consists in the "mapping, exploration, and transformation of structures and conceptual spaces."[17] It starts when "a base or source domain is mapped onto a target so that inferences easily available in the source are exported to the target." The integration network (or blend) is the new conceptual space emerging from this mapping, "a scenario that draws from the two analogues but ends up containing more," as in the "Iron Lady" epithet coined for Margaret Thatcher in the 1980s.[18] All this entails a number of operations: "Building an integration network involves setting up mental spaces, matching across spaces, projecting selectively to a blend, locating shared structures, projecting backward to inputs, recruiting new structure to inputs or the blend, and running various operations in the blend itself."[19] There is more than one reason why Turner and Fauconnier's theory seems especially apt to describe the cognitive workings of *etymegoreia*: it questions linguists for their scientistic gloating over "core meaning"[20] and takes

15. Mark Turner and Gilles Fauconnier, *The Way We Think* (New York: Basic Books, 2002).
16. Ibid., 18.
17. This line of research recalls Lakoff and Johnson's seminal work on metaphor, *Metaphors We Live By* (Chicago: University of Chicago Press, 1980), but special emphasis is laid here on the fact that blending is not to be reduced to a set of formal operations: "Form can be grasped but does not equate with meaning." Turner and Fauconnier, *The Way We Think*, 6.
18. Ibid., 20.   19. Ibid., 35, 44.
20. "A powerful and, at first, highly promising feature of form approaches such as generative grammar was the possibility of postulating successive invisible levels of form (such as deep

them to task for trying to formalize all figurative thought;[21] it shows
how irrelevant the issue of "falsity" is, since a viable course of action
may well be derived from counterfactual statements. It even confesses
to being "unscientific" since the blends it puts forward cannot be predicted or determined on the basis of falsifiable algorithms. Also, the
"mental spaces" Turner and Fauconnier bring up are very much like
the "loci" of classical rhetoric we find at work in allegorical etymology. As a sustained metaphorical process of "bundling together,"[22] Etymegoreia may well be one of the terrains on which cultures carry on
and refine their "unconscious cognitive exploration"[23] and where "the
sudden interlocking of two previously unrelated skills or matrices of
thought"[24] takes place to generate ground-breaking blends.

It may be worth looking at one final example of how premodern
etymologies fit the cognitive models we have seen above: let us compare Vico's etymology of *pater* (father) with the reconstruction of *pater* found in Peter Davies' popular etymological manual *Roots: Family
Histories of Familiar Words*.[25] The kind of tree diagrams used by Davies

---

structure, or logical form) behind the superficial appearance. Mysteries of formal organization at
one level would thus be explained in terms of regularities at a higher one. This technique is what
we described earlier as looking for more armor inside the armor. In itself it is not as absurd as it
sounds—a warrior could have additional protection under his topsuit of armor, and hidden layers of form are a plausible explanatory technique. The absurdity would come from assuming that
the *only* thing that can lie behind a form is yet another form. [. . .] Of course, traditional lines of
inquiry before this century had often accepted, even gloated over, the powerful role of metaphor
in scientific discovery, artistic creativity, and childhood learning, but the acceptance was entirely
canceled during the ascendancy of form approaches. What analytic philosophers gloated over
now was the complete exclusion of figurative thought from "core meaning." Core meaning is, as
the formally minded philosopher sees it, the part of meaning that can be characterized formally
and truth-conditionally. [. . .] Inevitably, these analytic approaches were blind to the imaginative operations of meaning construction that work at lightning speed, below the horizon of consciousness, and leave few formal traces of their complex dynamics." Ibid., 14–15.
     21. "Matching and aligning the elements of two domains, finding the common schemat-
ic structure that motivates an analogy between them, are now recognized as formidable feats
of imaginative work to which the current state of computational modeling cannot do justice."
Ibid. 12.
     22. Here I am thinking of Quintilian's definition of *allegoria* as "*metaphora continuata*."
     23. Turner and Fauconnier, *The Way We Think,* 73.
     24. Ibid., 38.
     25. Peter Davies, *Roots: Family Histories of Familiar Words* (New York: McGraw-Hill, 1981),
142–43.

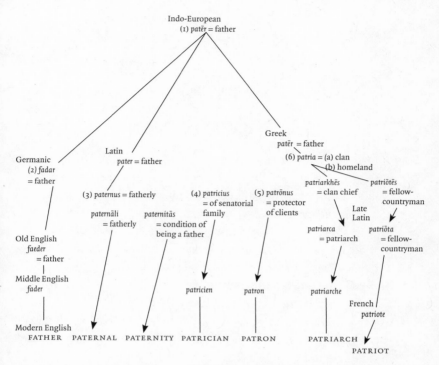

FIGURE 6. A tree diagram of the *pǝter root. Peter Davies, *Roots: Family Histories of Familiar Words* (New York: McGraw Hill, 1981), 143. Reproduced with permission of the McGraw-Hill Companies.

(figure 6) illustrates the formalized procedure of scientific etymology, more concerned with tracing supposed morphophonemic roots of a word (petǝr) than with querying its semantic clusters. It seems the modern etymologist still aims at breaking linguistic utterances down into discrete, analyzable units to be studied in isolation. While acceptable from a linguistic viewpoint, this kind of etymology would more aptly be defined as an "atomology," for it cuts up and muddles the set of historical meanings and the constellation of rhetorical senses a word belongs to, while also encouraging the surreptitious rift between synchronic and diachronic features that Sweetser disapproves of.

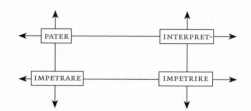

FIGURE 7. The term
pater in a Vichian reconstruction.

The etymological "holograms" we find in Varro and Vico openly differ from Davies' tree diagrams: they can be described as complex, multidirectional networks (figure 7) that in true Vichian fashion favor induction and synthesis over deduction and analysis. These "neural networks"—to use a term common among cognitivists and artifical intelligence researchers—are foreground parallel allegorical process- es based on insight over serial—Cartesian or Boolean—binary logic.[26] And networks set up provisional, open-ended links between words (*pater—patrare—intepret . . .*) rather than feature-based, static frame- works: single lexical entries are then woven into a narrative—in Vich- ian terms a myth, or an allegory—that, like Turner's "blend," may be the indicator of a paradigm shift.

In the case of *pater*, Vico detects connections between lexical nodes (*pater* → *impatrare* to make → *impetrire* to divinate → *interpret*) that pro- duce a cultural blend probably at work in ancient Latin societies: the semantic feature of hierarchy (*pater*, God; *pater*, noble founder) and the pragmatic need to ensure communication with it (*impetrire* as divinate/

26. This is how neural networks are conceived in current artificial intelligence (AI) re- search. AI researchers try to model databases as typical situations or *scripts* to be analyzed by a parallel net of processing units—a neural network. For a discussion of this "connectionist" model and its limits, as well as of other cognitive models that may bear upon literary studies see Patrick Hogan, *Cognitive Science, Literature, and the Arts: A Guide for Humanists* (London: Rout- ledge, 2003). This is what Hogan has to say about "connectionism": "Connectionism . . . is essentially the idea that the mind is a brain that created knowledge by building connections between nodes in a vast network. Inputs [. . .] to the network activate some nodes, inhibit oth- ers, and over time begin to produce a stable pattern of response across the network." Hogan, *Cognitive Science*, 49ff. The relevance of Vico's *New Science* for AI research has been demonstrated by Marcel Danesi, *Vico*, 143ff.

interpret as "being among the fathers"). Modern etymologizing would concede on morphological grounds that the first three words are related—*pater, impatrare, impetrire*—but would ignore the metaphorical leap that might have metathetically (*etr* → *ret*) led to *interpret*, and would rather relate the latter word to an isolated Indo-European **per* root.

If we keep in mind Sweetser's and Turner's cognitive models we see that a network is a good descriptor of the "bundle-like" structuring of *etymegoriea*. But we can look for further evidence elsewhere, in the volume *Psycholinguistique Textuelle: Une approche cognitive de la compréhension et de la production des texts*. Pierre Coirier, Daniel Gaonac'h, and Jean Passerault focus on psycholinguistic mechanisms at work in the production and the comprehension of texts. One of them has to do with the fact that readers or writers tend to draw upon coherent, sketchy representations of common knowledge, "scripts" that allow them to place separate linguistic utterances within a familiar cognitive domain (*domaine referential*).[27] Quoting Schank, Coirier and his colleagues note that "scripts represent complex causal links [that] provide information on the world with reference to a recurrent situation."[28] And in words that recall the etymological model discussed above, they add that "the global cognitive system at work in comprehension appears as a complex conceptual network (*réseau*) of hierarchical encapsulations (*emboîtments*) and cross links."[29]

All this matters, first because it sheds light on cognitive patterning that often eludes scientistic etymologizing. If, as it seems, humans build models of the world not in a linear fashion but by bundling together experiences in linguistic "scripts" that blend within integrated semantic networks—Coirier's *intégration sémantique*[30]—then the explanations given by scientific etymology must be, if not completely at fault, at least severely partial. The current uneasiness of academia in

27. Pierre Coirier, Daniel Gaonac'h, and Jean Michel Passerault, *Psycholinguistique Textuelle: Une approche cognitive de la compréhension et de la production des texts* (Paris: Armand Colin, 1996), 62–64.

28. Coirier et al., *Psycholinguistique*, 62.   29. Ibid., 67.

30. Coirier et al., *Psycholinguistique*, 55–56.

coping with etymological matters and the efforts to redefine etymology's scope on the part of dedicated scholars bear witness to this. For us, etymologizing is inherently "scriptural" because it aims to restore, reactivate, and use the historical and political scripts of a given word, and also because it weaves its own "word (hi)stories" against the theological scripts of religion and the teleological scripts of philosophy.

And then also, scripts lead us to glance at *etymegoreia* through the diaphanous realms of remembrance and desire. In *The Art of Memory*, Frances Yates quotes the famous example from the Sophistic fragment *Dialexeis* (400 BC) to show that the *ars memorativa* relied on a primitive etymological dissection of the word to be committed to mind.[31] And in her pioneering monograph on memory in medieval culture, Mary Carruthers cites Raymond Di Lorenzo to suggest that "much of what we suppose to be allegory . . . [may very well be] a mnemonic heuristic,"[32] a script, as seems to be the case with the fourfold scheme of patristic exegesis.[33] From a cognitivist perspective this makes sense. "The stereotyped order of scripts," Coirier says, "is an important factor of recollection."[34] In fact, using Schank's acronym, scripts can be defined as MOPS (*Memory Organization Packets*): cognitive frames we use to chart experience flexibly, and not with reference to a unique set or sequence of events. So for instance, we MOP experience when, in an action like "phoning," we not only envision objects or actions associated with "phoning" but activate broader scripts, for example, "communicating" of which "phoning" is only a component.[35] This is where Coirier's image of the complex cognitive network (*réseau*) comes in,

31. Among the prescriptions of the *Dialexeis* we read "what you hear, place on what you know. For example Χρύσιππος [Chrysippus] is to be remembered: place it on χρυσος [gold] and ἵππος [horse]. Another example: we place πυριλάμπης [glowworm] on πύρ [fire] and λάμπειν [shine]." Quoted in Yates, *The Art of Memory*, 44.

32. Mary Carruthers, *The Book of Memory: A Study of Memory in Medieval Culture*, Cambridge Studies in Medieval Literature (Cambridge: Cambridge University Press, 1992), 142.

33. Ibid., 168.

34. "L'ordre stéréotypé du script constitue un facteur important du rappel." Coirier et al., *Psycholinguistique*, 66.

35. Eco's semiotic discussion of *scripts* and *frames*, mentioned in chapter 3 of this book, develops along similar lines.

together with the idea of Russian-doll "encapsulation" (*emboîtment*). The connection between this *boîte* (or "box" in which one places ideas and expectations) and the Ciceronian *locus* (the place where one stores or finds [*invenit*] arguments, also a feature of *etymegoreia*) is striking. Francois Goyet devoted a whole article to analyzing the *Locus ab etymologia* in the Renaissance tradition and concluded that it can be seen as an "imperfect definition" (*définition imparfaite*), something that rhetoricians would call "description."[36] Our ability to remember, or recollect (*rappel*), is directly related to the ability to establish viable *routes* between the various scripts, or *loci*, of reality. As Schank notes, memory is not the passive receptacle of perceptive experience but a "dynamic" process:[37] I am arguing that allegorical etymology is one of the territories where dynamic remembering takes residence.

To be sure, a word origin like Thomas Cistercensis's *flos* (flower), which uses acronyms to fixate the properties of the flower in easily memorizable ciphers (*flos: Fundens Late Odorem Suum*—widely effusing its scent)[38] is more "mnemonic" than "memorative": it is already a symptom of the technicized, literalistic drift into form that started with the *expositiones* of the late Middle Ages and reached its climax in the Renaissance. I am thinking here, instead, of allegorical etymologizing in Plato, Varro, Isidore, and Vico—to name just the few landmarks my study has touched—where etymologies are memorative mainly because they recollect the motivational routes cemented in words and produce blends—or scripts—that become the common reservoirs (*loci communes*) of complex cognitive experiences.[39] This is

36. Francis Goyet, "Le *locus ab etymologia* à la Renaissance," in Chambon and Lüdi, *Discours étymologiques*, 173–84. Etymology sets the common ground for argumentation, but it shies away from clear-cut delimitation, which is probably why seventeenth-century logicians quickly wearied of etymologizing.

37. As a matter of fact, the task that information technologists seem to be facing at the moment is not finding ways of storing large amounts of information: the Internet already provides a virtually limitless complex of "memorized" data. It is, rather, that of finding efficient ways to organize information in coherent wholes to be conveniently retrieved.

38. Quoted in Zamboni, *L'etimologia*, 26.

39. K. Ruthven alludes to the heuristic value of allegorical etymology when he notes that "in studying examples of pseudo-etymology one begins to suspect that certain ideas have been

probably the kind of "bundling together" Anton Maria Salvini talked about in his *Apologia sopra le etimologie* of 1737: "Nor did I really learn what the art of memory was, which the ancients had described and celebrated when they talked about putting images on places [*luoghi*], until I started to learn languages on the basis of etymologies. . . . Now, it is no trifling matter that etymologies should allow one to reflect, to combine, to retain, and to fasten (as if in a pleasant *bundle* [fascetta]) languages that share a common way of thinking, and a certain affinity of expression."[40]

In questioning postmodernist appropriations of allegory as the dizzy figure of forgetfulness, and in reading allegory *also* as the trope of unification and recollection ("gathering together into one"), my study has attempted to shed light on how memory and allegory merge. And it has zeroed in on one distinctive *locus* where this merging occurs: allegorical etymology, or *etymegoreia*. But there is another side to *etymegoreia* that postmodernism, in its frequent reconnoiters of language and allegory, has encroached upon and given vent to: it is the domain of volition, the province of desire. For, we have seen, etymology itself demands that we take the *allos* of allegory not only as conveying "the multiple, the many, the diverse" but also "the Other, the different, the interlocutor": the distant aim of our knowing and the "true," but removed, object of our longing.[41] We return to the arcane sense-

---

suggested by the fortuitous similarity of historically unrelated words." Ruthven, "The Poet as Etymologist," 31. And if, he argues, individual details can be shaped etymologically, there is reason to believe that etymology may have shaped (and may continue to shape) broad cognitive structures. I agree with Ruthven, but I would complement his claims (which in some sense reformulate the *nomen est omen* adage) with the observation that allegorical etymology also is shaped by cognitive and experiential structures (i.e., *nomina sunt consequentia rerum*). These are the two axes (introduced in chapter 2) on which one can base an interpretation of allegorical etymology.

40. [Né prima imparai che cosa era l'arte della memoria, descritta, e celebrata dagli antichi, del porre le immagini sopra i luoghi. Se non quando mi misi ad imparare lingue sopra etimologie. . . . Or non è poco frutto questo dell'Etimologie, il riflettere, il combinare, il ritenere, e in un grazioso quasi fascetto legare più lingue, che tutte hanno tra loro un comune vincolo di pensare, e una leggiadra amistà nello esprimersi], quoted in Ludovica Koch, ed., *Etimologia: Pratiche e Invenzioni* (Naples: I.U.O., 1983), 29.

41. Longing, need, and desire within the linguistic constructs of *etymegoreia* would need

histories we came upon with *con-templatio* and *inter-pretatio*; to the "fanciful" etymologizing of *desiderium* from *de-sidera*—the stars from which Latin augurs are said to have drawn their omens—and of *consider* from *cum-sidera*, the "dwelling with the stars," which may stand for "regaining one's own points of reference in the territory of the possible and uncertain encounter with the Other."[42] As it professes to trace *etyma*—the "true" senses and "original" directions of our language—*etymegoreia* in fact takes on and distils allegory's persistent struggle to grant this "Other" harbor and voice and to give this yearning a name, without congealing either into the recesses of language or laying either open to the entrenchments of ideology. Literature has always accepted that such a quest must be endless, and its outcome precarious. And postmodernism has justly sought to qualify and query the ideological modes of that time-honored injunction. Our research of *etymegoreia* was meant to heed both concerns. The gaps it has not bridged,[43] and the theoretical venues it has opened up[44] are many. But in the uncanny

---

to be discussed at length following Jacques Lacan's suggestions about le *manque-à-être*. See for instance, Jacques Lacan, "Psychanalyse et Médecine," *Cahiers du Collège de Médecine* 12 (1966), 36–38. The cognitive functioning of *etymegoreia* could also, I think, be profitably investigated by thinking of desire in terms of a need for cognitive closure. A. W. Kruglanski and D. M. Webster, "Motivated Closing of the Mind: Seizing and Freezing," *Psychological Review* 103 (1966), 263–83.

42. As Maria Giovanna Garuti puts it: "A look at the Latin etymology of the two words reveals that desire is condemned to frustration or, worse, to envy, precisely because it is projected around the stars (de sidera), that is, onto the impossible or unreachable. Considering (cum sidera), on the other hand, means dwelling with the stars, regaining one's own points of reference in the territory of the possible and uncertain encounter with the Other." Garuti's analysis of the notion of system (and the related concepts of plurality-in-unity, of systemic nodes, of boundary, and of encountering "the Other") seems to substantiate, from an anthropological viewpoint, some of the claims we have made with regard to the two main senses of allegorical etymologizing. Maria Giovanna Garuti, "Working In and With Groups: Cultural References," http://www.continents.com/garuti.htm (accessed November 17, 2004). See also Darby Costello, "Desire and the Stars," http://www.ancientsky.com/desire.htm (accessed November 17, 2004).

43. A much more in-depth analysis of Isidore's etymologies is called for, but I would also have gladly taken a closer look at Renaissance etymologizing and especially at Hermeticism (and the relation between etymology and iconography).

44. The gist of our research may be compressed in the following series of statements, each of which would benefit from expanded discussion: (1) Allegorical etymology (*etymegoreia*) establishes multiple routes of approximation between a given word and the range of its possible meanings. (2) It is "allegorical" (a *diversiloquium*) because it does not aim at reconstruct-

word histories of the past it has caught sight of the fleeting junctures where the forms of language cross, at once, the cautious trails of history and the numinous paths of desire.

---

ing linear, isolated *etyma* but sets up open scripts across ample cognitive, narrative schemas. (3) Because it combines a diachronic (historical) and a synchronic (metahistorical) outlook, allegorical etymology is synthetic. (4) Since it works by establishing or finding *loci* of invention, allegorical etymology is related to rhetoric (as a form of *amplificatio* or *expositio*) and to memory (as a topical technique of *collectio* and *recollection*). (5) Finally, allegorical etymology is epistemological (*nomina sunt consequentia rerum*), because it yields conceptual blends that become part of shared knowledge; and (6) eschatological (*nomen est omen*), because it sets up scenarios of cognitive closure (Kruglanski) that respond to the projections of desire.

SELECTED BIBLIOGRAPHY

The present bibliography is by no means exhaustive. Nor is it intended as a comprehensive aid to scholars interested in etymology or allegory. Its scope is, for practical reasons, loosely restricted to major texts analyzed and discussed in this study. I have attempted to include everything of potential relevance but, given the wide range of subjects, I have omitted references to articles or works that I only incidentally touched upon.

Agamben, G. Stanze. La parola e il fantasma nella cultura occidentale. Turin: Einaudi, 1977.

Aitchison, Jean. Language Change: Progress or Decay? Cambridge: Cambridge University Press, 2001.

Allen, Don Cameron. Mysteriously Meant: The Rediscovery of Pagan Symbolism and Allegorical Interpretation in the Renaissance. Baltimore: Johns Hopkins University Press, 1970.

Amsler, Mark. Etymology and Grammatical Discourse in Late Antiquity and the Early Middle Ages. Amsterdam: Benjamins, 1989.

Anttila, Raimo. Historical and Comparative Linguistics. Amsterdam Studies in the Theory and History of Linguistic Science. Series IV: Current Issues in Linguistic Theory. 2nd rev. ed. Philadelphia: Benjamins, 1989.

Asher, R. E., and J. M. Y. Simpson eds. The Encyclopedia of Language and Linguistics. 1st ed. Oxford: Pergamon Press, 1994.

Attridge, Derek. Peculiar Language: Literature as Difference from the Renaissance to James Joyce. London: Methuen, 1988.

———. "Language as History/History as Language: Saussure and the Romance of Etymology." In Post-Structuralism and the Question of History, edited by Geoff Bennington and Robert Young, 90–126. Cambridge: Cambridge University Press, 1989.

Auerbach, Erich. Scenes from the Drama of European Literature. Theory and History of Literature, vol. 9. Minneapolis: University of Minnesota Press, 1984.

Augustine. De Doctrina Christiana. Edited by Joseph Martin. Corpus Christianorum Series Latina 32. Turnhout: Brepols, 1962.

———. Sancti Aurelii Augustini episcopi De civitate dei libri XXII. Edited and translated by Philip Levine. Loeb Classical Library. Cambridge, Mass.: Harvard University Press, 1966.

———. De Dialectica. Edited by Jan Pinborg. Translated by B. Darrell Jackson. Dordrecht: Reidel, 1975.

Baierlein, Ralph. Thermal Physics. Cambridge: Cambridge University Press, 1999.

Bakhtin, Mikhail. Esthétique et théorie du roman. Translated by Daria Olivier. Paris: Gallimard, 1978.

———. Problems of Dostoevsky's Poetics. Edited and translated by Caryl Emerson. Minneapolis: University of Minnesota Press, 1984.

Baldinger, Kurt. *Festschrift Walther von Wartburg zum 80. Geburtstag. 18 Mai 1968*. Tübingen: Niemeyer, 1968.

―――. "L'étymologie hier et aujourd'hui." In *Die Faszination der Sprachwissenschaft: ausgewählte Aufsätze zum 70. Geburtstag*, 40–69. Tübingen: Niemeyer, 1990.

Baldinger, Kurt, and Roger Wright. *Semantic Theory: Towards a Modern Semantics*. Oxford: Blackwell, 1980.

Bass, Alan. "Introduction." In *Writing and Difference*, by Jacques Derrida. Translated by Alan Bass. London: Routledge, 1978.

Battistini, Andrea. "Vico e l'etimologia mitopoietica." *Lingua e Stile* 9 (1974): 31–66.

Baxter, Timothy M. S. *The Cratylus: Plato's Critique of Naming*. Philosophia Antiqua 58. Leiden: Brill, 1992.

Belardi, Walter. *L'etimologia nella storia della cultura occidentale*. 2 vols. Rome: Dipartimento di Studi Glottoantropologici Università di Roma "La Sapienza," Editrice il Calamo, 2002.

Benedetti, Marina. "Etymology between Typology and History." In *Il cambiamento linguistico*, edited by Marco Mancini, 209–62. Rome: Carocci, 2003.

Benjamin, Walter. *The Origin of German Tragic Drama*. London: Verso, 1985.

Bennington, Geoff, and Robert Young, eds. *Post-structuralism and the Question of History*. Cambridge: Cambridge University Press, 1989.

Bloch, Howard. *Etymologies and Genealogies: A Literary Anthropology of the French Middle Ages*. Chicago: University of Chicago Press, 1980.

Bloom, Harold, Paul de Man, Jacques Derrida, Geoffrey H. Hartman, and J. Hillis Miller. *Deconstruction and Criticism*. New York: Seabury Press, 1979.

Bloomfield, Leonard. *An Introduction to the Study of Language*. Amsterdam Studies in the Theory and History of Linguistic Science, Series II. Vol. 3, *Classics in Psycholinguistics*. New ed. Amsterdam: Benjamins, 1983.

Boccaccio, Giovanni. *Genealogie deorum gentilium libri*. Edited by Vincenzo Romano. Bari: Laterza, 1951.

Borchardt, Frank. "Etymology in Tradition and in the Northern Renaissance." *Journal of the History of Ideas* 29, no. 3 (1968): 415–29.

Bottiroli, Giovanni. *Retorica: L'intelligenza figurale nell'arte e nella filosofia*. Turin: Bollati-Boringhieri, 1993.

―――. *Jacques Lacan: Arte, Linguaggio, Desiderio*. Bergamo: Bergamo University Press, 2002.

Breazeale, Daniel, ed. and trans. *Philosophy and Truth: Selections from Nietzsche's Notebooks of the Early 1870s*. Atlantic Highlands, N.J.: Humanities Press, 1979.

Bright, William, ed. *The International Encyclopedia of Linguistics*. Oxford: Oxford University Press, 1992.

Bussmann, Hadumod. *Routledge Dictionary of Language and Linguistics*. Edited and translated by Kerstin Kazzazi and Gregory Trauth. London: Routledge, 1996.

Bynon, Theodora. *Historical Linguistics*. Cambridge: Cambridge University Press, 1977.

Carravetta, Peter. *Prefaces to the Diaphora: Rhetorics, Allegory, and the Interpretation of Postmodernity*. West Lafayette, Ind.: Purdue University Press, 1991.

Carruthers, Mary. *The Book of Memory: A Study of Memory in Medieval Culture*. Cambridge Studies in Medieval Literature. Cambridge: Cambridge University Press, 1992.

Cavazza, Franco. *Studio su Varrone etimologo e grammatico*. Florence: La Nuova Italia, 1981.

Chambon, Jean-Pierre, and Georges Lüdi, eds. *Discours étymologiques*. Freiburg: Max Niemeyer Verlag, 1991.

Chance, Jane. *Medieval Mythography*, vol. 1. Gainesville: University Press of Florida, 1994.

Cicero. *Tusculan disputations*. Loeb Classical Library. rev. ed. Cambridge, Mass.: Harvard University Press, 1945.

———. *Ad. C. Herennium de ratione dicendi*. Translated by Harry Caplan. London: Heinemann, 1954.

———. *De senectute, De amicitia, De divinatione*. Loeb Classical Library. Cambridge, Mass.: Harvard University Press, 1964.

———. *De re publica, De legibus*. Loeb Classical Library. Cambridge, Mass.: Harvard University Press, 1970.

———. *Topica*. Loeb Classical Library. Cambridge, Mass.: Harvard University Press, 1976.

Cochrane, Robertson. *Wordplay: Origins, Meanings, and Usage of the English Language*. Toronto: University of Toronto Press, 1996.

Coirier, Pierre, Daniel Gaonac'h, and Jean Michel Passerault. *Psycholinguistique Textuelle: Une approche cognitive de la compréhension et de la production des texts*. Paris: Armand Colin, 1996.

Colish, Marcia. *Stoic Tradition from Antiquity to the Early Middle Ages: Stoicism in Christian Latin Thought Through the Sixth Century*. Leiden: Brill, 1990.

Collart, Jean. *Varron, grammairien latin*. Publications de la Faculté des lettres de l'Université de Strasbourg, fasc. 121 (1954).

Costello, Darby. "Desire and the Stars." http://www.ancientsky.com/desire.htm (accessed November 17, 2004).

Crowley, Terry. *An Introduction to Historical Linguistics*. 2nd ed. Auckland: Oxford University Press, 1992.

Crystal, David, ed. *Encyclopedic Dictionary of Language and Languages*. Cambridge: Cambridge University Press, 1992.

Curtius, Ernst Robert. *European Literature and the Latin Middle Ages*. Translated by Willard R. Trask. New York: Pantheon Books, 1953.

Dahlmann, Hellfried. *Varro und die hellenistische Sprachtheorie*. Berlin: Weidmann, 1964.

Danesi, Marcel. *Vico, Metaphor, and the Origin of Language*. Advances in Semiotics. Bloomington: Indiana University Press, 1993.

Davies, Peter. *Roots: Family Histories of Familiar Words*. New York: McGraw-Hill, 1981.

de Lubac, Henri. *Exégèse médiévale: les quatres sens de l'écriture*. Paris: Aubier, 1959.

de Man, Paul. "The Rhetoric of Temporality." In *Interpretation: Theory and Practice*, edited by Charles S. Singleton, 173–209. Baltimore: Johns Hopkins University Press, 1969.

———. *Allegories of Reading: Figural Language in Rousseau, Nietzsche, Rilke, and Proust*. New Haven, Conn.: Yale University Press, 1979.

———. *The Resistance to Theory*. Minneapolis: University of Minnesota Press, 1986.

Del Bello, Davide. "Forgotten Paths: The Making of Vico's Etymology." *Semiotica* 113 (1997): 171–88.

Della Corte, Francesco. *Varrone, il terzo gran lume romano*. Florence: La Nuova Italia, 1970.

Derrida, Jacques. *Of Grammatology*. Translated by Gayatri Spivak. Baltimore: Johns Hopkins University Press, 1976.

———. *Writing and Difference*. Translated by Alan Bass. Chicago: University of Chicago Press, 1980.

———. *Dissémination*. Translated by Barbara Johnson. Chicago: University of Chicago Press, 1981.

———. "Plato's Pharmacy." In *Dissémination*. Translated by Barbara Johnson, 63–171. Chicago: University of Chicago Press, 1981.

———. *Glas*. Translated by John Leavey. Lincoln: University of Nebraska Press, 1986.

———. *Memoires for Paul de Man*. New York: Columbia University Press, 1986.

———. "La guerre of Paul de Man." Published in the French edition of the conferences under the title *Mémoires*. 1988.

Desbordes, Françoise. "La Pratique Étymologique Des Poètes Latins à l'Èpoque d'Auguste." In Chambon and Lüdi, *Discours étymologiques*, 149–59.

Diab, Mohammad. *Lexicon of Orthopaedic Etymology*. Amsterdam: Harwood Academic Publishers, 1999.

Dietrich, Paulus. *De Ciceronis ratione etymologica*. Jena: Typis G. Nevenhahni, 1911.

Dihle, A. "Analogie und Attizismus." *Hermes* 85 (1957): 170–205.

Donawerth, Jane. *Shakespeare and the Sixteenth-Century Study of Language*. Urbana: University of Illinois Press, 1984.

Donker, Marjorie. *Dictionary of Literary-Rhetorical Conventions of the English Renaissance*. Westport, Conn.: Greenwood Press, 1982.

du Marsais, César. *Les Tropes*. Paris: Belin-le-Prieur, 1818.

Duret, Claude. *Trésor de l'histoire des langues de cet univers*. 1613.

Eco, Umberto. *Semiotics and the Philosophy of Language*. Advances in Semiotics. Bloomington: Indiana University Press, 1984.

———. *The Search for the Perfect Language: The Making of Europe*. Translated by James Fentress. Cambridge: Blackwell, 1995.

Eco, Umberto, Richard Rorty, Jonathan Culler, and Christine Brooke-Rose. *Interpretation and Overinterpretation*. Edited by Stefan Collini. Cambridge: Cambridge University Press, 1992.

The Encyclopedia of Language and Linguistics. Edited by R. E. Asher and J. M. Y. Simpson. 1st ed. Oxford: Pergamon Press, 1994.

Engels, Friedrich. *The Origin of the Family, Private Property, and the State* [Ursprung der Familie, des Privateigentums und des Staats], in *Marx Engels Werke*, Band 21. London: Electric Book Co., 2001.

Ernout, Alfred, and Antoine Meillet. *Dictionnaire étymologique de la langue latine: histoire des mots*. 4th ed. Paris: Klincksieck, 1967.

Fletcher, Angus. *Allegory: The Theory of a Symbolic Mode*. Ithaca, N.Y.: Cornell University Press, 1964.

Förstemann, Ernst. "Über deutsche Volksetymologie." *Zeitschrift für vergleichende Sprachforschung* 1 (1852): 1–27.

Foucault, Michel. *Fearless Speech*. Edited by Joseph Pearson. Los Angeles: Semiotext(e), 2001.

———. *The Order of Things: An Archaeology of the Human Sciences*. London: Routledge, 2002.

Fowler, Harold. "Preface." In *The Cratylus*. Loeb Classical Library. Cambridge, Mass.: Harvard University Press, 1971.

Franken, Gereon. *Systematische Etymologie: Untersuchungen einer 'Mischsprache' am Beispiel des Shakespeare-Wortschatzes*. Anglistische Forschungen 228. Heidelberg: Universitatsverlag C. Winter, 1995.

Fraunce, Abraham. *Arcadian Rhetorike*. London: Imprinted by William How for Thomas Gubbin and T. Newman, 1588.

———. "The Lavviers Logike Exemplifying the Praecepts of Logike by the Practise of the Common Lawe." London: Imprinted by William How for Thomas Gubbin and T. Newman, 1588.

Freud, Sigmund. *The Uncanny*. Translated by David McLintock. New York: Penguin Books, 2003.

Garuti, Maria Giovanna. "Working in and with Groups: Cultural References." http://www.continents.com/garuti.htm (accessed November 17, 2004).

Gellius, Aulus. *Noctes Atticae*. In *The Attic Nights of Aulus Gellius*. Translated by John C. Rolfe. 3 vols. Loeb Classical Library. Cambridge, Mass.: Harvard University Press, 1927.

Genette, Gérard. *Mimologics = Mimologiques: voyage en Cratylie*. Translated by Thaïs Morgan. Lincoln: University of Nebraska Press, 1995.

Gessner, Konrad. *Mithridates*. 1555.

Gilson, Simon. *Dante and Renaissance Florence*. Cambridge: Cambridge University Press, 2005.

Goethe. *Über die Gegenstände der bildenden Kunst*. 1797.

Goyet, Francis. "Le locus ab etymologia à la Renaissance." In Chambon and Lüdi, *Discours étymologiques*, 173–184.

Grabbe, Lester. *Etymology in Early Jewish Interpretation: The Hebrew Names in Philo*. Brown Judaic Studies 115. Atlanta, Ga.: Scholars Press, 1988.

Grimm, Jacob. *Deutsche Mythologie*. Berlin: Dummlers, 1875.

Guichard, Estienne. *L'harmonie etymologique des langues*. In Umberto Eco, *The Search for the Perfect Language: The Making of Europe*. Translated by James Fentress. Cambridge, Mass.: Blackwell, 1995.

Guiraud, Pierre. *Structures étymologiques du lexique français*. 2nd ed. Paris: Larousse, 1967.

———. *Dictionnaire des étymologies obscures*. Paris: Payot, 1982.

Hanson, R. *Allegory and Event: A Study of the Source and Significance of Origen's Interpretation of Scripture*. London: S.C.M. Press, 1959.

Harington, John. "An Apology for Ariosto: Poetry, Epic, Morality." In Vickers, *English Renaissance*, 302.

Hauser, Alan, and Duane Watson, eds. *A History of Biblical Interpretation*. Grand Rapids, Mich.: William B. Eerdmans, 2003.

Hogan, Patrick. *Cognitive Science, Literature, and the Arts: A Guide for Humanists*. London: Routledge, 2003.

Holkot, Robert. *English Friars and Antiquity in the Early Fourteenth Century*. Oxford: Oxford University Press, 1960.

Innocenti, Carlo. *L'immagine significante: studio sull'emblematica cinquecentesca*. Padua: Liviana, 1981.

The International Encyclopedia of Linguistics. Edited by William Bright. Oxford: Oxford University Press, 1992.

Irvine, Martin. *The Making of Textual Culture: "Grammatica" and Literary Theory, 350–1100*. Cambridge Studies in Medieval Literature 19. Cambridge: Cambridge University Press, 1994.

Isidore. *Etymologiae*. In *Isidori Etymologiarum Libri XX*. Edited by Lindsay. 2 vols. Oxford Classical Texts. Oxford: Oxford University Press, 1911.

Jameson, Fredric. *The Political Unconscious: Narrative as a Socially Symbolic Act*. Ithaca, N.Y.: Cornell University Press, 1981.

Jardine, Lisa, and Anthony Grafton. *From Humanism to the Humanities: Education and the Liberal Arts in Fifteenth- and Sixteenth-Century Europe*. Cambridge, Mass.: Harvard University Press, 1986.

Johnson, Barbara. *The Critical Difference: Essays in the Contemporary Rhetoric of Reading*. Baltimore: Johns Hopkins University Press, 1981.

Johnson, John. *The Academy of Love Describing the Folly of Young Men and the Fallacie of Women*. London: Printed for H. Blunden, 1641.

Joseph, John. *Limiting the Arbitrary: Linguistic Naturalism and Its Opposites in Plato's Cratylus and the Modern Theories of Language*. Amsterdam: Benjamins, 2000.

Joseph, Miriam, C.S.C. *Shakespeare's Use of the Arts of Language*. New York: Columbia University Press, 1947.

Klinck, Roswitha. *Die lateinische Etymologie des Mittelalters*. Medium aevum; philologische studien, Bd. 17. Munich: W. Fink, 1970.

Koch, Ludovica, ed. *Etimologia: Pratiche e Invenzioni*. Naples: I.U.O., 1983.

Kosko, Bart. *Fuzzy Thinking: The New Science of Fuzzy Logic*. New York: Hyperion, 1993.

Kruglanski, A. W., and D. M. Webster. "Motivated Closing of the Mind: Seizing and Freezing." *Psychological Review* 103 (1966): 263–283.

Lacan, Jacques. "Psychanalyse et Médecine." *Cahiers du Collège de Médecine* 12 (1966): 34–61.

———. *Speech and Language in Psychoanalysis*. Translated by Anthony Wilden. Baltimore: Johns Hopkins University Press, 1981.

Lakoff, George, and Mark Johnson. *Metaphors We Live By*. Chicago: University of Chicago Press, 1980.

Lallot, Jean. "L'Étymologie en Grèce Ancienne d'Homère aux Grammariens Alexandrines." In Chambon and Lüdi, *Discours étymologiques*, 135–48.

Law, Vivien. *The History of Linguistics in Europe from Plato to 1600*. Cambridge: Cambridge University Press, 2003.

Lepschy, Giulio. *History of Linguistics*. Longman Linguistics Library. London: Longman, 1994.

Liddell, Henry George, and Robert Scott. *A Greek-English Lexicon*. 9th ed., with a 1996 supplement. New York: Oxford University Press, 1940.

Lotman, Juri. "On the Metalanguage of a Typological Description of Culture." *Semiotica* 3 (1975): 97–123.

———. *Universe of the Mind: A Semiotic Theory of Culture*. Translated by A. Shukman. Bloomington: Indiana University Press, 1990.

Lurati, Ottavio. "Étymologie et anthropologie culturelle." In Chambon and Lüdi, *Discours étymologiques*, 305–19.

Madsen, Deborah. *Rereading Allegory: A Narrative Approach to Genre*. New York: St. Martin's, 1994.

Malkiel, Yakov. *Theory and Practice of Romance Etymology: Studies in Language, Culture and History*. London: Variorum Press, 1989.

———. *Etymology*. Cambridge: Cambridge University Press, 1993.

Mancini, Marco, ed. *Il cambiamento linguistico*. Rome: Carocci, 2003.

Marrou, Henri. *Histoire de L'éducation dans L'antiquité*. Paris: du Seuil, 1950.

Mazzotta, Giuseppe. *The New Map of the World: The Poetic Philosophy of Giambattista Vico*. Princeton, N.J.: Princeton University Press, 1998.

———. *Cosmopoiesis: The Renaissance Experiment*. Toronto: University of Toronto Press, 2001.

McKee, Richard. *The Clan of the Flapdragon and Other Adventures in Etymology*, by B. M. W. Schrapnel, Ph.D. Tuscaloosa: University of Alabama Press, 1997.

McMahon, April. *Understanding Language Change*. Cambridge: Cambridge University Press, 1994.

Meyer-Lübke, Wilhelm. *Romanisches Etymologisches Wörterbuch*. 3rd ed. Heidelberg: Winter, 1930–1935.

Miller, Joseph. "The Critic as Host." In Harold Bloom, Paul de Man, Jacques Derrida, Geoffrey H. Hartman, and J. Hillis Miller. *Deconstruction and Criticism*. New York: Seabury Press, 1979.

Mondésert, Claude. *Legum Allegoriae, Book I–III*. Paris: Éditions du Cerf, 1962.

Mooney, Michael. *Vico and the Tradition of Rhetoric*. Princeton, N.J.: Princeton University Press, 1985.

Moss, Ann. *Renaissance Truth and the Latin Language Turn*. Oxford: Oxford University Press, 2003.

Mucciolo, John M., ed. *Shakespeare's Universe: Renaissance Ideas and Conventions: Essays in Honour of W. R. Elton*. Aldershot, England: Scolar Press, 1996.

Mulcaster, Richard. *Elementarie*. In Jane Donawerth. *Shakespeare and the Sixteenth-Century Study of Language*. Urbana: University of Illinois Press, 1984.

Muller, F. *De veterum imprimis Romanorum studis etymologicis*. Utrecht: A. Oosthoek, 1910.

Murphy, James J., ed. *Renaissance Eloquence: Studies in the Theory and Practice of Renaissance Rhetoric*. Berkeley: University of California Press, 1983.

Nietzsche, Friedrich. "On Truth and Lies in the Extramoral Sense." In *Philosophy and Truth: Selections from Nietzsche's Notebooks of the Early 1870s*, edited and translated by Daniel Breazeale, 77–97. Atlantic Highlands, N.J.: Humanities Press, 1979.

Nordtug, B. "Subjectivity as an Unlimited Semiosis: Lacan and Peirce." *Studies in Philosophy and Education* 23 (2004).

Ohly, Friedrich. *Geometria e Memoria: Lettera e allegoria nel Medioevo*. Translated by Bruno Argenton. Bologna: Il Mulino, 1985.

Ong, Walter. *Rhetoric, Romance, and Technology*. Ithaca, N.Y.: Cornell University Press, 1971, 1980, 1990.

Orphica Argonautica. Edited by E. Abel. Leipzig: 1885.

The Oxford Companion to the English Language. Edited by Tom McArthur. Oxford: Oxford University Press, 1992.

The Oxford English Dictionary on Historical Principles on CD-ROM. 2nd ed. rev. Oxford: Oxford University Press, 2002.

Palatino, Giovambattista. *Sonetto Figurato*, in *Libro di M. G. B. Palatino cittadino romano nel quale s'insegna a scrivere ogni sorta di lettera Antica e Moderna di qualunque nazione, con le sue regole e misure e essempio et con un breve discorso et util de le cifre*. Rome: Blado, 1547.

Palmer, F. R. *Semantics*. 2nd ed. Cambridge: Cambridge University Press, 1981.

Pépin, Jean. *Mythe et allégorie; les origines grecques et les contestations judéo-chrétiennes*. Philosophie de l'esprit. Aubier: Editions Montaigne, 1958.

Peter of Poitiers. *Allegoriae super tabernaculum Moysi*. Edited by Philip S. Moore and James A. Corbett. Notre Dame, Ind.: University of Notre Dame, 1938.

Pfaffel, Wilhelm. *Quartus gradus etymologiae: Untersuchungen zur Etymologie Varros in "De lingua Latina."* Beitrage zur klassischen Philologie Heft 131. Konigstein: Hain, 1981.

Pinborg, Jan. "Das Sprachdenken der Stoa und Augustins Dialektik." *Classica et Mediaevalia* 23 (1962): 148–77.

Pisani, Vittore. *L'etimologia: Storia, questioni, metodo*. Brescia: Paideia, 1967.

Pitra, Jean Baptiste. *Spicilegium Solesmense, complectens Sanctorum Patrum scriptorumque ecclesiasticorum anecdota hactenus opera selecta e Graecis Orientalibusque et Latinis codicibus*. Graz, Austria: Akademische Druck, 1962.

Plato. *Cratylus*. Translated by Harold Fowler. Loeb Classical Library. Cambridge, Mass.: Harvard University Press, 1926.

———. *Fedro [Phaedrus]*. Translated by Giovanni Reale. Milan: Rusconi, 1993.

Plett, Heinrich. "The Place and Function of Style." In Murphy, *Renaissance Eloquence*, 356–74.

———. *Rhetoric and Renaissance Culture*. Berlin: de Gruyter, 2004.

Praz, Mario. *Studi sul concettismo*. Florence: Sansoni, 1946.

Preminger, Alex, and T. V. F. Brogan, eds. *The New Princeton Encyclopedia of Poetry and Poetics*. Princeton, N.J.: Princeton University Press, 1993.

Proclus. *Lezioni sul "Cratilo" di Platone*. Translated by Francesco Romano. Symbolon 7. Catania: Università di Catania, 1989.

Puttenham, George. "English Poetics and Rhetoric." In Vickers, *English Renaissance*. Chapter 7, "Figures and Figurative Speech," 295–303.

Qiao, Zhang. *Fuzzy Linguistics*. Dalian Shi: Dalian ch'ban she, 1998.

Quintilian. *Institutiones oratoriae*. In *The Institutionio oratoria of Quintilian*. Translated by H. E. Butler. 4 vols. Cambridge: Cambridge University Press, 1933–36.

Ramsey, Ian. *Models and Mystery*. London: Oxford University Press, 1964.

———. *Religion and Science: Conflict and Synthesis, Some Philosophical Reflections*. London: S.P.C.K., 1964.

Reale, Giovanni. *Per una nuova interpretazione di Platone: Rilettura della metafisica dei grandi dialoghi alla luce delle "Dottrine non scritte."* 11th ed. Milan: Vita e Pensiero, 1991.

Reitzenstein, Richard. *Geschichte der griechischen Etymologika*. Leipzig: 1897.

———. *Etymologika*. In "Paulys Real-Encyclopadie der classischen Altertumswissenschaft." 6 vols. Stuttgart: J. B. Metzler, 1907.

Richard of St. Victor. *Excerptiones*. Patrologiae cursus completus, series latina, ed. J. P. Migne.

Riganti, Elisabetta. *Lessico latino fondamentale*. Bologna: Patron, 1989.

Roberts, Francis. *Mysterium & Medulla Bibliorum the Mysterie and Marrow of the Bible, viz. God's Covenant with Man in the First Adam before the Fall, and in the Last Adam, Iesus Christ, after the Fall, from the Beginning to the End of the World: Unfolded & Illustrated in Positive Aphorisms & Their Explanation*. London: Printed by R. W. for George Calvert, 1657.

Rollinson, Philip B. *Classical Theories of Allegory and Christian Culture*. Duquesne Studies. Language and Literature Series, vol. 3. Pittsburgh, Pa.: Duquesne University Press, 1981.

Rorty, Richard. "Is Derrida a Transcendental Philosopher?" In *Essays on Heidegger and Others*. Philosophical Papers, vol. 2. Cambridge: Cambridge University Press, 1991, 119–28.

Rosiek, Jan. "Apocalyptic and Secular Allegory, or How to Avoid Getting Excited—Walter Benjamin and Paul de Man." *Orbis Litterarum* 48 (1993): 145–60.

Ross, Alan S. C. *Etymology: With Especial Reference to English*. Fairlawn, N.J.: Essential Books, 1958.

Routledge Dictionary of Language and Linguistics. Hadumod Bussmann. Edited and translated by Kerstin Kazzazi and Gregory Trauth. London: Routledge, 1996.

Ruthven, K. "The Poet as Etymologist." *Critical Quarterly* (1978): 9–37.

Salmon, Vivian. *Language and Society in Early Modern England: Selected Essays 1981–1994*. Amsterdam: Benjamins, 1996.

Saussure, Ferdinand de. *Cours de linguistique générale*. Edited by Rudolf Engler. Wiesbaden: Harrassowitz, 1967.

———. *Course in General Linguistics*. Translated by Wade Baskin. London: Fontana, 1974.

———. *Course in General Linguistics*. Edited by Charles Bally and Albert Sechehaye. Translated and annotated by Roy Harris, with the collaboration of Albert Riedlinger. LaSalle, Ill.: Open Court, 1986.

Cours de linguistique générale. Edited by Charles Bally and Albert Sechehaye. Paris: Payot, 1989.
————. *Troisième cours de linguistique générale (1910–1911): d'apres les cahiers d'Emile Constantin*. *Saussure's third course of lectures on general linguistics (1910–1911): from the notebooks of Emile Constantin*. Edited by Eisuke Komatsu. Oxford: Pergamon Press, 1993.
Schaeffer, John. *Sensus communis: Vico, Rhetoric, and the Limits of Relativism*. Durham, N.C.: Duke University Press, 1990.
Schank, Roger. *Scripts, Plans, Goals and Understanding: An Inquiry into Human-Knowledge Structures*. Hillsdale, N.J.: Lawrence Erlbaum Associates, 1982.
Schanze, Helmut. "Problems and Trends in the History of German Rhetoric to 1500." In Murphy, *Renaissance Eloquence*, 105–25.
Schelling, Friedrich. *Philosophie der Kunst*. 1802.
Schlegel, Auguste-Guillaume. *De l'étymologie en général*. Leipzig: 1846.
Schröter, Robert. *Studien zur varronischen Etymologie*. Köln: Erster Teil, 1959.
————. "Die varronische Etymologie, Varron." *Entretiens sur l'antiquité classique* 9 (1963): 81–116.
Schweickard, Wolfgang. "'Etymologia est origo vocabulorum...': Zum verständnis der Etymologiedefinition Isidors von Sevilla." *Historiographia Linguistica* 12 (1985): 1–25.
Seebold, Elmar. *Etymologie: Eine Einführung am Biespiel der deutschen Sprache*. Munich: Beck, 1981.
Seznec, Jean. *The Survival of the Pagan Gods: The Mythological Tradition and Its Place in Renaissance Humanism and Art*. Translated by Barbara F. Sessions. Princeton, N.J.: Princeton University Press, 1995.
Simonetti, Manlio. *Biblical Interpretation in the Early Church: An Historical Introduction to Patristic Exegesis*. Translated by John A. Hughes. Edinburgh: T. & T. Clark, 1994.
Singleton, Charles S., ed. *Interpretation: Theory and Practice*. Baltimore: Johns Hopkins University Press, 1969.
Smalley, Beryl. "Some Latin Commentaries on the Sapiential Books in the Late Thirteenth and Early Fourteenth Centuries." *Archives d'histoire doctrinale et littéraire du moyen âge*, vols. 25–26. Paris: J. Vrin, 1950–51.
Spenser, Edmund. "Allegory and the Chivalric Epic." In Vickers, *English Renaissance*, 297–301.
Spevack, Marvin. "Etymology in Shakespeare." In *Shakespeare's Universe: Renaissance Ideas and Conventions: Essays in Honour of W. R. Elton*. Edited by John M. Mucciolo, 187–94. Aldershot, England: Scolar Press, 1996.
Stahel, T. H. "Cristoforo Landino's Allegorization of the *Aeneid*: Books iii and iv of the *Camaldolese Disputations*." Ph.D. diss., Johns Hopkins University, 1986.
Struever, Nancy. "Vico, Valla, and the Logic of Humanistic Inquiry." In *Giambattista Vico's Science of Humanity*, edited by Giorgio Tagliacozzo and Donald Philip Verene, 173–85. Baltimore: Johns Hopkins University Press, 1976.
Sweetser, Eve. *From Etymology to Pragmatics: Metaphorical and Cultural Aspects of Semantic Structure*. Cambridge Studies in Linguistics 54. Cambridge: Cambridge University Press, 1990.
Swiggers, Pierre. "Le travail étymologique: typologie historique et analytique, perspectives, effets." In Chambon and Lüdi, *Discours étymologiques*, 29–46.
Tagliacozzo, Giorgio, and Donald Philip Verene, eds. *Giambattista Vico's Science of Humanity*. Baltimore: Johns Hopkins University Press, 1976.
Taylor, A. E. *Plato: The Man and His Work*. London: Methuen, 1960.

Tejaswini, Niranjana. "Deconstructing Allegory: Reading Paul de Man." *Indian Journal of American Studies* 19 (1989): 93–98.

Thomson, N. S. *Chaucer, Boccaccio and the Debate of Love*. Oxford: Oxford University Press, 1999.

Todorov, Tzvetan. *Theories of the Symbol*. Translated by Catherine Porter. Ithaca, N.Y.: Cornell University Press, 1982.

Trabant, Jurgen. *Vico's New Science of Ancient Signs*. Translated by Sean Ward. London: Routledge, 2004.

Trask, Robert Lawrence. *Historical Linguistics*. London: Arnold, 1996.

Trinkhaus, Charles. "The Question of Truth in Renaissance Rhetoric and Anthropology." In Murphy, *Renaissance Eloquence*, 207–20.

Turner, Mark, and Gilles Fauconnier. *The Way We Think*. New York: Basic Books, 2002.

Ursini, Flavia. *Etimologia, cultura e lessico dialettale*. Macerata: Pacini, 1979.

van Helmont, Mercurius. *Alphabeti veri naturalis Hebraici brevissima delineatio*. 1667.

Varro, Marcus Terentius. *De lingua Latina*. Translated by Roland Kent. Loeb Classical Library. Rev. and repr. ed. Cambridge, Mass.: Harvard University Press, 1951.

Vendryes, Joseph. "Pour une Étymologie Statique." *Bulletin de la Société de Linguistique de Paris* 49 (1953): 1–19.

Verene, Donald. *Vico's Science of Imagination*. Ithaca, N.Y.: Cornell University Press, 1981.

Vickers, Brian, ed. *Appropriating Shakespeare: Contemporary Critical Quarrels*. New Haven, Conn.: Yale University Press, 1994.

———. *English Renaissance Literary Criticism*. Oxford: Oxford University Press, 1999.

———. "The Royal Society and English Prose Style: A Reassessment." In *Rhetoric and the Pursuit of Truth: Language Change in the Seventeenth and Eighteenth Century*. Papers read at a Clark Library Seminar, March 8, 1980.

Vico, Giambattista. *The New Science of Giambattista Vico*. Translated by Thomas Goddard Bergin and Max Harold Fisch. Ithaca, N.Y.: Cornell University Press, 1976.

Vygotsky, Lev. *Thought and Language*. 1934. Translated by Alex Kozulin. Cambridge, Mass.: MIT Press, 1986.

Walde, Alois, and Johann B. Hoffman. *Lateinisches Etymologisches Wörterbuch*. 3rd ed. Heidelberg: Winter, 1939–65.

Wartburg, Walther von. *Etymologica*. Tübingen: Niemeyer, 1958.

Watkins, C. *The American Heritage Dictionary of Indo-European Roots*. Boston: Houghton-Mifflin, 1985.

Whitman, Jon. *Allegory: The Dynamics of an Ancient and Medieval Technique*. Oxford: Clarendon, 1987.

Wilson, Thomas. *An English Rhetoric Book III on Elocution*. In Vickers, *English Renaissance*, 73–124.

Yates, Frances Amelia. *The Art of Memory*. London: Pimlico, 1992.

Zamboni, Alberto. *L'etimologia*. Bologna: Zanichelli, 1976.

Zumthor, Paul. *Langue, texte, énigme*. Paris: Éditions du Seuil, 1975.

INDEX

Abraham, 68. *See also* Abram
Abram, 67, 68
abusio, 75, 76, 84
Accademici Occulti, 127, 128
Achilles, 150
additio, 81
adiectio, 81
adnotatio, 104, 105, 107
Aelius Stilo, 74, 83
Aeschylus, 48, 56
Agamben, Giorgio, 129
Agamemnon, 35, 36, 59, 60, 62, 64
ager, 87, 89
Alan de Lille, 99
alchemy, 119, 146
aletheia, 61
Alexandrian etymologizing, 66, 158
alieniloquium, 36, 56, 108
allegorism, 37, 49, 95, 98, 100, 104
allegory: xiv, xv, xvi, 66, 114, 118, 143, 145,
    147; in Benjamin, 140; as commodity,
    138; as *continua metaphora*, 69, 92; as *dark
    conceit*, 120; and deconstruction, 136–139;
    and duplicity, 121, 122; and emblem,
    126n42; and enigma, 108; and etymology,
    34, 37, 38–43, 45–48, 54, 56, 58, 59, 61;
    as *fair semblant*, 122; and irony, 139; in late
    18th century, 138; as in medieval exegesis,
    45–47; metonymy, 40; as Other speaking,
    85, 94, 106, 137; and Renaissance culture,
    118–120, 129; and symbol, 70n68
Ambrose, 67, 104, 109
amicus, xiii, 46, 110, 111
anagogical, 44, 103
anagogy, 45
analogia, 73, 84
anecdotes, 12, 114
anomalia, 84
Apollo, 49, 50, 64
aquilex, 153

arbitrariness, xv, 13, 16–21, 53, 55
Arcadia, 123
Arcadian Rhetorike, 124
argumentation, 64n, 77, 167n30
Aristotle, 38, 78, 105, 117, 139
arithmos, 82
ars memorativa, 166
Artemis, 64
artes liberales, 79, 96, 98
artificial intelligence, 64, 87n41, 164n26
Astyanax, 55, 64
Atreus, 63
Atropos, 50
Attridge, Derek, 11n35, 15n41, 17n47, 18n50,
    24, 25
auctoritas, 81, 84, 95
Auerbach, Erich, 104
Augustine, 71, 72, 74; *De Dialectica*, 74–76,
    106n42; and etymology, 75, 77, 80
Augustine, of Dacia, 45

Bakhtin, Mikhail, 40, 85
Balbus, 116
Baldinger, Kurt, 9, 10, 17n47, 28, 156n2
Bass, Alan, 141n26
Battistini, Andrea, 152n62
Baxter, Timothy, 51, 54, 55, 57, 58, 59, 61
Belardi, Walter, xvin7, 87n40
Benedetti, Marina, 32n104
Benjamin, Walter, 137, 138, 140, 141n22, 145
Bennington, Geoff, 17n47
Benveniste, Émile, 12, 20
bestioni, 151
binary logic, 18n51, 164
Bloch, Edward, 106
Bloom, Harold, 2n3
Bloomfield, Leonard, 19n57, 28
Boccaccio, Giovanni, 116n1
boîte, 167
Boolean, 18, 164

181

Bopp, Franz, 5
Borchardt, Frank, 116n1
Bottiroli, Giovanni, 91n49, 98, 126n40,
	157n3
Bréal, Michel, 5
Breazeale, Daniel, 155n70
bundle, 27, 106, 112, 157, 158, 168

caduceus 147, 151
caelum, 90, 91, 93
Cain, 69
calatis comitiis, 153
Carravetta, Peter, 151
Carruthers, Mary, 166
Cartesianism, 41, 140, 164
Cavazza, Franco, 44n31, 51n13, 53–55, 57,
	58, 73, 77, 78, 79, 80, 82n28, 84n31,
	85n39
Chambon, Jean Pierre, 29
Christian exegesis, 66, 67, 79, 96, 102, 103,
	107n44, 109
Chrysippus, 49, 50, 73, 80, 166n31
Cicero, 38, 72–75, 77, 80; cited by Isidore,
	104, 105; cited by John Johnson, 125n36;
	cited by Vico, 146; definition of etymology
	as nota, 77, 78, 107n44; on Latinitas, 79,
	84; on locus, 155, 167; Topica Ad Heren-
	nium 38n14; on veriloquium 43, 107n43
Cleanthes, 49, 73, 84
cognition 18, 92n53, 156; and metaphor,
	156, 161
cognitive, 9, 14, 32, 38n17, 70, 92, 98, 107,
	151, 161; allegory, 42; blending, 157;
	closure, 168n41, 170; hermeneutics, 136;
	mapping, 159; model, 152, 164n26; net-
	work, 166; frames, 166; science, 165
coincidentia oppositorum, 145
Coirier, Pierre, 165, 166; on scripts, 166n34
Colish, Marcia, 73n7
colligere, 105, 106
columbarium, 155n70
commutation, 81
compounding, 61
conceptual blending, 161
connectionism, 164n26
contemplari, 154
contrarium, 76, 80
conventionalism, 17, 52, 81, 109
correptio, 81
cosmology, 57, 65, 68

Crates, of Mallus, 80
Cratylus, xiv, 16n44, 34, 47; etymologies in,
	50, 51, 52, 53, 132
crus, 75
Curia Calabra, 86, 87
Curtius, Ernst Robert, xiii, 48, 95, 97n5,
	156n1

daemon, 116n1
dark conceit, 120, 121
Davies, Peter, 162, 163, 164
de Lubac, Henri, 104n35
de Man, Paul, xiv, 18n51, 38n17, 135, 136; on
	allegory, 137, 138, 139, 140, 143, 150; and
	Benjamin, 145; and Derrida, 141; on tem-
	porality, 140, 151; and Vico, 150
De Saussure, Michel, 13, 14, 16, 18, 19, 25,
	157n3; on folk etymology, 15; on mime-
	tism, 17
degnità, 146, 148n50, 153n65
Della Corte, Francesco, 72n2, 85
demogorgon, 116n1
demos, 116n1
Denkform, 95, 114, 94
derivation, xiii, 74, 109, 110
derivation, 8n24, 24, 35, 61, 87, 89, 101, 107,
	116n1
Derrida, Jacques
Desbordes, Françoise, 72, 73
Descartes, René, 84, 126
desiderium, 169
Di Lorenzo, Raymond, 166
diachronic phonetics, 5, 12
diachrony, 3, 23
Dialexis, 166
Dietrich, Paul, 73, 74, 80, 84n35
Diez, Friedrich, 5; definition of etymology, 6
différance, xiv, 38n17, 140, 141
Dihle, Albrecht, 84
Dionysus, 50, 79
discursive practice, 96, 100, 117
Dissémination, 141, 142
Distich, 45, 103
diversiloquium, 36, 56, 150, 151, 157, 158,
	169n44
divine language, 147
Don Cameron, Allen, 118n6
du Marsais, César, 43n29
Durkheim, Émile, 27
dynamis, 63

Forgotten Paths: Etymology and the Allegorical Mindset was designed and typeset in Quadraat by Kachergis Book Design of Pittsboro, North Carolina. It was printed on 60-pound Natures Natural and bound by Thomson-Shore of Dexter, Michigan.